CONDUCTING
POLITICAL
RESEARCH

CONDUCTING POLITICAL RESEARCH

E. TERRENCE JONES
University of Missouri–St. Louis

HARPER & ROW, PUBLISHERS
New York   Evanston   San Francisco   London

Standard Book Number: 06-043428-7

Library of Congress Catalog Card Number:
75-165026

TO MY PARENTS

CONTENTS

PREFACE

During the past two decades, teachers of politics have increasingly come to realize that one of the most important skills they can give their students is the ability to develop new knowledge. Facts can be forgotten or become obsolete, but the ability to seek and test new explanations can be used again and again. Many of us employ a body of logic and methods—generally called the scientific method—in our own search for knowledge. We can do our students and ourselves a great service by passing on this mode of knowing.

In order to help fulfill this purpose, this book presents a reasonably comprehensive treatment of research methods for political science students who have no previous training in statistics and only a normal high school mathematical background. Without going into excessive technical detail, it covers all of the primary topics associated with ongoing political research: research design, measurement, sampling, data collection, coding, data analysis, and statistical inference. In addition, an introductory chapter on the philosophy of science helps locate the research enterprise in the larger framework of science by showing the dynamic relationship between theory and research and by comparing the scientific method with other modes of seeking knowledge. The final chapter, a case study in political research, demonstrates how the various elements of the research process interrelate.

The book's organization reflects the steps in a typical research project. Thus each chapter relates quite closely with its predecessor and successor, and these interrelationships are emphasized in the text. At all times the student is not only told how to do something, but he is also shown why certain methods are preferable in certain situations and how each method helps answer questions about political phenomena. Since no procedure is foolproof and since the competent investigator is aware of the limitations of his research, the risks associated with any approach are pointed out. Throughout the book, research methods are presented as tools for aiding understanding, not as substitutes for clear thinking. Moreover, in order to demonstrate the applicability of the techniques to political research and to exemplify the interaction between abstract methods and political phenomena, most of the examples are drawn from major political science research studies.

The book's coverage is sufficiently broad so that it can stand alone as the text in a research methods course or, where instructors wish to emphasize certain techniques while maintaining a moderate breadth of coverage, it can serve as the core text. Since the book assumes little background, it can be used at any level.

Like all authors, I have accrued the usual share of debts. Fortunately, most can be repaid in words rather than money. I am indebted to the Literary Executor of the late Sir Ronald A. Fisher, F.R.S., to Dr. Frank Yates, F.R.S., and to Oliver & Boyd, Edinburgh, for permission to reprint Tables IV and V from their book *Statistical Tables for Biological, Agricultural and Medical Research* (6th ed., 1963). Data and questionnaires from the Inter-University Consortium for Political Research provided many of the book's examples. Linda Sagun stoically typed and retyped the manuscript with admirable dispatch and accuracy, Phyllis Wood provided her artistic skills in the construction of the book's figures, and Peggy Braden orchestrated the secretarial services. My students at Kansas State University and the University of Missouri—St. Louis, by a judicious combination of blank stares and enlightened faces, taught me which explanations work best. My wife and colleague Ruth fulfilled both roles to the utmost, my son Mark generously thought that writing books was a fine thing for fathers to do and thus excused me from many play sessions, and my parents, as always, provided much encouragement. My thanks to everyone.

E. T. J.

**CONDUCTING
POLITICAL
RESEARCH**

1 HOW DO WE KNOW?

Between the time we were born and the present day each of us has accumulated a body of knowledge, a set of things which we know to be so. How did we learn the things we did and how shall we go about decreasing our ignorance? Without engaging in a complete dissection of all the possible ways of knowing, we can distinguish three broad methods for seeking knowledge. An understanding of these will give us a better perspective on the approaches used to know politics.

WAYS OF KNOWING

The first way of knowing—called *empiricism*—is to rely on what our senses tell us. Through a combination of hearing and seeing we came to know the sound of a locomotive; more generally, through these two senses, we learned to associate certain sounds with certain objects. Our senses also provided the means for learning about various relationships between temperature and objects (e.g., stoves are often hot), or between smells and animals (e.g., at certain times, skunks stink). At the same time that we have been learning so much through sense experience, we have also discovered that our physical faculties can sometimes be misleading. The most obvious example of this is the optical illusion involving two lines which, although apparently of unequal lengths, are actually identical; through careful manipulation of the material surrounding the two lines, our senses can be fooled. A mirage is another example of a confusing sense experience. The fact that the sun seems to revolve around the earth is still another. Although it can be argued that these and other instances of individuals being misled by their senses can ultimately be resolved after careful examination of the facts, the point is that our senses of and by themselves do not seem to be the perfectly complete providers of knowledge.

Another source of knowledge is mental reflection; this method—known as *rationalism*—emphasizes ideas more than material substances. We accept certain things as being true because they seem to have logical interconnections. Since our lives are so full of sense experience, it is difficult to give a pure example of rationalism. Perhaps the best illustration is mathematics. Most of us learn that the probability of getting a head when tossing a coin is one half, by rationalizing that with a two-sided coin each side has an equal chance of occurring. We reason this result without recourse to sense experience; we did not toss the coin a large number of times and keep track of the number of heads and tails. The conclusion that the probability is one half simply seems logical and is accepted on these grounds alone. When confined to the world of abstractions (and mathematics is an abstract world), the mind seems to do rather well; its knowledge is quite reliable. This is probably so because, in the abstract realm, the mind both makes the rules of the game (i.e., decides what the logic shall be) and plays the game. But when one attempts to apply apparently correct logic to the world of nature, then many purely rational conclusions prove to be false. From a purely rationalistic viewpoint it might be logical to expect that when political power is concentrated in one person, the other members of the society will be oppressed. But our senses tell us that there have been occasions when concentration of political power has not led to oppression.

A final method for knowing relies on our emotions or, to speak a bit more plainly, our gut reactions. When the thing we know has some religious or theological connotation, this method is called *fideism*; we have faith, we believe. In our early years, we accepted the existence of Santa Claus, we knew his reality, because we had faith in what our parents told us. We had not physically sensed Santa Claus (if we discount the department-store and street-corner varieties) nor had we concluded that his existence was logical. Similarly, for most of us the belief or the nonbelief in a Supreme Being was not arrived at through our senses or our mind; we simply have faith that He does or does not exist. Nor is our love for a fellow human based as much on senses or mind as it is on a gut emotional feeling; we know that we are in love with somebody and we do not need our eyes or our mind to tell us so. The insufficiency of faith as a method for knowing is pointed up in the common phrases "blind faith" and "love is blind." Knowledge gained by faith has a tendency to be more firmly embedded than knowledge arrived at through the other two methods and, as a result, is not as subject to revision on the basis of new evidence.

In addition to using empiricism, rationalism, and fideism separately as a means of knowing, we frequently employ them in combination. Our mind and senses often work together in the knowledge-gathering process. Based on a series of sense experiences, our mind arrives at a logical explanation; for example, seeing the sun rise each day combined with the mental proposition that things which always occur will continue to happen leads to the knowledge that the sun has risen and will continue to rise every day.

Empiricism and fideism are also common knowledge-gathering partners. If our sense experience tells us that what a certain person says always turns out to be the case, then we have faith in additional pronouncements by this person, even when we do not have immediate confirmation of his statements. Students' faith in their teachers is one example of this process. They accept as definite knowledge the teacher's comments about facts which they have not personally experienced.

Finally, rationalism and fideism sometimes work together to produce knowledge. Many individuals' belief in a Supreme Being is part faith, part reason. Given the existence of human beings and, on larger terms, a universe, they think it reasonable that somebody must have started or created the whole setup. By an act of faith, they then close the gap between this incomplete logical proposition and the knowledge of the existence of some supernatural creator.

The next step in this analysis of knowledge-seeking methods would apparently be a critical discussion of each approach, leading to a final decision concerning the proper approach or combination of approaches to use in our continual search for knowledge. A bit of reflection, however, should indicate that to do so would be to enter into a vicious circle from which there is no clear-cut escape, since we would have to decide first what method to use in order to know which method to apply to politics. If we decided on the basis of which approach made the most mental sense, then we would be using rationalism to judge the issue; if we decided on the basis of which approach would be best able to cope with the material world, then we would be employing empiricism in the selection process; if we decided on the basis of faith, then we would be using fideism as a selection device.

Thus we are in a quandary. Although it is relatively easy to distinguish among the various ways of obtaining knowledge, it is seemingly impossible to make any well-defined decision about which to use. One answer—the one to be followed here—is to confine the discussion to the current dominant method for seeking knowledge: the scientific method. Although this solution is not overly satisfying in that no ultimate justification for it exists, it is not an arbitrary approach. Both because of its widespread use in many areas of human endeavor and its numerous successes in securing new knowledge, the scientific method deserves close attention.

THE SCIENTIFIC METHOD

As is the case with so many words, "science" (and hence the scientific method) has several overlapping meanings. It is sometimes used in a narrow sense to refer to the activities of certain specified fields of study such as physics and chemistry; in other instances it is applied broadly to all efforts to increase knowledge. It has described both the product of investigations and the procedures employed in those investigations. In order to pinpoint the meaning of science for this particular book, it is again necessary to confront the problem of which knowledge-seeking method to use. Should we, on the basis of mental reflection, construct an ideal meaning for science? Should we empirically examine what scientists do when they "scientize" and base our definition on the results of our examination? Or should we, in a leap of faith, jump to some attractive definition? The choice here involves a combination of the rational and empirical modes of knowing. We shall define science as a mental reconstruction of what actual scientists do. The empirical component of this definition becomes quite evident when we ask which scientists are to serve as the basis for our meaning of science. The answer—those scientists who have had the most success in gathering new knowledge—indicates the definition's emphasis on empirical results. The rational element of the definition involves what is done with the product of the survey of successful scientists. We do not simply accept our sense experiences of successful "scientizing," but in addition, seek a logical (i.e., mentally satisfying) order in our observations. This mental reconstruction, as one might expect, takes a good deal of the life out of science but, for this price, gives us a relatively generalized version of scientific activity.

What, then, do successful scientists do? What kind of logical procedure do they employ? In broad terms, the scientific method moves in a cyclical fashion from sense observations to "theory," to a more complete test of the explanation's correspondence to reality, to an adjusted theory and so forth in a never-ending process. There is a constant movement between fact and theory.

This broad procedure can be divided into five steps, but the following explanation should not be regarded as the one and only scientific method. The purpose is to exemplify the scientific process, not, as if it were possible, to set it in concrete.

1. Getting an Idea. One becomes interested in a particular segment of reality. The inspiration might come from past scientific investigations, personal experience, the need to achieve, or any number of other sources. (Example: On the basis of some volunteer work in a recent political campaign, a student becomes intrigued by the relationship between a person's wealth and his political party affiliation.) This idea about reality might be expressed rather precisely (Example: In the United States at the present time, the wealthier a person, the more likely he will be a Republican.), or somewhat vaguely (Example: Is there any connection between wealth and political party affiliation?).

2. Getting the Facts. In as systematic a fashion as possible, the relevant segment of reality is specified, observed, and measured. In order that the ultimate findings might have the greatest possible validity, care is taken to avoid misleading sense observations. Each segment of reality is carefully defined in terms of measurable aspects of the real world, and an objective procedure is developed for carrying out these measurements. Throughout the getting-the-facts process, each operation is critically evaluated in order to minimize measurement errors. (Example: Wealth is operationally defined as a person's annual income; party affiliation is considered to be the

response to the question: "On the whole, do you consider yourself a Democrat, a Republican, or what?" A random sample of citizens is drawn, and the measurements of wealth and party affiliation are collected by experienced interviewers.)

3. Summarizing the Facts. The results of the above procedures are described as precisely as possible. In many instances, this description not only gives the kinds of relationship which exist between the relevant segments of reality, but also states the probability that chance—and nothing else—could have produced the relationship. (Example: Dividing the sample into low-, medium-, and high-income groups, 20 percent of the low-income population are Republicans, 50 percent of the middle-income group are Republicans, and 70 percent of the high-income segment are Republicans. Overall, the wealthier a person, the more likely he will be a Republican. A statistical test indicates that this result would occur by chance less than once in a hundred times; hence, the risk associated with concluding that there is a nonrandom relationship between wealth and party affiliation is less than 1 percent.)

4. Explaining the Facts. Once a certain relationship has been empirically verified, the next step is to offer an explanation. This is the most creative aspect of the scientific method, and as such there is no hard-and-fast procedure for accomplishing it; one simply cannot tell a person how to be original. In logical terms, the movement from the summarization of the facts to an explanation is inductive inference. *Inductive reasoning* moves from the particular to the general and, unlike its counterpart (*deductive reasoning*), it is not subject to a definite set of logical rules. More than one explanation can be offered for any particular set of facts. The goal is to arrive at an explanation which is sufficiently general to explain both the findings in the particular instance as well as other findings in other settings. Pursuing this goal to its ultimate limit, the final end of science is to arrive at a single generalization which will explain everything. Failing the achievement of this rather utopian aim, the intermediate purpose is to create explanations which cover as much reality as possible. (Example: The problem is to provide a general explanation for the fact that wealthier people tend to be Republicans. One explanation can be rooted in the generalization that like attracts like. Since the active party workers and candidates in the Republican Party tend to be wealthier than their Democratic counterparts, then according to the like-attracts-like generalization, the wealthier elements of the citizenry are more likely to be affiliated with the Republican Party. But this, of course, is not the only possible explanation. Another one can be based on the proposition that the more material goods a person has, the more likely he is to support parties which are most oriented toward maintaining the status quo. Since Republicans in the United States are more oriented toward the status quo than are Democrats and since the wealthier persons have more material goods, then the wealthier a person, the more likely he will belong to the Republican Party.)

5. Testing the Explanation. After its foray into the theoretical realm of explanation, the scientific method returns to the facts. Any explanation, including the two used in the example above, covers more than the original set of facts; all have implications for other segments of reality. For the most part, deductive reasoning is used in order to enumerate the smaller conclusions implicit in the generalization; unlike induction, deduction is a necessary, logical movement from premise to conclusion. This is the primary place of mathematics (as a set of abstract logical systems) in the scientific method. In many instances, the possible conclusions inherent in any particular statement or set of statements are not immediately apparent. One often needs assistance—the kind of assistance provided by a mathematical system—in extracting the logical implications. Once these implications have been deduced, one or several are chosen for testing; they provide the "idea" mentioned in the first step of the scientific process. The circle is thus completed, and a never-ending cycle has been instituted in the search for the best possible generalization. (Example: From the principle that like attracts like, one can deduce that countries with similar domestic characteristics [governmental forms, economic systems, etc.] should be friendlier to each other than countries with dissimilar characteristics. The pursuit of this particular line of thinking might lead to a more specific statement concerning what kinds of similarities, if any, provide mutual attraction. Based on the notion that the amount of material goods possessed by an individual is positively related to the degree of his attachment to status quo political organizations, it can be deduced that in Great Britain the wealthier individuals would be more apt to support the Conservative Party—the most status quo party—than would the poorer citizens. Note that in reaching both of these particular conclusions, nothing new has been added to the original generalization; what has happened is that specific examples of "like," "possession of material goods," and "status quo political organizations" have been substituted for the general terms.)

The scientific method, as this brief outline indicates, is not a pure case of one of the ways of knowing; instead, it combines strong doses of empiricism and rationalism with just a touch of fideism. It is empirical in that it always treats correspondence with the real world as the final test of any proposition; it is rational in that it seeks to organize sense observations into mentally satisfying forms (induction) and rationally manipulate these forms to arrive at new notions about reality (deduction); it is slightly fideistic in that underlying the entire search for generalizations is the belief that there is a nonrandom, discoverable order in the real world.

SCIENCE: SOME GENERAL COMMENTS

No single outline of the scientific method can adequately convey its meaning. Some aspects need to be amplified and others qualified. The following points should be kept in mind in attempting to gain a fuller understanding of the meaning of science.

First, science is a human activity. Because it is, the reconstructed nature of the outline of the scientific method should be emphasized. As Abraham Kaplan has noted:

. . . a reconstructed logic is not a description but rather an idealization of scientific practice. Not even the greatest of scientists has a cognitive style which is wholly and perfectly logical, and the most brilliant piece of research still betrays its all-too-human divagations. The logic-in-use is embedded in a matrix of an *alogic-in-use*, even an *illogic-in-use*. The reconstruction idealizes the logic of science only in showing us what it *would* be if it were extracted and refined to utmost purity.[1]

The scientific method, as outlined above, is a general explanation quite like the generalizations discussed in the fifth and final step. As is the case with most generalizations, it explains the facts—in this instance, what successful scientists do—only imperfectly; its saving grace is that it appears to explain the facts better than any alternative explanation. Because the most successful scientists during the past few centuries have been physicists, the reconstruction of scientific logic is largely a reconstruction of physicists' logic. Although, at this point in time, one cannot say with any certitude that this kind of scientific logic will not be equally applicable to the life and social sciences, it might well be that future developments in these two areas will result in major changes in the reconstructed scientific method or in entirely new and different scientific methods.

In addition, the abstract nature of the scientific method merely presents the bones of science. Certain parts of the flesh deserve mention. First, because science is a historical activity, certain pet theories are dominant at any given time in any particular field. These preeminent points of view—often called *paradigms*—tend to determine the kinds of problems investigated and the kinds of explanations provided. Frequently, their influence as explanatory devices carries over into other fields. The Newtonian paradigm, for example, not only dominated physics during the eighteenth and nineteenth centuries, but it also had its influence on political thinking; the whole notion of separation of powers and of checks and balances—the principle behind much of the American Constitution—has a Newtonian action-and-reaction air about it. Because the utilization of scientific theory in political science is a relatively recent development, no single paradigm dominates the study of politics in the same way that Newton's view did and Einstein's view does dominate physics. Nevertheless, certain ways of looking at the political world are more common than others; viewing politics as an interrelated system (*systems analysis*) and a high degree of concern for the functional implications of specific political structures (*structural-*

---

[1] Abraham Kaplan, *The Conduct of Inquiry*, San Francisco, Chandler, 1964, pp. 10–11.

functionalism) are two modes of analysis frequently used in modern political science.

A second piece of flesh to be added to the scientific method's bones is the feelings and emotions of scientists. The pursuit of scientific knowledge, like all human endeavors, is influenced by the fears, jealousies, and ambitions of individual human beings. Sometimes these factors help the development of knowledge, as when the sour personality of Scientist A encourages his colleagues to examine his new explanation quite closely (and thus quickly eliminate its weak points), or when the personal rivalry between Scientist B and Scientist C causes both to work feverishly on a critical aspect of their field. At other times, however, personal feelings can hinder the search for knowledge, as when a young scientist is denied research funds because his seniors do not consider him sufficiently "respectful" of his elders. Although personal feelings can partially influence who gets what in science, it is difficult for them to constitute an absolute roadblock to scientific progress, since the ultimate test of any generalization is how well it accords with the facts. Since one of the scientific method's major characteristics is that any test can be repeated by other investigators, such systematic repetition can determine the validity of any generalization.

Another aspect of the humanity of science is that the mind of a scientist does not always operate in the step-by-step fashion indicated by the outline of the scientific method. Frequently, for example, investigators begin getting the facts with only the haziest of ideas guiding their search; then, after an initial immersion in the factual world, they step back, formulate a more precise hypothesis, and proceed onward. At other times, a particular project is abandoned as fruitless after one or two steps; many times scientists get an idea, begin collecting the factual information, and—after a preliminary examination of the data—decide that the original idea was not as attractive as when it first appeared.

Another important qualification is that science is not a universal method for knowing. Once a successful tool or technique has been developed there is always a danger that it will be overused. The scientific method is no exception to this rule. Having achieved major accomplishments in many knowledge-seeking endeavors, there is the temptation to believe that it is the sole method for gaining all knowledge. Yet a brief inspection of the nature of the scientific method reveals that it is inherently incapable of covering all the varied interests of man. The scientific method begins and ends with the empirical world; scientific generalizations must always be subjected to a factual test. In order to do this, each of the key words or phrases in the generalization must be defined in terms of observable phenomena. Much of what captures man's attention, however, cannot be defined in empirical terms. For example, there is no universally acceptable definition of what is absolutely good or absolutely evil. Although most of us, in our heart of hearts, are quite positive that certain actions are good and others bad, the scientific method gives us no way of proving—to the satisfaction of our fellow men—that our particular notions are the correct ones. More generally, the scientific method can tell us what *is* the case but it cannot tell us what *ought* to be the case; it can tell us why a man votes the way he does but it cannot tell us whether his vote is, in and of itself, a good or bad action.

The inability of the scientific method to decide questions of right and wrong does not mean that science has no role to play in discussions of "values." Many value questions do not deal with disagreements over absolute or final ends, but rather concern themselves with the best method for achieving some desired goal. Here the scientific method can be most helpful in providing a way for determining the best alternative. For example, the scientific method is unable to state whether democracy is good, but it can be applied to the search for the most practical strategy for achieving democracy. In addition, the scientific method enters into the area of values through studies of the distribution of moral positions in various populations, analyses of the internal consistency of moral philosophies, and the implications of various existing factors in the attainment of certain desired goals. For example, one can scientifically examine the ability of democracy (as well as other kinds of political systems) to achieve economic equality and stability.

The fact that the scientific method cannot decide questions of absolute right and wrong does not mean that science denies the existence of such absolutes. Indeed, such an interpretation would imply that the scientific method could decide such questions, since some empirical proof would be required in order to support the denial of absolute right or wrong. All one can say is that the scientific method of and by itself is not the appropriate way of knowing such matters.

To be a scientist is to be a special kind of man. All professions have their peculiar characteristics, but science, because it is not as much an occupation as it is a way of thinking, implies a rather definite set of mental attributes. Three of these attributes deserve special mention.

First, the scientist is objective. As far as it is humanly possible, he tries to prevent his personal desires from influencing the results of his research. Such an effort is not easy, especially when, as is the case of political scientists, the subjects of his studies are other men. In order to maintain an adequate level of objectivity, the scientist must be honest with himself; he must constantly seek to recognize his own biases and vigilantly guard against the danger of their interfering with his findings.

Second, the scientist is more skeptical than most men. No explanation is sacred and no finding is above questioning. The moment the scientist accepts some result as final is the moment he stops being a scientist. All knowledge is tentative and the job of advancing understanding is a never-ending one.

Third, the scientist is curious. For him the world is one big question waiting to be answered. Like the young child, he never stops asking why. Once he can explain a particular set of facts, he immediately embarks on a search for an explanation for the first explanation.

Science is not a particular set of tools or techniques. A frequent fallacy is to confuse the scientific method with techniques often used by scientists. According to this misconception, an individual is acting "scientifically" when he uses complex statistical formulas or employs a computer; conversely, if he does not utilize certain popular tools, he is not proceeding in a scientific way. But, of course, one cannot guarantee the scientific quality of his research by using esoteric instruments; like all things, they can be used well or poorly. One common slogan in computer centers is "garbage in, garbage out." This point is especially important since a large portion of this book will be devoted to techniques which many political scientists find useful. To become a good scientist, one must not only master the techniques' intricacies but also use them well.

Ideal scientific theory is not a haphazard set of generalizations. Although in most individual research studies the immediate objective is the discovery of a single suitable generalization, this is not the final goal of science. Once several generalizations have been constructed and relatively well-tested, the next step is to find a more general theorem which will explain the more specific generalization; given the existence of a set of theorems, each of which covers several generalizations, the next goal is to discover a single explanation for the theorems. The scientific enterprise, in short, is always trying to tie the whole package together.

Such a developed theoretical structure, it should be noted, does not currently exist in political science or, for that matter, in many of the natural and social sciences. But in acting scientifically, the political scientist attempts to proceed in a cumulative manner. He does not act in isolation, but instead takes what others have done and builds upon their work.

The usefulness of the scientific method for the study of politics is an open question. Although scientific qualities can readily be detected as early as the days of ancient Greece, the widespread, conscious use of the scientific method by political scientists is essentially a post-World War II phenomenon. Like any new development, this one has its supporters and its opponents. Some think that political science came of age only with the incorporation of the scientific method; others regard the intrusion of science as the beginning of a tragic end. Rather than repeat all the arguments and counterarguments engendered by the role of science in the study of politics, let us simply acknowledge their existence here. In the final analysis, science's place in political science will be decided by the results it achieves, not by a debater's scoreboard. In your analysis, the usefulness of the material presented in the remainder of this book can serve as an intermediate test.

EXERCISES

1 Give an example of knowledge you have obtained through each of the following modes of knowing: empirical, rational, fideistic, empirical-rational, empirical-fideistic, and rational-fideistic.

2 In our early childhood, most of us have at some time used a rough version of the scientific method to obtain new knowledge. Using the five-step framework (getting an idea, getting the facts, etc.) outlined in this chapter, briefly describe a situation where you employed the scientific method.

3 In order to get a better understanding of how scientists seek new knowledge, read an account of an actual discovery. Such descriptions can be found in histories of science and biographies of scientists. One excellent study is James Watson's autobiographical account of his work on the DNA molecule in *The Double Helix* (New York, Atheneum, 1968).

2 PLANNING POLITICAL RESEARCH

The first two steps of the scientific method are getting an idea and getting the facts. This chapter discusses procedures for stating ideas as precisely as possible and presents general strategies for testing the empirical validity of the ideas. Succeeding chapters will cover concrete procedures for implementing the strategies formulated at this stage of the research process.

Like most activities political research works best when planned ahead. Although one is frequently tempted to rush out and start collecting facts, such empirical enthusiasm is quite apt to yield only highly inconclusive results. What elements, then, make up a pre-research checklist? The following items, while not exhaustive, give the major preliminaries for any research effort:

1. What is the general topic?
2. What is already known about the topic and how well is it known?
3. What kind of question about the topic is to be answered?
4. What is the operational meaning of each term in the question?
5. What is the best strategy for getting an answer to the question?

CHOOSING A TOPIC

In most ways the choice of a topic depends on the investigator's interests and values; nonetheless, some general criteria have been put forth for evaluating the relative worth of topics. These criteria, which are themselves value statements not subject to empirical proof, include the importance of the topic for the development of scientific theory (Value: knowledge for its own sake); how increased knowledge of the topic will improve the social, economic, or political well-being of mankind (Value: maximizing some version of the good life); how many others are investigating the topic (Value: conformity); how few others are investigating the topic (Value: individuality); the amount of inconsistency in previous investigations (Value:

clear up ambiguous areas of knowledge); and the ease with which the topic can be studied (Value: pragmatism, or hunting where the ducks are).

WHAT IS KNOWN?

There are several reasons why it is useful to review past research in a particular area before proceeding with one's own efforts. If a certain question has been thoroughly researched, there is little purpose in repeating the same process unless one suspects that he has discovered a situation where a well-established generalization does not hold. If there have been only a few studies in the area, then it is highly useful to repeat an investigation in order to test the confidence we might place in a certain finding. This process—called *replication*—comprises a major portion of scientific activity; a creative researcher who comes up with a new finding is followed by other scientists' backing-and-filling replications aimed at ascertaining the validity of the original finding. If there have been almost no studies on the topic, then two lessons can be drawn. First and most obvious, the topic might be a fruitful area for new work; since little is now known, there must be much to learn. In a second and a more cautious vein, lack of work in a given area might be an indication that there are few meaningful relationships to be found or that there are some inherent obstacles to serious research (relevant data are unavailable); others have tried, failed, not published their negative findings (scientific journals are generally unreceptive to reports on failures to discover some kind of nonrandom relationship), and have gone on to other things.

In addition to learning the substantive knowledge available on any given topic, a review of the scholarly literature can acquaint one with the methodological procedures which have been used. How have other investigators measured the key terms? What strategies or research designs have they employed? What statistical techniques have they used to analyze the results? Not only is it much more pleasant to learn from others' errors than from one's own, it is also eminently sensible to profit from others' methodological successes. To repeat an earlier statement, science is a cumulative endeavor. If our knowledge of politics is to grow rapidly, then we must incorporate in our work the findings and procedures of other investigators.

Where do you look for reports on past work on a particular topic? First, ask a professor or colleague for references to any books on the topic; the card-catalogue subject index at any library can also provide initial references. Second, the *International Encyclopedia of the Social Sciences* publishes review essays by leading scholars; these essays are an excellent means to an understanding of how a topic is interpreted, to a summary of significant research findings, and to references for leading works.

In the rapidly moving world of scientific research, however, both books and encyclopedias are inevitably somewhat out-of-date. In order to acquaint ourselves with the latest research in a particular area, we must consult the periodical literature. Fortunately, several guides exist to this massive and widely scattered body of material. The following bibliographic indexes reference the relevant articles and, in most instances, provide a one-or-two paragraph summary of the research: *The ABC Guide to Recent Publications in the Social and Behavioral Sciences, International Bibliography of Political Science, International Political Science Abstracts, Psychological Abstracts, Public Affairs Information Service, Social Sciences and Humanities Index* (formerly *International Index*), *Sociological Abstracts,* and the *Universal Reference System.*

ASKING THE QUESTION

We can distinguish three kinds of reasons for undertaking a scientific investigation of a topic.[1] First, we might wish to gain some preliminary understanding of the topic before proceeding with a more structured research project. (Example: What are some of the more important factors influencing legislators' policy decisions?) Second, we might want to obtain a very precise description of a specific phenomenon. (Example: What percentage of the population voted for the Democratic presidential candidate in the last election?) Third, we might want to test whether there is a certain kind of relationship between two or more phenomena, or as it is generally called, test a causal hypothesis. (Example: A person's socioeconomic status positively affects his loyalty to the national political system.) Although only the last of these questions is truly scientific in that it is the only one which attempts to explain why something does or does not occur, getting some kind of feel for the phenomena and precise descriptions of single variables are necessary precursors for many scientific investigations. For example, if one is interested in testing some general statements about the relationship between legislative committees' formal and informal structures and their policy decisions, then it might be very useful to do a case study of how a single committee made one decision. This case study can then be an excellent springboard for the formulation of more specific hypotheses for testing. Such case studies are especially helpful if you have had little personal contact with the topic or if the scholarly literature on the topic is vague or nonexistent. Another fine procedure for gaining familiarity with the topic is to talk with individuals who have had a good deal of experience in the area. In the legislative-committee example, it might be useful to conduct informal interviews with staff members. In these instances, one should not be overly concerned with interviewing a representative sample, but should concentrate on people who have a high degree of familiarity with the topic and the ability to articulate their experience with clarity.

Precise descriptions of specific phenomena also fulfill important scien-

---

[1] The following classification of scientific questions is based on one given in Claire Selltiz et al., *Research Methods in Social Relations,* rev. ed., New York, Holt, Rinehart and Winston, 1963, chaps. 3 and 4.

tific functions. First, accurate knowledge about the extent to which a particular phenomenon is present or absent often serves as a spur to explain its relative frequency. (Example: You see a table listing the percentage of the gross national product spent on military functions for every nation; you note that this percentage varies a great deal. Why?) Second, in order to test hypotheses (the third type of question), we must be able to provide precise empirical measurements for their terms. Previous efforts aimed at describing single phenomena can then be enormously useful for the hypothesis-tester either by providing him with the necessary measurements or by furnishing him with a workable procedure for gathering the information.

Finally, let us examine the most common way of expressing the third type of question: the *hypothesis*. Hypotheses are if-then statements; if something (*X*) occurs, then something else (*Y*) will also occur. The if-terms are referred to as *independent variables* and the then-terms are called *dependent variables*. There are several variations on the simple if-then theme. First, the hypothesis can be deterministic (if *X*, then *Y* always occurs) or probabilistic (if *X*, then *Y* is likely to occur). Second, a probabilistic hypothesis can be stated vaguely, as above, or quite specifically (if *X*, then the probability of *Y* occurring is between 70 and 80 percent). Third, there can be more than one independent variable (if X_1 and X_2, then *Y*) or more than one dependent variable (if *X*, then Y_1 and Y_2). Fourth, conditional independent variables can be added (if X_1 or X_2 is present and if X_3 is absent, then *Y*; if X_1, and if X_2 is greater than 10, then *Y*). Fifth, the hypothesis can be phrased in more-less terms (the more *X* is present, the more *Y* is present; the less *X* is present, the more *Y* is present).

OPERATIONALIZING THE TERMS

The critical test for any scientific proposition is how well it fits the facts. Thus, once a hypothesis has been stated in if-then terms, it becomes necessary to relate the crucial words in the hypothesis to real-world phenomena. Given the variety of meanings that can be attached to any word, this is far from an automatic process. It is rarely obvious that a particular term in a hypothesis has one and only one way of being measured; typically, there is a near infinity of possible definitions. The problem is to decide which one or combination of definitions from this set of possibilities is most appropriate for your research purposes.

Hypotheses, then, are generally composed of rather abstract terms. If these terms are quite absract, we will call them concepts; if they are somewhat abstract, we will call them variables; if they are quite specifically related to the real world, we will call them *operational definitions* or indicators. In general, every concept contains several variables, and for every variable there are a number of possible operational definitions.

Concepts can be defined in two ways. First, their meaning can be expressed in terms of other concepts (e.g., Concept A is the absence of Concept B.). Conceptual definitions, although useful in clarifying relationships between concepts, do not of and by themselves link concepts to empirical phenomena. In order to do this, we must use conceptual definitions to break down the concepts into smaller concepts—variables—and then define the variables in operational terms.

Figure 2.1 summarizes the relationship between concepts, variables, conceptual definitions, operational definitions, and the empirical world. This diagram also implies other important distinctions. First, note that concepts, variables, and conceptual definitions are in the theoretical world; thus, in a scientific sense, they are neither right nor wrong because they are not directly related to the empirical world. This leads to an important qualification about scientific tests: Relationships between concepts are not tested directly, but rather indirectly through the test of a relationship between operational definitions of the concepts. Hence, no single test of a hypothesis can show that two concepts are unrelated; you can only indicate that certain operational definitions are not associated with each other. A large number of negative tests, involving a wide variety of operational definitions for a certain set of concepts, is required before one can rather confidently state that there is no relationship between or among the concepts. Second, the fact that concepts and variables do not relate directly to the real world does not mean that they are meaningless; quite to the contrary, they are essential to scientific development because they enable many different empirical phenomena to be grouped under one term. They are the means by which science can move from the enormous diversity of the real world to more concise explanations of that world. Third, the sepa-

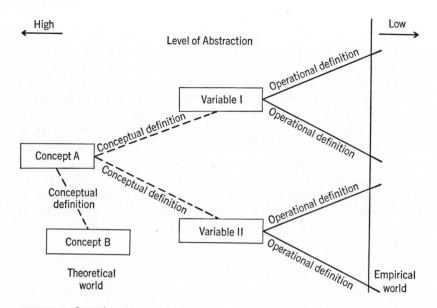

FIGURE 2-1 Operationalizing concepts

ration in Figure 2.1 of the scientific world into theoretical and empirical parts reflects a division of labor among scientists. Some investigators spend most of their time in the empirical world testing hypotheses; their trips into the theoretical world are generally restricted to a search for new hypotheses to test. Other scientists—often called theorists—devote most of their efforts to the theoretical world. They attempt to clarify existing concepts and variables, develop new concepts and variables, and specify more precisely the interrelationships between various parts of the theoretical world; for them, the empirical world is a source of ideas for their theorizing. This book is devoted to empirically-oriented scientific work, and to techniques for testing hypotheses.[2] But this is not all there is to science, nor necessarily the most important aspect of science; as David Easton has written, "Research untutored by theory may prove trivial, and theory unsupported by data, futile."[3] Finally, Figure 2.1, like all attempts at conveying real-world processes, should not be treated as a sacred schema. Some concepts are more vague than others and where a concept ends and a variable begins is often an arbitrary distinction. The diagram is intended simply as a device for clarifying the process of moving from a theoretical proposition to an empirical test.

Let us amplify the procedure for operationalizing a concept by taking a typical hypothesis stated in conceptual terms: "The higher the level of education in a country, the more democratic that country will be." If we wish to test this proposition, we must develop measurements for the key terms: "level of education," "country," and "democratic." The term "country" presents only a few minor definitional problems (Example: Is Formosa a separate country?), so we will concentrate on "level of education" and "democratic." The first step in operationalizing these concepts is to specify alternative means for translating them into empirical indicators. This list of choices can then serve as a base for discussing which indicator or set of indicators best fulfills the purposes of a particular research project. Figures 2.2 and 2.3 present dissections for "level of education" and "democratic." In each instance, the concept is first divided into several variables and then operational definitions are given for each variable.

Turning to Figure 2.2 we see that education might be interpreted as exposure to formal schooling, actual amount of knowledge concerning a particular topic, or possession of certain basic skills (e.g., reading and writing). Each of these variables captures part of the meaning of education, but none exhausts its implications. The decision as to which variable or combination of variables to use depends primarily on a consideration of which aspect of education is apt to be most critical in the attainment and

[2] An excellent book on the theorizing process is Arthur L. Stinchcombe, *Constructing Social Theories*, New York, Harcourt Brace Jovanovich, 1968.
[3] David Easton, "The Current Meaning of 'Behavioralism'," in James C. Charlesworth (ed.), *Contemporary Political Analysis*, New York, Free Press, 1967, p. 16.

Concept   Variables   Operational Definitions

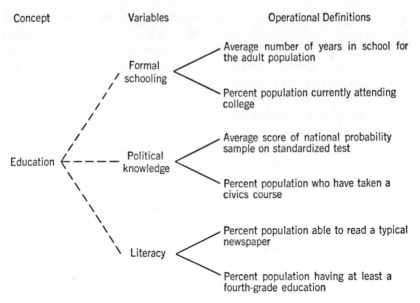

FIGURE 2-2   Operationalizing education

maintenance of democracy. Is it formal schooling, political expertise, or literacy? We must make the choice. The important point is that this choice should be made only after a careful consideration of the alternatives.

After selecting which variable(s) to employ, the next decision is which operational definition to use. In addition to taking into account the most appropriate indicator for the meaning you wish to assign to the variable in the particular research project, two other criteria are relevant: expense and accuracy. Which measurement will require the least time and money to collect? Which indicator can be measured most accurately? For example, if you have decided on "amount of political knowledge" as a variable, two possible operational definitions are the mean score for a representative sample of the national adult population on a twenty-item test and the percentage of the national adult population who have taken a civics course lasting a minimum of one semester at the high school level or above. Quite clearly, the second indicator would be less expensive to measure, since it could probably be obtained directly from governmental figures or extrapolated from current enrollment data. The national test indicator, on the other hand, most likely cannot be obtained from secondary sources and would necessitate a national survey in each country; the cost, of course, would be quite high. If the criterion is accuracy, however, then the survey instrument might be preferable. The government figures on civics enrollments might in some cases be inflated, and more importantly, it would be difficult to ascertain the degree of inaccuracy. Moreover, one would have to assume that all civics courses were comparable in their impact on political knowledge. Thus the choice of an indicator is governed by appropriateness for research purposes, collection cost, and accuracy. In the final analysis, one tries to maximize the appropriateness and accuracy within established cost constraints.

An operational breakdown of democracy (see Figure 2.3) is presented for two reasons. First, it illustrates how a major political concept can be decomposed into operational indicators so that one can, to take this instance, measure how democratic a country is. For example, electoral equality—an important characteristic of a democratic state—might be measured by the percentage of the adult population that possesses the franchise, the extent to which the nation's chief legislature is apportioned on a one-man–one-vote basis, and the degree to which all ideas have a chance to be heard as indicated by the number of separately-owned newspapers. Second, highly abstract concepts like democracy can rarely be adequately measured by a single indicator. More frequently, it is necessary to take several indicators and combine them into an overall index. Deane Neubauer, for example, combined three electoral equality indicators and two political competition indicators in his examination of the conditions encouraging democracy.[4]

[4] Deane E. Neubauer, "Some Conditions of Democracy," *American Political Science Review, 61* (December 1967), 1002–1009.

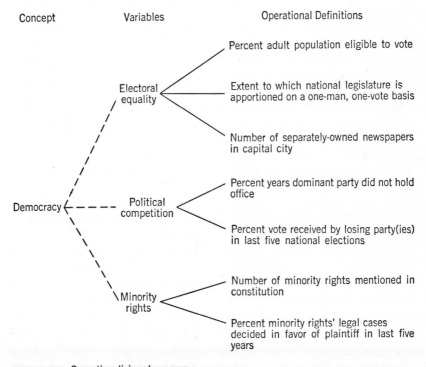

FIGURE 2-3 Operationalizing democracy

FORMULATING A STRATEGY

The initial step in formulating a strategy for testing hypotheses is to decide who or what subjects will be tested, or in more technical words, at what level the analysis will take place. Frequently, the level of analysis will be stated in the hypothesis. (Example: The higher a nation's gross national product, the more politically stable it will be.) In some instances, however, a hypothesis can apply to several levels. (Example: "The more education, the more political conservativism" can refer to countries, regions, cities, a group of political leaders, mass publics, or other levels.) In such cases, the level from which the subjects will be chosen must be determined.

Once the appropriate level of analysis has been specified, the next step is to obtain the most representative sample of the level as is financially possible. In cases where every member of the level—known as *universe* or *population*—will be included in the study, the representativeness problem vanishes; nothing is more representative than a complete enumeration. Although full inclusion of the members of a population is sometimes feasible (e.g., all fifty American states, all members of a legislature), more often it is patently impossible. If, for example, the universe is all adult Americans, some kind of sample must obviously be used; even if the universe is markedly smaller (say, all students at a major university), a representative sample is often preferable in order to maintain quality of measurement. It is easier to conduct competent interviews with 200 people than with 20,000. Fortunately, procedures have been developed for selecting (or drawing) representative samples; these techniques will be presented in Chapter 4. Here only two points need to be made. First, unless a representative sample is drawn, we cannot generalize from the particular subjects studied to any larger population. Second, financial considerations often prohibit sampling the ideal population (say, the entire national population); in such instances, we should not haphazardly assemble a set of subjects, but should attempt to construct a representative sample for some smaller population (e.g., a city or a neighborhood). The research should be designed so that the results can be generalized to as large a population as possible.

Now that the concepts have been operationalized, the level of analysis established, and the units for analysis chosen, we are ready for the actual testing process. In order to infer that one or more independent variables causes one or more dependent variables, it is necessary to show three things: (1) the independent variable(s) occurred before the dependent variable(s); (2) the independent variable(s) and the dependent variable(s) vary together in some consistent, nonrandom manner; (3) no other independent variable(s) could cause the same observed variation in the dependent variable(s). Many scientists are reluctant to use the word "cause" in the sense that one variable "causes" another; instead, they prefer euphemisms such as "is related to" or "helps determine." Without involving ourselves in a philosophical discussion of causality, here we are limiting the meaning of cause to a relationship where the three conditions mentioned above are relatively well-fulfilled. We will now discuss each of these conditions in turn.

In many cases, the fact that the independent variable temporally pre-ceded the dependent variable is quite obvious: A childhood experience (e.g., attending parochial school) is hypothesized as the cause of a particular adult behavior (e.g., voting for a Democratic candidate for President), or the investigator introduces an independent variable (e.g., reading a speech and testing its impact on the subject's political attitudes). In other instances, however, things are not that apparent. For example, if we were interested in explaining why some American cities have a mayor-council form of gov-ernment and others have a council-manager form, we might posit one or more socioeconomic characteristics, say the proportion of the population having a college education, as being positively related to having a council-manager form of government. We then might take a sample of cities, measure current governmental forms and the present proportion of the population having a college education (both measurements are easily available from published sources), and proceed with the remainder of the analysis. In doing so, however, we would have failed the time-order test. Most decisions about city governmental forms were made decades ago; thus the dependent variable most typically occurred between 1900 and 1930. The independent variable, however, was obtained from current census data (circa 1970). Since it is logically impossible for a 1970 event to cause a 1920 event, the research design must be changed. Two modifi-cations are possible. The first is to ascertain the last date on which each city made a decision concerning governmental form and then measure the independent variable as of that date (or as close before it as past records allow). The second modification (in the event that the above information is unavailable) is to assume that the 1970 independent variable measure-ments are in all likelihood highly correlated with the earlier (but unavail-able) values of the independent variable. If this tack is taken, then the earliest available data should be used (i.e., 1950 would be better than 1970) in order to strengthen similarity between available sets of data having as much as a fifty-year time gap.

This kind of study—where a socioeconomic independent variable is posited as the cause of a political dependent variable—reveals a wide-spread tendency of political scientists to bypass the time-order problem by assuming that socioeconomic variables are empirically prior to political variables: a man's income determines his political party affiliation, a na-tion's racial composition affects its political stability, and so forth. There is, of course, nothing wrong about making assumptions if their implications are carefully considered and if it would be inordinately expensive or prac-tically impossible to pin down the time order within the research design One should, however, not allow a proposition which seems sensible in most instances to turn into a universal guideline; there are cases, one suspects, where the political variable does causally precede the socioeconomic factor, and one should be alert to this possibility.

Another type of research presenting time-order problems is an investigation into the relationship among two or more attitudes. In examining whether a general attitude (e.g., political liberalism) causes another more specific attitude (e.g., opinion on a current policy matter), the most common practice is to measure both variables on the same survey (i.e., at the same time), and to assume that the more general factor precedes the more specific one. This, however, is not necessarily the time order; conceivably, the subject's reaction to the most recent issue, especially if that issue had an immediate impact on his living conditions (e.g., old people and Medicare), might have substantially changed his liberalism score. A better strategy would be to apply the general liberalism test prior to the public appearance of the specific issue, and then, once the issue had come to the fore, retest the subjects in order to obtain their issue opinions. This procedure has some ancillary disadvantages (e.g., locating the subject for the second test), but it does clarify the time sequence.

Although the best means for ensuring that the independent variable(s) occurred prior to the dependent variable(s) is for the investigator to introduce both variables to the subjects, this procedure is often impossible in political research. The kinds of concepts and variables which interest most political scientists are ones like voting and stability. We as political researchers clearly have no control over when an election is held or when a revolution will occur; we must take them as we find them and accept the time-order ambiguities that sometimes result. Whenever possible, however, the research design should pinpoint the time sequence; when this is not feasible, the secondary evidence—drawn from either the study itself or other similar research endeavors—should be gathered to support the assumption that the independent variable occurred before the dependent variable.

Ascertaining the degree and form of *covariation* is the least troublesome aspect of research design; once the relevant variables have been measured, a variety of statistical techniques exist for determining how much they vary together. Nonetheless, there are two important considerations at this stage of the research process. First, we should have a relatively precise idea about what specific kind of common variation is being predicted by the hypothesis. For variables which can be measured in more-and-less terms (Example: Conservativism—an individual can be more conservative or less conservative than someone else; or material goods—a person can have more goods than another man.), there are three major kinds of covariation:

1. For the entire range of values for both variables, an increase in the independent variable causes an increase in the dependent variable and a decrease causes a decrease. This kind of covariation is called a *direct relationship*. (Example: The more material goods a man has, the more politically conservative he will be; conversely, the fewer goods he possesses,

the less conservative are his opinions. Since the hypothesis covers the entire range of values, the man with the most goods should be the most conservative, the individual with the next highest amount of goods should be the second most conservative, all the way down to the subject with the least material goods who should be the least conservative.)

2. For the entire range of values, an increase in the independent variable causes a decrease in the dependent variable, and similarly a decrease causes an increase. This type of covariation is known as an *inverse relationship.* (Example: The more material goods a man has, the less politically conservative he will be; conversely, the less goods he possesses, the more conservative are his opinions. Then, using the same logic as in the first example, the man with the most goods should be the least conservative, and so on.)

3. For one set of the entire range of values of the independent or dependent variable or both, there is no common variation (i.e., no nonrandom relationship); for the other set of values, there is a direct or inverse relationship. This type of case is generally called a *threshold relationship* since one or both of the variables must be above or below a specified threshold value in order for a nonrandom relationship to occur. (Example: The more material goods over $50,000 a man has, the more conservative he will be; below $50,000, there is no consistent relationship between amount of material goods and political conservatism. This hypothesis, then, predicts that a man with $40,000 in goods is just as likely to be more conservative than the man possessing $1,000 in goods as he is to be less conservative; for all subjects having $50,000 and more, the relationship is the same as that given in the first example.)

Other kinds of variations for more-or-less variables involve more precise specifications of the major types listed above. The primary remaining distinction is between *additive variations,* where a constant increase or decrease in the independent variable results in a constant increase or decrease in the dependent variable (Example: For the entire range of values —for every 1 percent increase in a nation's literacy rate its average voting turnout increases by 2 percent.) and *nonadditive variations,* where a specified increase or decrease in the independent variable causes the dependent variable to increase or decrease at an increasing or decreasing rate. (Example: An increase in a nation's literacy from an absolute level of 30 to 40 percent causes voting turnout to increase 12 percent; when literacy goes from 40 to 50 percent, turnout increases 24 percent.).

For variables which cannot be measured in more-or-less terms (e.g., political party affiliation—a person is a Democrat, a Republican, or an Independent; race—a person is white or nonwhite), there are three major types of covariation:

1. The occurrence of the independent variable causes the occurrence of the dependent variable, and nonoccurrence causes nonoccurrence. (Example: All nonwhites are Democrats and all whites are not Democrats.)

2. The occurrence of the independent variable causes the nonoccurrence of the dependent variable, and nonoccurrence causes occurrence. (Example: All nonwhites are not Democrats, and all whites are Democrats.)

3. The occurrence of the independent variable causes the occurrence of the dependent variable, but nonoccurrence of the independent variable is not related to nonoccurrence of the dependent variable. (Example: All non-whites are Democrats, but whites are equally likely to be Democrats or non-Democrats.)

The second consideration regarding common variation is to design the study so that the independent and dependent variables have an opportunity to vary. For example, if one is interested in a relationship between sex and political party affiliation, then the subjects should be chosen so that all possible values of the two variables occur (male, female, Democrat, Republican). Although this advice seems commonplace, failure to follow it has caused grief to more than one investigator. The point is especially pertinent for those examining phenomena which seldom occur. For example, you might be interested in testing whether there is a correlation between the degree of permissiveness of parents and the likelihood of their son's belonging to a radical student organization. If you planned to investigate this proposition on a campus where political radicalism was relatively rare (e.g., 2 to 4 percent of the student body) and financial exigencies limited the sample to 100 students, a typical unweighted sample would yield only 2 to 4 radical organization members. This, of course, is not a secure base for drawing conclusions about the causes of student radicalism; the dependent variable (membership in radical organizations) does not vary sufficiently, with over 95 out of 100 subjects having the same value or score (nonmembership in radical organizations). The design would yield firmer conclusions if more radical organization members were included. Techniques for increasing the number of empirically rare cases in a sample without invalidating the representativeness of that sample will be presented in Chapter 4.

If one has shown that the independent variable(s) preceded the dependent variable(s) and that the two sets of variables varied together in the specified manner, he has still not closed the logical circle essential for inferring causality. He still must show that nothing else could have caused the changes in the dependent variable.

The research situation at this point of the design process can be expressed as $X_1 \rightarrow Y$ where the direction of the arrow (from X_1 to Y) indicates that the time order has been established and the existence of a solid arrow shows that there is common variation. What other arrangements of variables might have yielded the same results? Some major possibilities are

$$X_1 \longrightarrow X_2 \longrightarrow Y \quad \text{(Intervening case)}$$

where the causal influence of X_1 on Y is transmitted through an intervening variable (X_2). If certain values of the intervening variable do not occur, then

X_1 does not influence Y. An obvious example is that of an individual who favors Medicare (X_1) which causes him to vote for a specified candidate (Y) only if he knows that the candidate favors Medicare (X_2); if the subject does not associate the candidate with a certain position on Medicare, then the developmental sequence is broken and the relationship between X_1 and Y does not occur.

Another possible arrangement is

where other independent variables (X_2 and X_3) also cause Y. (Example: Either having a father who was a Democrat or belonging to a labor union will cause a man to be a Democrat.)

Another common arrangement is

$$\text{If } X_2, \text{ then } X_1 \longrightarrow Y \quad \text{(Conditional case)}$$

where X represents the condition(s) under which X_1 causes Y. For example, a negative relationship between income and participation in riots might hold for American blacks but not for whites. Incorporating a second condition, it might hold for American urban blacks but not for rural blacks nor all whites.

A final arrangement is

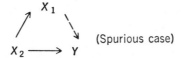

where some common factor (X_2) causes both X_1 and Y, and where the common variation between X_1 and Y (broken arrow) is totally a product of the common cause. In this instance, X_1 is not the direct cause of Y, and thus the relationship is called spurious. (Example: A relationship between the value of a man's house and his party affiliation might stem from their common relationship to his income; a high income might cause a man to have an expensive home and a Republican party affiliation.)

If we are to have much confidence in our findings, we must find some way of including these additional factors in our research design. The first step is to decide what factors might be acting as intervening, alternative, conditional, or spurious causes. Although we clearly cannot include every possibility in our study, we can attempt to incorporate the more obvious ones, and even if practical obstacles prevent this, we should go through this reflective process in order to realize how much our results should be qualified.

We can help anticipate intervening variables by asking precisely how the independent variable would cause the dependent variable; for example, how would having a high income cause a man to be a Republican? It might be that high income causes more concern about maintaining possessions, that the GOP is viewed as the party most likely to keep wealthy people wealthy, and thus that rich people are Republicans; it might be that high incomes cause political conservatism which causes a Republican affiliation; or it might be that there are no intervening variables.

Alternative causes are best foreseen by asking what else might cause the variation in the dependent variable. Your original review of the scholarly literature might provide some answers; personal experience might give you some more; and long, deep reflection might yield the remainder. Since political scientists rarely find that there is only one cause for a particular phenomenon, the need for including in the research design as many alternative possibilities as is practically feasible is quite evident.

Specifying conditional variables is best accomplished by asking whether the relationship would hold in all places, at all times, and for all groups, or whether it would be more likely to occur under one or more of these circumstances. If the answer is Yes, you have identified a possible conditional factor.

Not incorporating intervening variables, additional causes, or conditional factors in one's research design means that one's findings will be incomplete but not totally incorrect. Ignoring possible spurious arrangements, on the other hand, is done at the risk of mistakenly concluding that there is a causal relationship. Thus it is especially important to anticipate factors that might invalidate one's findings. A good starting point is to ask whether there is any factor which might cause both the independent and the dependent variables and whether that factor acts directly on the dependent variable (i.e., the orginal hypothesized cause is not an intervening variable). Say, for example, that your original hypothesis is that the higher the educational level, the more democratic a nation. What might cause a high level of education and democracy? One likely answer is economic development; thus you should structure your research design so that this possibility can be checked.

Once the possible confounding factors have been identified, what can be done to prevent them from clouding the findings? One general strategy is to randomize all factors except the independent and dependent variables. This approach—called *randomization*—aims at making the idea of all-other-things-being-equal a reality; if all other things really are equal, none of them could have any impact on the hypothesized relationship. Thus, for example, if your hypothesis stated again was that education was positively related to democracy, you would divide the set of nations into a specified number of groups according to their democratic score. In order to keep the example simple, let's say we have two groups on the democratic index: high and low. In order to assume randomization in this situation, both of these groups must have approximately the same distribution of values on every other possible confounding factor except for the independent variable: education; in other words, each group must have roughly identical distributions of GNP, colonial backgrounds, etc. It is, of course, highly unlikely that this will be the case; the two sets of nations will have different distributions on many other variables besides education.

This example points out the general inapplicability of the randomization strategy in the testing of political hypotheses, for in order to randomize all extraneous factors the investigator must be able to manipulate some of the phenomena. Using a fanciful version of the above example, in a randomized test the nations would be like marbles in one bucket; two groups of nations would then be randomly chosen from the main bucket and placed in two separate containers. Since the two groups had been chosen purely at random, thereby avoiding any intentional or unintentional selection bias, one can justifiably assume that each container had the same distribution of scores on both the dependent variable and all the possible confounding factors. Next, the investigator would apply a specified dose of education to the marbles in one of the two containers. Finally, after waiting a certain period of time in order that the independent variable (education) might have an opportunity to evoke the hypothesized causal impact, the investigator would measure democracy scores for the two containers to see if the education-treated group had a significantly higher democratic score than the group which did not receive the education dose.[5]

Designs using randomization, then, demand that the investigator be able to do two things: randomly assign subjects to different groups and manipulate the independent variable(s). In the above example, it is absurd to think that anyone could apply doses of education to a nation for the purpose of conducting a scientific test. Exceedingly rare is the political science hypothesis where both of these strategies can be used and where randomization strategy can be employed. Nonetheless, since it is such a powerful technique, you should be alert for those few cases where it can be applied. If, for example, you are interested in the impact of a piece of propaganda on certain political attitudes, you could randomly assign the subjects to two groups, expose one group to the technique, and then measure the attitudes.

Since randomization is generally impossible to achieve in political research, the only other available strategy is to measure any variable which might affect the meaning of the relationship between the original independent and dependent variables. Once measured, the possible arrange-

[5] This method of achieving randomization is one of many kinds of randomized designs. For an excellent exposition of this general type of research design, see Donald L. Campbell and Julian C. Stanley, *Experimental and Quasi-Experimental Designs for Research*, Chicago, Ill., Rand McNally, 1966.

ments (intervening, alternative, conditional, spurious) can be tested for their validity. It should be realized, however, that this strategy runs a poor second to randomization. Costs prevent the measurement of every conceivable confounding factor, and even if an unlimited budget were available, no one could possibly anticipate them all anyway; commonly, only the most obvious confounding factors can be included in the research design. The beauty of the randomization strategy is that it does not require that everything be thought out in advance.

CONCLUDING COMMENTS

After formulating strategies for testing hypotheses, we can now see that we require certain tools for implementing our research design. The remaining chapters will provide most of the necessary armament. Chapter 3 will present methods for measuring variables. Chapters 4 and 5 will discuss the major means for collecting the required information. Chapter 6 will explain statistical measures for describing single variables so that one can ascertain how each variable's values are distributed. Chapter 7 will present techniques for determining the amount of common variation between a single independent variable and a single dependent variable. Chapter 8 will explain methods for determining how two or more independent variables are associated with a dependent variable. Chapter 9 will show how to go about calculating the risk involved in concluding that a certain amount of common variation in a sample of subjects means that the variables are really related for the entire population. Finally, Chapter 10 will describe, from beginning to end, a political research project in order to demonstrate how the various elements of the research process interrelate.

In constructing a research design in political science, we should modestly accept the fact that there is no such thing as a definitive test—one which proves once and for all that a relationship is or is not so. Illusions of finality are dreams for several reasons. First, as we have already seen, relationships between concepts are not tested directly but rather through specified operational definitions of those concepts. Thus no single test can prove or disprove a conceptual relationship; it can only add or subtract from the evidence relating to such a relationship. Second, at least at the present state of development in the study of politics, all relationships are partially if not completely time-bound and culture-bound. Generally, they apply only to certain times and places in man's earthly existence. Third, and connected with the second point, there is one dimension of man's existence which is impossible to test: his future experience. Even though some proposition might have been tested (and never disproved) for every time and place up until now, there is no airtight guarantee (just an extremely high probability) that the proposition will hold true tomorrow; we simply cannot know for certain until tomorrow's test comes.

EXERCISES

1 Develop a ten-item bibliography, including both books and articles, for one of the following concepts: political participation, political alienation, political party identification, political modernization, and liberal policy attitudes. For each citation, give a one-paragraph summary of the material.

2 Develop three alternative ways of operationalizing one of the concepts listed above.

3 Suggest one alternative, one intervening, one conditional, and one spurious cause for each of the following two-variable hypotheses:
   a. the more political information a person has, the greater the likelihood that he will participate in political activities;
   b. the greater the proportion of college graduates in a city, the more likely that it will have a city-manager form of government; and
   c. the wealthier a nation, the more likely that it will be politically stable.

4 Develop a research design: State the hypothesis, operationalize the terms, and formulate the testing strategy.

3 MEASURING POLITICAL PHENOMENA

Measurement is a crucial step in the scientific process, for we cannot test the relationships between phenomena unless we can measure them. As we saw in the preceding chapter, each concept or variable in the hypothesis must be operationally defined in order to provide a set of procedures for measuring the relevant segment of reality. For example, the operational definition "number of years of formal education" tells us that a person who spent three years in a school should receive a score of 3, and so forth. Thus when we measure something, we are assigning numerals to things according to rules provided by the operational definition. This chapter will consider the different levels at which measurement can occur, discuss methods for combining individual measures into more comprehensive indexes or scales, and present procedures for determining the amount of confidence we can place in a measurement instrument.

LEVELS OF MEASUREMENT

When we set out to measure phenomena, we quickly discover that not all of them can be measured in the same way. If the variable is family income, we can employ numbers in the manner we have been taught to use them: We can say that one person has an income of $10,000, another an income of $7,000, and a third an income of $3,000, and then make a valid statement that the last two incomes add up to the first. On the other hand, if the variable is political party identification, the numbers cannot be employed in the same fashion; even if we assign 1 to a Democrat, 2 to a Republican, and 3 to an Independent, it does not make sense to conclude that one Democrat plus one Republican equals one Independent, even though arithmetically $1 + 2 = 3$.

This example points up the fact that numbers can be used in different ways in the measurement process. Broadly speaking, they can be used first merely as symbols or names (*nominal measurements*) for particular groups such as political parties; second, numbers can be used to signify ordered relationships (*ordinal measurements*), as when we assign a liberalism score of 5 to one man and a score of 3 to another, thereby indicating that the first is more liberal than the second, even though we do not know how much more liberal he is; third, numbers can be used to express relative differences or intervals (*interval measurements*) between things, as in the statement that the interval between $3,000 and $4,000 (i.e., $1,000) is the same as the interval between $5,000 and $6,000; finally, numbers can be employed to express ratios between objects (*ratio measurements*), as in the statement that a 20-year-old man is twice as old as a 10-year-old boy. Let us take each of these four measurement levels and examine its characteristics in more detail.

Nominal categories are the simplest form of measurement since they merely involve dividing the phenomena into distinct groups and assigning a unique symbol (generally but not necessarily a numeral) to each group. In this measuring process all members of the same group are considered equal to each other and different from the members of the remaining groups. Thus all you need do to apply nominal measurements is to be able to categorize the phenomena so that each instance of it falls into one and only one group. Dividing nations into democratic and nondemocratic, sex into male and female, and race into white and nonwhite are examples of nominal measurement. When a complete classification of the phenomena into substantive categories is impossible, a catch-all category for the otherwise unclassifiable cases can be constructed.

Although nominal measurements hardly seem like measurements at all (and, indeed, a few purists deny them measurement status), certain arithmetic techniques can be applied to them. The cases in each category can be counted (e.g., there are 250 Democrats, 150 Republicans, and 100 Independents in the sample), ratios between categories can be computed (e.g., the ratio of Democrats to Republicans is 250:150 or 5:3), and the percentage of total cases in one category can be calculated (e.g., 100/500 or 20 percent of the sample are Independent). Moreover, as we shall see in succeeding chapters, there are statistical techniques for determining the degree and the significance of the relationship between two or more nominally measured variables. Two nominal scores, however, cannot be added, subtracted, multiplied, divided, or used in greater-than ($>$) or less-than ($<$) comparisons.

Like nominal measurements, ordinal measurements name or categorize things; in addition, they rank the categories so that for any pair you can say that one category is greater than (or less than) another. Thus in order to measure something on the ordinal level, you must be able both to categorize the variable so that each case falls into one and only one category *and* to rank the categories from highest to lowest. For example, we can ordinally measure liberalism by asking individuals whether they agree or disagree with three statements expressing liberal positions. We can then assign a score based on the number of agree responses, a score which might range from 3 (agrees with all three statements) for the most liberal to 0 (disagrees with all the statements) for the least liberal. Note that the choice of numbers to signify ordinal categories is partially arbitrary. Although the set 3, 2, 1, 0 is used here, any set in which the number assigned to the most liberal is greater than the second most liberal, and so forth, is acceptable; thus, in the current example, the set 24, 17, 9, 5 would be equally appropriate.

Any operation that can be applied to nominal measurements can be used with ordinal ones; hence, cases can be counted, ratios and percentages calculated, and, for two or more ordinal variables, the degree and significance of relationships determined. Moreover, although two ordinal scores cannot be added, subtracted, multiplied, or divided, greater-than and less-than comparisons can be made between them. (Example: One cannot say that a liberalism score of 1 plus a liberalism score of 2 equals a liberalism score of 3 because this operation assumes that there are constant units of liberalism—an assumption that is not well supported by the measuring instrument.)

Interval measurements not only categorize and order phenomena, they also provide a constant unit of measurement so that the extent of the difference between one score and another can be given. Thus, in order to use interval measurements, you must be able to categorize the variable so that each case falls into one and only one category, order the categories from highest to lowest, *and* measure the differences or intervals between categories in constant terms. Ratio measurements, in addition to having the above characteristics and requirements, have a nonarbitrary or natural zero point.

The distinction between interval and ratio is best exemplified in the measurement of temperature. The Fahrenheit scale is an interval measurement, since its zero point (0° Fahrenheit) does not mean that there is no heat; thus, while one can say the intervals on the Fahrenheit scale between, respectively, 0° and 30°, and between 30° and 60° are equal (i.e., a degree is a constant unit of measurement), it does not make sense to state that 60° is twice as hot as 30° (i.e., 60/30 = 2), since a natural zero is required before one can calculate ratios. The Kelvin scale, on the other hand, is a ratio measurement since it does have a natural zero point; 0° Kelvin (−278° Fahrenheit) does signify the complete absence of heat, and thus with the Kelvin scale, one can specify intervals and compute ratios. Since almost all the variables in political research which meet the interval requirements also fulfill the ratio criteria, we will not distinguish between the two in the remainder of the book but simply refer to both as *metric measurements.*

Metric measurements, of course, are numbers in the everyday sense of the term. They can be added, subtracted, multiplied, divided, and used in greater-than or less-than comparisons. The most frequently found metric political variables are percentages formed from nominal or ordinal measurements. For example, Democrat and Republican are nominal scores but the percentage of Democrats or Republicans in some collectivity (e.g., a county) is a metric measure.

You might have noticed how the requirements for each level of measurement are cumulative. Numbers can do three kinds of things: name, order, and specify intervals (i.e., have constant units) and ratios (i.e., have a natural zero). Nominal measurements only name, ordinal measurements name and order, and metric measurements name, order, and specify intervals and ratios. The mathematical operations appropriate for each level are also cumulative. For two nominal scores, the only appropriate mathematical operations are $=$ (equal) and $\neq$ (not equal); for ordinal scores, the legitimate operations are $=$, $\neq$, $>$, and $<$; and for metric scores, all normal mathematical operations (the above together with $+$, $-$, $\cdot$, and $\div$) are applicable.

The first set of comparisons (name, order, etc.) provides the key to understanding at what level a particular phenomenon can be measured. If all you can do is categorize it, then you must measure it nominally; if you can both categorize and order the phenomenon, then you can measure it nominally or ordinally; if you can categorize, order, and specify intervals and ratios, then you can use any level of measurement. The general rule is to use as high a level as possible since the higher the measurement level, the more information you have about the phenomenon. The second set of comparisons (appropriate mathematical operations) gives you guidelines for determining which statistical technique can be applied to your data. For example, if the technique requires that you be able to add and subtract the scores, then it can only be applied to phenomena that have been measured on the metric level; on the other hand, if the technique only calls for categorization, then it can be used for all three levels of measurement. On the whole, the higher the measurement level, the more powerful the statistical techniques which can be applied in the sense of providing fuller and more precise information. This fact reinforces the rule that one should measure at as high a level as possible.

INDEXES AND SCALES

If, as we suspect, many of the phenomena relevant for political research are very complex, then no single indicator is likely to be capable of capturing their central meaning. In cases like this, we must combine several individual indicators into either an overall *index* or an overall *scale* in order to do an adequate measuring job. In our usage of the terms, an index refers to a situation where there is no statistical evidence that the composite indicators are interrelated; conversely, a scale is a set of statistically interrelated indicators.

In constructing an index, two decisions must be made: What indicators shall make up the index? How shall they be combined? In deciding which indicators to include, the goal is to have each major aspect of the phe-nomenon represented. In effect, we must go through a process equivalent to operationalizing a concept: state the concept, divide it into variables, and operationally define each variable. Once the concept has been dis-sected, you must determine how the components shall be combined. Should each aspect or variable receive equal weight, or should certain variables be given more emphasis? In order to clarify these two index-construction de-cisions as well as review the three measurement levels, let us in turn examine a nominal, ordinal, and metric index.

A nominal index is a *typology*. If the index involves two variables (A and B) and each variable has two categories (1 and 2), then there are four pos-sible combinations or types (A_1B_1, A_1B_2, A_2B_1, and A_2B_2). Therefore, once the component variables and their categories have been enumerated, the com-bination rule for a nominal index always is all possible combinations. For example, let's say we want to measure the power structure (our concept) in political systems, and that according to the conceptual scheme the two component variables are the political leadership's ideology—categorized as either compatible (members of the elite have similar ideologies) or as con-flicting (elite members have different ideologies)—and the distribution of political power among citizens—categorized as either broad or narrow.[1] Combining these two variables, we have four possible combinations, repre-sented by the four blocks or cells in Figure 3.1. Finally, if we wish, we can devise appropriate descriptive terms (e.g., consensual mass) for each combination or type.

A nation's social homogeneity is an example of a concept which can be measured by an ordinal index, since a country could be more or less socially homogeneous. We might be interested in testing whether a nation's social homogeneity is positively related to its political stability. Excluding economic differences from our conceptual definition, let us say that the three major aspects (variables) of social homogeneity are religion, race, and language; on straight definitional grounds, the greater the tendency for the nation to have the same religion, race, and language, the more socially homogeneous it is. Next, we must operationally define the variables. For each of the three variables, let us assign a score of 3 to nations where 85 percent or more of the population have the same religion (race, lan-guage), 2 where more than 50 percent but less than 85 percent of the population have the same religion (race, language), and 1 where less than 50 percent of the population have the same religion (race, language). Thus, a nation which is 90 percent Catholic, 60 percent white, and where the most common language is spoken by 35 percent of the population would have a religious homogeneity score of 3, a racial homogeneity score of 2, and a linguistic homogeneity score of 1. In combining these three indi-

[1] This example is taken from Robert E. Agger, Daniel Goldrich, and Bert E. Swanson, *The Rulers and the Ruled*, New York, John Wiley, 1964, pp. 73–78.

	Distribution of Political Power among Citizens	
Political Leadership's Ideology	Broad	Narrow
Compatible	Consensual mass	Consensual elite
Conflicting	Competitive mass	Competitive elite

FIGURE 3-1 A nominal index
SOURCE: Robert E. Agger, Daniel Goldrich and Bert E. Swanson, *The Rulers and the Ruled,* New York, John Wiley, 1964, Figure 3-1, p. 73, with the permission of the publisher.

cators into a social homogeneity index, we might wish to weight one factor (say, religion) more than the others on the grounds that religious differences are most important for social homegeneity; if we do this and if we decide that religion is twice as important as either race or language, then our combination rule or equation would be:

$$\text{Social homogeneity score} = 2\,(\text{Religious score}) + (\text{Linguistic score}) + (\text{Racial score})$$

On the other hand, if we did not have any reasons for considering one aspect more critical than another, then the most sensible rule would be to weight them all equally, in which case the combination rule would be:

$$\text{Social homogeneity score} = (\text{Religious score}) + (\text{Linguistic score}) + (\text{Racial score})$$

In the latter instance, the social homogeneity index would go from 9 (3 on all variables, reflecting high homogeneity) down to 3 (1 on all variables, indicating low homogeneity). One major difficulty with this and most other ordinal and metric indexes lies in the interpretation of the intermediate scores—(in the homogeneity example, those between 4 and 8). Suppose that a particular nation had a social homogeneity score of 5. There are six different combinations of religious, racial, and linguistic scores (3-1-1, 1-3-1, 1-1-3, 2-2-1, 2-1-2, 1-2-2) that total five. Hence, the index assumes that all six of these combinations result in precisely the same amount of social homogeneity; moreover, when you are only given the total index score, you have no way of knowing which combination of the component factors compose it. Most ordinal and metric indexes, in sum, treat different combinations of the component variables as equal and discard information about the specific indicators.

Finally, let us consider a metric index. One of the most common explanatory concepts in political research is socioeconomic status (SES), a phenomenon which is certainly complex enough to require an index. How might we construct a metric SES index? First, we have to determine the major aspects of SES. Let us choose income, education, and occupation, so that the higher an income, the more education, and the more prestigious occupation a man has, the higher his SES. In order to avoid the problem of determining the occupational prestige of students and housewives, the index is aimed only at heads of households. Next, we need operational definitions for each variable. Let us make the income indicator the annual family income in dollars, the education indicator the number of years the head of the household attended school, and the occupational indicator the mean prestige rating (from 0 to 100) given it by a recent national sample.[2] (Although one cannot be certain that the prestige units are equal [e.g., that the interval between a prestige-ranking of 10 and 20 equals the interval between 30 and 40], investigators frequently assume that such extended ordinal measurements constitute metric indicators, since it is likely that the prestige units are roughly equal. We make such an assumption here.) Finally, in order to obtain the SES index, we must formulate a combination rule. Assuming that each component deserves equal weighting, the combination rule would be:

$$SES = \text{Income score} + \text{Education score} + \text{Occupation score}$$

Unlike the social homogeneity index, however, we cannot simply add up the three scores, since each is measured in different units: income in dollars, education in years, and occupation in prestige scores. We first must find a common yardstick for all three. Since the occupation scores might be the most difficult to transform, and since they are already arrayed from

---

[2] Such a set of ratings can be found in Albert J. Reiss, Jr., et al., *Occupations and Social Status*, Glencoe, Ill., Free Press, 1961.

0 to 100, the most workable procedure is to transform income and education scores into quasi-prestige units which range from 0 to 100. One way of doing this is to ask what is the relative standing among American household heads of individuals with a specified income and education. Suppose a person's income is $7,100. If we can find out how many household heads make less than $7,100, then we have pinpointed his relative income position. Turning to the U. S. Census figures (national surveys giving educational and income distributions could also be used), suppose we find that 69 percent make less than $7,100. Thus, this person ranks higher than 69 percent of the population, and by deduction, lower than 31 percent of the population; therefore, on a 0-100 index, we can assign him a score of 70 which indicates his relative position. (These scores are known as *percentiles* since they divide any distribution of scores into 100 equal groups.) Once the relative positions for income and education have been determined, then the three scores can be added together to obtain the SES index. Again, note that different combinations of the three variables can yield the same SES score.

Although indexes enable us to combine several separate indicators into one overall measure, thereby giving us a better chance to capture a complex phenomenon, they are less than satisfactory in two ways. First, we are uncertain whether the components of any index are empirically interrelated or whether, instead, an index is unwittingly and arbitrarily combining apples and stones. Second, the fact that a single value of an index can frequently represent several different combinations of the component indicators often makes for imprecise measurement. For these reasons, some kind of scale should be used instead of indexes whenever possible; however, situations occur when it is impossible or impractical to use scales. In such cases, we should gather as much evidence as possible about the interrelationships among the index components (e.g., by using the measures of association presented in Chapter 7 to discover the degree of covariation between the components).

Cumulative or *Guttman scales* not only combine several individual indicators into one measure, but they also provide a means for testing the proposition that the index's components are interrelated and produce a measuring instrument which yields a unique score for each combination of indicators.[3]

Let us begin our discussion of the cumulative scale by tracing the logic behind it. If we think that a certain concept—say, white Americans' integration sentiments—forms a scale, then graphically we are stating that

[3] This method of combining indicators was developed by Louis Guttman; hence the name Guttman scales. For the original exposition of the technique, see Guttman, "The Basis for Scalogram Analysis," in Samuel A. Stouffer *et al.* (eds.), *Measurement and Prediction*, Princeton, N.J., Princeton University Press, 1950, pp. 60–90.

there is a single line or dimension whose polarities are pro-integration and anti-integration:

Anti-integration ——————————— Pro-integration

If an integration scale actually exists, then each American would be located at some point on the line. For example, Rufus Redneck (RR), Charlie Middleclass (CM), Goody Intentions (GI), and Whitey Liberal (WL) might have these positions:

Anti-integration ——————————— Pro-integration

Cases (people) RR   CM   GI   WL

Finally, if there is an integration scale, then any question dealing with integration would intersect the line at a specific point. For example, the question "Do you think blacks should be sent back to Africa?" (Question A) might intersect the line close to the anti-integration end since we might expect only a few people to take an anti-integration position on this question; Rufus might agree, but the other three gentlemen would probably disagree. Say we have five integration questions ranging from a pro-integration answer for the back-to-Africa item (Question A) where most white people would give an integrationist response, to a question (Question E) where most white people would be expected to take an anti-integrationist position: "If you were a father, would you allow your daughter to marry a black or would you forbid her to do so?" The questions might intersect the integration dimensions in the following manner:

Item (question)   A   B   C   D   E

Scale score   0 . 1 . 2 . 3 . 4 . 5

Anti-integration ——————————— Pro-integration

Cases (people) RR   CM   GI   WL

According to this model, if we asked each of the four persons to answer all five questions, we would expect Rufus to given an anti-integrationist response to all five, Charlie to give a pro-integrationist response to A and B and an anti-integrationist response to C, D, and E, Goody to be pro-integrationist on A, B, and C and anti-integrationist on D and E, and Whitey to be pro-integrationist on all questions except E. More generally, we would expect any individual to respond positively to any question which cuts the line to the left of his position and to respond negatively to any question which cuts the line to the right of his position. We would then assign an integration scale score to each individual based on the number of pro-integration responses; in this example, Rufus would get 0, Charlie 2, Goody 3, and Whitey 4. These scores are ordinal measurements, since we do not know the extent to which Charlie's integrationist sentiments exceed Rufus's, although we can normally make these ordinal measurements more precise by including more questions in the scale. In addition, there is a unique score for each combination of items; the only way to get a score of 2, for example, is to give a pro-integrationist response to Questions A and B and an anti-integrationist response to C, D, and E.

Up to this point, the discussion has been entirely hypothetical. How can we determine whether this model fits reality? The key test is whether the questions we have selected actually cut the hypothesized dimension in some consistent order. If the model outlined above is empirically correct, then only certain sets of responses can be given. Anybody giving an anti-integrationist response to Question A (the back-to-Africa item) should, according to the model, also give an anti-integrationist response on all of the remaining questions. The correct sets of responses, if the questions are actually ordered in their likelihood of receiving a pro-integrationist answer from A (lowest likelihood), to B (next lowest likelihood), on up to E (highest likelihood), are:

| | Questions | | | | | |
Set of responses	A	B	C	D	E	Scale score
I	−	−	−	−	−	0
II	−	−	−	−	+	1
III	−	−	−	+	+	2
IV	−	−	+	+	+	3
V	−	+	+	+	+	4
VI	+	+	+	+	+	5

where a − indicates an anti-integrationist response and a + indicates a pro-integrationist answer. If a person does not have one of these sets of answers (say, he gives a pro-integrationist response only on C), then for this particular respondent, the questions divide the line in a different order (A, B, D, E, C). If, for all respondents, there is no consistent order in which the questions are ranked, then one cannot support the assumption that a scale exists; one must either abandon the assumption that there is an integration-sentiment scale or begin a search for a new set of questions which might form a one-dimension (or unidimensional) scale. According to conventional practice, the consistent order assumption can be accepted when:

1. The number of responses fitting the assumed pattern (known as *scalar responses*) is 90 percent or more of the total number of possible responses. This percentage is called the *coefficient of reproducibility* (CR).

2. The number of non-scalar responses is 40 percent or less of the total number of responses which can be classified as non-scalar. This percent-

age, known as the *coefficient of scalability* (CS) and generally expressed as one minus the ratio of actual-to-total possible nonscalar responses (i.e., CS must be 60 percent or more), is necessary because some sets of questions will by chance alone approximate or achieve a CR $\lesseqgtr$ .90.

Given this background, let us now go through the entire process of constructing a cumulative scale. The first step is to decide on a concept. For our example, we shall continue with white Americans' integration sentiments, which can be conceptually defined as "the willingness (of whites) to allow blacks to take part in various types of activities."[4] In specifying a supposedly scalable concept, we should define not only the concept itself but also the population to whom the concept applies (e.g., all white adult Americans). Some concepts might scale for some populations but not for others; for example, an integration scale appropriate for whites might appear nonsensical when applied to blacks, or a score suitable for Americans might not be relevant for Malaysians.

Once the concept and population have been specified, the second step is to select, from the universe of all possible items, a subset that will cut the line or dimension from one end to the other. The more items used, the more numerous the cuts; the more cuts, the more possible scores; the more scores, the more precise the measurement. In the above example, five items yielded six scores; in general, the number of possible scores is the number of items plus one. Collection costs, however, place an upper limit on the number of items which can be included. Assuming that one is interested in collecting information on several concepts in any research project, it is rather difficult to justify devoting a large amount of effort to measuring any one concept; so there are rarely more than twenty items employed—five to ten being the typical number. In addition to deciding on how many items to include, the different pro–anti splits must be determined; in graphic terms, the cuts have to be arrayed across the entire line. If this is not done, then the scale has large areas where there is no differentiation, where it would be difficult to distinguish between a mild or strong anti-integrationist. In order to maximize the chances of having a set of items which spread across the continuum and form a scale, one common selection practice is to apply a large number of items (30 to 50) to a small group of people (20 to 40) and then to choose a small subset of items which fit the criteria; this procedure assumes that the results achieved for the small sample will hold for the larger population. In our example, we will use the eight items given in Table 3.1.

The responses to these questions have been categorized as either pro-integration (*) or anti-integration (no asterisk) because the procedures for constructing cumulative scales are much simpler when there are only two

---

[4] The scale example is taken from Paul Sheatsley, "White Attitudes Toward the Negro," *Daedalus*, 95 (Winter, 1966), 217–238; minor changes have been made in the scale for pedagogical purposes.

TABLE 3.1 GUTTMAN SCALE OF INTEGRATION SENTIMENTS

Percentage giving pro-integration response (*)	Item or question
80	1. Do you think *a) Negroes should have as good a chance as white people to get any kind of job? or b) White people should have the first chance at any kind of job?
70	2. Generally speaking, do you think there should be separate sections for Negroes in streetcars and buses? *a) No b) Yes
60	3. Do you think Negroes should have the right to use the same parks, restaurants, and hotels as white people? a) No *b) Yes
55	4. Do you think white students and Negro students should go to *a) the same schools or b) separate schools
50	5. How strongly would you object if a member of your family wanted to bring a Negro friend home to dinner? a) Quite a bit or somewhat *b) Not at all
40	6. White people have a right to keep Negroes out of their neighborhoods if they want to, and Negroes should respect that right. a) Agree *b) Disagree
30	7. Do you think there should be laws against marriage between Negroes and whites? *a) No b) Yes
20	8. Negroes shouldn't push themselves where they're not wanted. a) Agree *b) Disagree

SOURCE: Paul Sheatsley, "White Attitudes Toward the Negro," *Daedalus, 95* (Winter, 1966), 234, Table 2, with permission of the publisher.

alternatives or a *dichotomy*; one can, however, form scales from three or more alternative responses.

After selecting the items and dichotomizing the alternatives, we obtain the responses from the subjects we are investigating. First, we check to see if the items' pro–anti distributions are spread out; in this case, the percentage of pro-integration responses go from 20 to 80 percent in fairly even intervals, so that if there is a scale, the cuts will be arrayed across most of the dimension. We then must calculate CR and CS to test the assumption that there is a scale and, if the scale assumption is upheld, assign scores to each case or respondent. Although computer programs and special mechanical devices (*scalogram boards*) have been devised in order to ease the burdensome calculation task, we shall use the old paper-and-pencil technique so that you can see how the computations are done. Table 3.2 displays the response patterns, so that the questions are ordered from left to right by the number of pro-integrationist responses, and the

TABLE 3.2 HYPOTHETICAL RESPONSE PATTERNS FOR AN INTEGRATION-SENTIMENT SCALE

Case	Question 1	2	3	4	5	6	7	8	Errors	+	−	Scale score
A	+	+	+	+	+	+	+	+	0	8	0	8
B	+	+	+	+	+	+	+	+	0	8	0	8
C	+	+	+	+	(−)	+	+	+	1	7	1	8
D	+	+	+	+	+	+	+	−	0	7	1	7
E	+	+	+	+	+	+	+	−	0	7	1	7
F	+	+	+	+	+	+	+	−	0	7	1	7
G	+	+	+	+	0	+	−	(+)	1	6	1	6
H	+	+	+	+	+	−	−	−	0	5	3	5
I	+	+	+	+	+	−	−	−	0	5	3	5
J	+	0	+	+	+	−	−	−	0	4	3	5
K	+	+	(−)	+	+	−	−	−	1	4	4	5
L	+	(−)	+	(−)	+	−	−	−	2	3	5	?
M	+	+	+	−	−	−	−	−	0	3	5	3
N	+	+	−	−	−	−	−	−	0	2	6	2
O	+	+	−	−	−	−	−	−	0	2	6	2
P	+	−	−	−	0	−	−	−	0	1	6	1
Q	(−)	+	−	−	−	−	−	−	1	1	7	2
R	−	−	−	−	−	(+)	−	−	1	1	7	0
S	−	−	−	−	−	−	−	−	0	0	8	0
T	−	−	−	−	−	−	−	−	0	0	8	0
								Total	7	81	76	
Total (+)	16	14	12	11	10	8	6	4	81			
Total (−)	4	5	8	9	8	12	14	16	76			
Total (+ or −)	20	19	20	20	18	20	20	20	157			
Errors	1	1	1	1	1	1	0	1	7			

Legend: + = pro-integrationist response
    − = anti-integrationist response
    0 = no answer
    ( ) = error

cases or respondents are ranked from top to bottom by the number of pro-integrationist responses. (The questions and cases could also be ranked in the reverse order, i.e., by the number of anti-integrationist responses.)

Our first step is to identify the error responses (i.e., those which do not fit the hypothesized scale pattern). The rule for counting errors is the minimum number of changes that must be made in order to turn an individual's set of responses into a perfect scale pattern. For example, Respondent Q has only one error since either changing his response to Question 1 from negative to positive or changing his Question 2 response in the opposite direction would give him a perfect scale pattern; conversely, two of Respondent L's answers (either on Questions 2 and 4 or on Questions 3 and 5) must be changed in order to get a perfect pattern. In all, there are 7 errors. Since the total number of plus-or-minus responses is 157, then the number of correct (i.e., fit the scale pattern) responses is 157 − 7 or 150 and

$$CR = \frac{150}{157} = .955$$

Since the CR is greater than .90, this scale passes the reproducibility test.

Calculating CS is a bit more complex since we must first determine the maximum number of errors (ME) that could occur. To do this, we compute the ME given the distribution of responses by items (the greater the difference between pro- and anti-response percentages, the fewer errors could occur), and the ME given the distribution of responses by individuals (the more extreme the individuals on either the pro- or anti- end, the fewer errors could occur); we then take the smaller of these two figures and divide it into the number of errors that actually did occur. For any particular dichotomous item, the ME is equal to the number of times the less popular alternative is selected; for example, the ME for Question 1 is 4. Why is this so? Because if you changed the four negative responses to Question 1 to positive answers, there would be no way in which errors could occur. Similarly, the MEs for Questions 2 through 8 are respectively 5, 8, 9, 8, 8, 6, and 4, for a total ME (Items) of 52. For any individual responding to a dichotomous item the ME is equal to the number of times an individual gave the less popular (for him) response; for example, Respondent D's ME is 1. The reasoning is the same as before: Only one of D's responses need be changed in order to make him a perfect scale type. If an item or individual has the same number of pro- and anti-responses (e.g., Respondent K), then either one can be considered the less popular. The total ME for all respondents is 31. Since the ME for the cases is smaller than the ME for the items, this indicates that the respondents are more extreme than the items and that we should use the ME (Cases) in our calculations. The formula for CS is

$$CS = 1 - \frac{Errors}{Maximum\ errors\ (Cases\ or\ Items,\ whichever\ is\ less)}$$

or, in this example

$$CS = 1 - \frac{7}{31} = .774$$

Since the CS is greater than the standard criterion of .60 (and since the CR > .90), we are justified in assuming that this set of items forms a scale. If the CR, the CS, or both fail to meet the .90 and .60 criteria, the scale can be salvaged by dropping the item which has the most errors and recomputing the two coefficients to see if they would then meet the standards. If eliminating one item does not yield a satisfactory CR and CS, the item contributing the next greatest number of errors can be dropped, and so forth. If after three or four successive item eliminations the remaining items still do not constitute a cumulative scale, then it is better to start anew.

The next job is to assign a scale score to each case. First, we arbitrarily decide that a high score shall indicate pro-integration and a low score anti-integration. For perfect scale types (Respondents A, B, D, E, F, H, I, M, N, O, S, and T), the scale score is simply the number of pro-integrationist responses. For respondents who did not answer one of the questions (e.g., Respondents J and P), who had one error (Respondents C, K, Q, and R), or who had both (Respondent G), the no-answer-or-error response is changed so that a perfect scale type occurs and the appropriate score is then assigned; if a perfect scale type would occur no matter how the no-answer-or-error response was changed (e.g., + + + + + 0 − −), then it should be assigned the value which gives it the score closest to the middle value (e.g., + + + + + − − − or 5). For respondents having two or more errors on an eight-item scale (Respondent L), or, more generally, for cases having more than 20 percent errors, it is best to eliminate them from the analysis on the grounds that the scale does not apply to them.

Up to now our discussion of cumulative scales has dealt entirely with the measurement of attitudinal concepts. Guttman scales, however, are also quite useful in the analysis of legislative and judicial roll-call voting behavior. Scaling is employed in these research areas in two ways. The first application corresponds quite closely with the use of scales in attitudinal measurement: One hypothesizes the existence of some concept (e.g., liberalism/conservatism), tests whether a single dimension underlies a set of votes chosen to represent that concept (e.g., medicare, aid-to-education, or social-security benefits, etc.) and if a dimension is found, scores the legislators or judges on that concept. In this application, the votes are treated as items or questions and the legislators or judges as cases or respondents.[5]

The second application arises when one is interested in discovering how

---

[5] For a legislative example, see Leroy Rieselbach, *The Roots of Isolationism*, Indianapolis, Ind., Bobbs-Merrill, 1967; for a judicial application, see Glendon Schubert, *The Judicial Mind*, Evanston, Ill., Northwestern University Press, 1965.

many empirically distinguishable issue-dimensions underlie a session or sessions of a legislature or court. For example, did most of the votes by the U.S. House of Representatives in 1967 fall along one dimension or were they scattered among many dimensions? In this context, scaling is used to measure the concentration/dispersion of conflict. On the whole, the scale-calculation procedures outlined above will be inappropriate for this kind of scale analysis since, among other difficulties, the number of items is too large (typically, over one hundred) for pencil-and-paper techniques. Instead, we must engage in a preliminary search in order to discover how votes are related to other votes. This means that for a legislative session involving 150 record votes one must measure the degree of relationship between each pair of roll calls.[6] If all the votes are strongly related to each other, this implies that there is only one dimension; if the votes fall into three or four major subsets of twenty to thirty votes each, with each subset containing votes that relate strongly to each other but weakly to votes in the other subsets, this means that three or four dimensions dominate; and if there are very few strong relationships between votes, this implies that almost every vote reflects a unique issue. Once subsets have been identified, one can then proceed to construct scales in the manner already outlined.

Cumulative or Guttman scales, in sum, are useful for measuring attitudinal concepts from questions or votes; the underlying logic is straightforward, only an ordinal measurement level must be assumed, and the calculation procedures—while somewhat burdensome—require no great mathematical skills. You should remember, however, that a cumulative scale is not conclusive proof that a certain concept exists. It could be that the particular set of items refers to some other concept or to two or more highly (but not perfectly) related concepts. In addition, the fact that a particular item fits into one scale does not mean that it is a pure reflection of the scale's concept and is hence totally unrelated to every other concept. Most items are sufficiently complex to contain two or more conceptual notions (Example: Some of the integration items might also fit on a sociability scale.). Thus, in this sense, cumulative scales oversimplify by considering only one of many possible concepts underlying a specific item.

Two other techniques—*item analysis* and *factor analysis*—can be used

---

[6] Measuring the degree of relationship between two variables will be covered in Chapter 7. The coefficient most commonly used for ascertaining the relationship between roll calls is Yule's Q. For an elaboration of the use of this coefficient in roll-call research, see Duncan MacRae, Jr., "A Method for Identifying Issues and Factions from Legislative Votes," *American Political Science Review*, 59 (December, 1965), 909–926; and Lee F. Anderson, Meredith W. Watts, Jr., and Allen R. Wilcox, *Legislative Roll-Call Analysis*, Evanston, Ill., Northwestern University Press, 1966, chap. 6. The latter work is a useful compendium of techniques for analyzing both legislative and judicial voting behavior.

to construct scales. Only a brief verbal description will be offered here.[7] Item analysis is a formalized version of testing the interrelationships among index components. The most common way of constructing an item-analysis scale is to select a set of items which might represent the concept, compute an overall score for a pretest group, correlate each item with the overall score, and use only those items which have strong relationships (as revealed by a measure of association) with the overall score. For this final set of highly correlated items, one can either assign them equal weight in the computation of the final scale score, or each item's weight can be proportional to the strength of its relationship with the overall score (i.e., the stronger the item's relationship, the more weight it is given in the final scale).

Factor analysis is not one specific set of procedures, but rather a variety of methods having similar characteristics. Whereas cumulative scaling is used more to find specific items to measure concepts which have already been posited, factor analysis is most often employed to induce concepts from a preexisting set of items. In general, factor analysis proceeds by taking a set of items, computing the degree of relationship between each pair of items, and statistically analyzing this set of intercorrelations (or *correlation matrix*) in order to ascertain how many empirically distinct dimensions underlie the items. Although it is similar to the second application of cumulative scaling to roll-call votes, it differs in that a specific item can conceivably be located on more than one dimension. For example, a factor analysis of legislative roll calls might yield two dimensions, which we decide to label "economic policy" and "welfare policy"; a particular item—say a vote on increasing social-security benefits—might be moderately related to the economic-policy factor and strongly associated with the welfare-policy factor. Assigning labels to factors is an inductive process. One inspects the items which are highly correlated with (or *loaded on*) a particular factor and induces (i.e., intelligently guesses) what the core meaning of these items might be. Thus, factor analysis can help identify the complexity or multidimensionality of specific phenomena.

The diversity of factor analysis comes in selecting which measure of association to use in computing the relationship between each specific item and

[7] Item analysis is rarely used in political research; factor analysis, on the other hand, is being increasingly applied in political investigations. The standard texts are Benjamin Fruchter, *Introduction to Factor Analysis*, New York, Van Nostrand-Reinhold, 1954; and Harry Harman, *Modern Factor Analysis*, Chicago, University of Chicago Press, 1960. Sample political applications can be found in G. R. Boynton, Samuel C. Patterson, and Ronald D. Hedlund, "The Structure of Public Support for Legislative Institutions," *Midwest Journal of Political Science, 12* (May, 1968), 163–180; John Grumm, "A Factor Analysis of Legislative Behavior," *Midwest Journal of Political Science, 7* (November, 1963), 336–356; and Richard I. Hofferbert, "Socioeconomic Dimensions of the American States: 1890–1960," *Midwest Journal of Political Science, 12* (August, 1968), 401–418.

in choosing the criteria for extracting factors from the correlation matrix. Concentrating on the latter differentiation, shall we use a method where none of the factors is related to each other (*orthogonal rotation*) or one where the factors are allowed to have some intercorrelation (*oblique rotation*)? How many factors do we wish to find? Would we like one major factor and three minor ones, or would we prefer four moderate factors? The point is that unless one carefully considers each of these criteria and fully realizes the implications of the particular brand of factor analysis being employed, he is quite apt to misinterpret his findings. Like any powerful weapon—and factor analysis is statistically potent—it should be used only by those who know it well.

RELIABILITY AND VALIDITY

The preceding discussion of measurement has dealt with choosing appropriate levels and developing indexes and scales which do justice to complex phenomena and which are, in the case of scales, internally related or homogeneous. Two important questions remain: Is the measurement reliable or consistent? Is it actually measuring what we think it is measuring? These two qualities of any measurement—called, respectively, *reliability* and *validity*—are especially critical in the measurement of human attitudes and behavior.

A reliable measurement consistently assigns the same score to the same phenomenon. For example, if we measure an adult's height on two successive days, a reliable yardstick will give us the same number of inches each day. There are two ways to construe reliability: internal consistency of items in a scale or index and external consistency of any measuring instrument. The first kind of reliability—internal consistency—refers to the tendency for the items in an index or scale to relate to each other, an aspect we have already discussed as the degree of interrelationship within an index or scale. We mention it here because some investigators refer to this property as reliability, and because, all other things being equal, the more interrelated a set of items, the more likely it is that the scale they form will yield reliable measurements.[8]

A measurement is externally consistent if it assigns the same score to identical phenomena measured at the same time (e.g., if two people are equally conservative, a reliable conservatism scale would give them the same score) or gives a very similar score to the same phenomenon measured at two different times (e.g., a conservative person should receive approximately the same score each time he is measured). In attempting to judge the external consistency of any measurement, we cannot use a test

[8] For more on this aspect of reliability, including formulas for computing homogeneity, see William A. Scott, "Attitude Measurement," in Gardner Lindzey and Elliot Aronson (eds.), *Handbook of Social Psychology*, 2nd ed., Reading, Mass., Addison-Wesley, 1968, vol. 2, pp. 256–257.

in which identical phenomena receive the same score, because we do not know whether the phenomena are identical until we have measured them. Instead, we must rely on a test-retest procedure on the same set of subjects in order to ascertain reliability. We must apply the measurement instrument at two different times and then compare the similarity or consistency of the scores. Again, measures of association such as those discussed in Chapter 7 are employed in these comparisons. Even this means of testing reliability has its problems. First, we cannot reasonably expect every subject to receive the same score each time; random measurement errors, resulting from factors like misunderstood items or variations in subject dispositions, are bound to occur. Accordingly, we cannot use perfect association as evidence for reliability and lack of complete association as the absence of reliability. Second, if the time between the two measurements is lengthy, difference in scores might be reflecting real changes (e.g., people can become more or less integrationist) rather than lack of reliability. Conversely, if the intervening period is quite short (say, a day or two), individuals remembering their responses on the first test while taking the second might artificially inflate the reliability. Third, it is not always possible to conduct two tests for all subjects. If, for example, the subjects were a national sample of 1,500 to 2,000, a second test would be a very expensive proposition.

What can we do about these three problems? First, judging what constitutes satisfactory reliability depends on the importance attached to fine discriminations (as opposed to rough differences) and the subjects' homogeneity on the variable being measured. If the subjects tend to have similar scores on the variables or if you are particularly interested in making close distinctions between subjects (e.g., between a strong conservative and a very strong conservative) or both, then you need higher reliability than if the subjects vary widely on the variable or if you are simply interested in separating extremes (e.g., strong conservatives and strong liberals). Second, in choosing a time interval for the two tests short enough to minimize the amount of actual change and long enough to maximize the subjects forgetting their answers to the first test, past practice indicates that two to four weeks is the best period for most variables. Third, when practical considerations prevent two tests for all subjects, one can employ a smaller group in order to gauge reliability. This preliminary group should not be a subset of the same subjects that will be tested in the actual study, since the fact that some of the subjects would have seen the test might contaminate the results. The reliability test group should, however, be sociologically similar to the actual study group since what is a reliable instrument for one group (e.g., college students) might not be a consistent device for another group (e.g., ghetto residents).

In the event that the reliability of an instrument is unsatisfactory, what can be done to increase it? The most common cure is to increase the number of items in the scale or index. This has the effect of decreasing the relative impact of random measurement errors and thereby enables one to make finer distinctions. Using a baseball analogy, the more times-at-bat of a player, the more reliable his batting average as a measurement of hitting skill.

Even though a measurement is reliable, it might not be valid; instead, it might be consistently measuring the wrong thing. How do we go about deciding whether we are measuring what we want to measure? The first judgment concerning validity is made by the person making the measurement. Quite obviously you do not use a particular measurement for a variable unless you think it actually measures that variable. Nonetheless, an individual's judgment, or a series of individual judgments (e.g., asking some experts about the measurement's validity) is not enough. We need some additional checks.

Since the only way we know something scientifically is to measure it, any validity test must involve comparing one measurement of the variable with one or more additional measurements of the variables, and seeing if the several measurements jibe. Thus any validity test is indirect, and when we question a measurement's validity, we are in effect questioning its relationship to other kinds of measurements. Three overlapping types of checks —not all of which are necessarily applicable in every case—are used to test validity. They are *discrimination of known groups, behavioral validation,* and *construct or conceptual validation.*

If a measurement is valid, it should discriminate between groups known (through previous research) to differ on the variable. For example, if we apply our integration-sentiment scale to Southern and non-Southern whites and find that Southerners are more pro-integrationist than non-Southerners according to the scale scores, we can make one of two conclusions: either that Southern whites are really more pro-integrationist or that the scale is not measuring integration sentiments. If past investigations have been unanimous in their findings, as is the case with Southerners being less integrationist, then the first suspect should be the scale. In general, a valid measurement will tend to yield expected differences between groups.

Another validity check, similar to discrimination between known groups, is the measurement's ability to identify subjects whose observed behavior corresponds to their score on the variable. For example, if your measurement instrument is designed to measure political radicalism, and you know five people who have participated in radical activities (even though they might not belong to radical organizations) and five who have never done so, then a valid radicalism measurement should distinguish between these two groups. In general, any valid measurement of a variable with behavioral implications should be able to predict that behavior with a high degree of accuracy.

The final validity check involves the correspondence between the variable or concept being measured and other variables or concepts which, according to one's theoretical notions, should relate with it. In discussing the operationalization process in Chapter 2, we saw that any concept or variable, in addition to being operationally defined, is also conceptually defined. What specific conceptual interrelationships exist are, of course, a function of the theory one is using. Our theory might hold that pro-integration sentiments are positively associated with liberal attitudes on welfare policies and negatively related to dogmatic tendencies. We could then check the validity of the integration measurement by seeing if it has the predicted relationship with the measurements of the other two variables.

It should be quite clear by now that any validity test is incomplete. Whether we check our measurements against sociological, behavioral, or attitudinal differences, we are always testing both a causal hypothesis (e.g., Southern whites are more integrationist than non-Southern whites, persons with radical attitudes are more apt to behave radically than persons without radical attitudes, pro-integrationists are more likely to be liberal on welfare issues and less apt to be dogmatic than anti-integrationists) and validity at the same time. If the predicted relationship does not occur, there is no definitive way of knowing whether we should reject the hypothesis or the measurement instrument. All we can do is rely on past experience. If the hypothesis has been frequently supported in the past and the measurement instrument is a new one, then rejecting the measurement is more sensible; if the hypothesis is new and the measuring device well-established, then the hypothesis should be rejected; if both are new or both are old, then welcome to the hard choices of scientific research. In short, maintaining scientific objectivity does not mean that one should leave all his past experience and knowledge on the shelf. The results of any particular measurement (or, for that matter, any test of a hypothesis), should be related to earlier findings in order to gauge its validity.

CONCLUDING COMMENTS

A measurement instrument is a tool, and like any new tool it should be given as many trial runs as possible before being employed in any real situation. You should not hesitate to try out your measurements on some small group in order to get preliminary information about item interrelationships, reliability, and validity. Precisely because new measuring devices are filled with uncertainties, employ existing instruments whenever possible. They are to be preferred not only because their advantages and limitations are better known, but also because it is easier to compare research findings when the same measurement instruments have been used. As is the case with any borrowed tool, you should read an instrument's directions before using it. In particular, you should gather as much information as possible about the instrument's homogeneity, reliability, and validity; this background material should include the groups for which the measurement was used (some measurements will not be applicable to all groups) and the wording of the specific items (some phrases and references to events will be dated). In addition to finding measurement instruments in substantive research reports,[9] several useful compendiums are available. The most prominent are Charles Bonjean, Richard Hill, and Dale McLemore, *Sociological Measurement* (San Francisco, Chandler, 1967); Delbert Miller, *Handbook of Research Design and Social Measurement* (New York, David McKay, 1964); John P. Robinson, Jerrold G. Rusk, and Kendra B. Head, *Measures of Political Attitudes* (Ann Arbor, Mich., Institute for Social Research, 1968); John P. Robinson, Robert Athanasiou, and Kendra B. Head, *Measures of Occupational Attitudes and Occupational Characteristics* (Ann Arbor, Mich., Institute for Social Research, 1969); John P. Robinson and Phillip R. Shaver, *Measures of Social Psychological Attitudes* (Ann Arbor, Mich., Institute for Social Research, 1969); and Marvin Shaw and Jack Wright, *Scales for the Measurement of Attitudes* (New York, McGraw-Hill, 1967).

EXERCISES

1 Construct a nominal index encompassing at least three variables with each variable having a minimum of three categories.

2 Construct an ordinal index encompassing at least three variables with each variable having a minimum of five ranks or scores.

3 Construct a metric index encompassing at least three variables.

4 For the following response-distribution to five questions, compute the coefficient of reproducibility, the coefficient of scalability, and the scale scores for each subject:

Subject	Question				
	1	2	3	4	5
Arthur	Yes	No	Yes	Yes	Yes
Beatrice	No	No	No	Yes	No
Candide	Yes	No	No	Yes	No
Delilah	Yes	Yes	Yes	Yes	Yes
Esmeralda	Yes	No	Yes	Yes	No
Fauntleroy	No	No	No	No	No
Grizzly	Yes	Yes	Yes	Yes	No
Horace	Yes	Yes	No	Yes	No
Ignatius	No	No	Yes	No	No
Junior	Yes	Yes	Yes	Yes	Yes

[9] See Chapter 2 for bibliographic indexes of political research.

4 CHOOSING THE SUBJECTS

The measurement process does not stop with the specification of indicators. After you have decided what the measurement instrument is going to be, you then must apply it. The application or collection part of measurement can be divided into three separate tasks: choosing the subjects, getting the information from the subjects, and storing the collected data. The subject-selection process will be described in this chapter, and the other two tasks will be presented in Chapter 5. In discussing the collection of data, we will necessarily repeat and elaborate on measurement itself since how data are collected affects how well phenomena are measured. A scale might have excellent homogeneity, reliability, and validity, but unless the subjects are properly selected and the scale is skillfully applied, the data will be worthless.

In Chapter 2, we briefly described the subject-selection procedure, noting that the major steps are specifying the level of analysis and selecting a representative set of units from that level. The complete list of all elements in the level of analysis is called the universe or population. Levels and possible universes where political analysis takes place include nations (e.g., all Latin American nations), states (e.g., all American states), communities (e.g., all American cities with a population over 25,000), various sets of individuals (e.g., all state legislators, all college students, all U.S. citizens), and verbal statements (e.g., all *New York Times* editorials, all arguments made in congressional debates, etc.).

Once the population or universe has been established, the job of selecting which units to include in the study begins. If the number of units in the population is small, then you can analyze all of them. Even when it is within the realm of practicality to include all the population's units, it may not be desirable to do so. For example, if the universe is composed of 1,000 persons, with the data being collected through face-to-face interviews, and only five experienced interviewers are available, it would be better to let the five interviewers work with a sample of 100 rather than to hire additional, less competent personnel to survey the entire group. In most instances, however, it is necessary to select a subset or sample. In selecting a sample, we want to choose our subjects in such a way as to make inferences with calculable levels of accuracy and risk for the entire population. In order to calculate accuracy and risk, we must have a *probability sample*, where every unit has a known chance of being selected. Nonprobability samples, where the chances of subject selection are unknown and where it is consequently impossible to infer with specified levels of accuracy and risk to any larger universe, are sometimes useful in answering exploratory questions. If our main objective is gaining new insights into some aspect of politics rather than obtaining precise descriptions or testing causal hypotheses, then the sampling criterion should be amount of new information and representativeness. This type of selection process is known as *purposive sampling.*

In the remainder of this section, we will cover the logic behind probability sampling and explain three types of probability samples (*simple random, disproportionate stratified,* and *multistage cluster*) frequently used in political research. The first part will concentrate on how many units to sample and the second part will deal with methods of choosing the units.

THE LOGIC OF PROBABILITY SAMPLING

Many people find it difficult to comprehend how a small sample can adequately represent a large population. They ask how something as complex and variable as the political attitudes of all Americans can be captured in a relatively small sample of 1,500 to 2,000 individuals? By using two intuitive explanations, thereby avoiding the formal mathematical rationale, let us try to eliminate this incredulity.

First, suppose that as part of a hypothesis test we need to know the percentage of American adults who identify with the Democratic party. Our variable, then, is a nominal one having two categories: Democrat and non-Democrat. Since we cannot contact every American adult, we need a sample. The question is: How large should the sample be? To answer this question, we need to know what factors affect our ability to estimate the variables' scores in the universe on the basis of sample data so that we can take these factors into account in determining the sample size. There are, in fact, three factors: how much the study's variables vary (*variability*), how accurate you wish the estimate(s) to be (*accuracy*), and how certain you want to be that the estimates are that accurate (*risk*). Let us see how each of these relates to sample size.

If everybody in the United States had the same value or score on a variable (e.g., either all Democrats or all non-Democrats), how large a sample would we need in order to get an accurate estimate of the population percentage? The answer is *One,* for if all the peas in the pod are alike, we need only examine one to know them all. In most cases, of course, everybody or everything is not alike; they vary to some extent. The more the study's variables vary, the more subjects will be needed for a sample, given constant levels of accuracy and risk; by the same logic, the less variation, the fewer subjects will be required. In this example, the fact that the variable has only two values limits the total possible amount of variability; the most highly variable situation would be one where half the population were Democrats and the other half non-Democrats. More generally, when the number of possible values of a variable is finite, the maximum variability is also finite. Even when a variable's values are potentially infinite, we generally only find a certain subset in the real world. For example, income can conceivably range from zero to infinity, but in fact there are relatively few incomes over $1 million, and most cluster in the $5,000 to $15,000 range. Put another way, although most things vary, few vary that much. This fact helps keep sample sizes relatively low. Note that a population's variability—not its absolute size—is the determining factor. If the variable values do not vary much, only a small sample is necessary even if the universe is composed of a billion units. Conversely, if variability is high, then a relatively large sample would be required even if the population were much smaller than a billion. On the whole of course, the larger the population, the greater the variation of most variables; but it is only in this indirect way that population size influences sample size.

Accuracy and risk are the remaining factors affecting sample size. The closer you want to be to the true universe figure and the more certain you want to be that we are that close, the larger the required sample size. Accuracy and risk levels will vary from project to project. If we are interested in predicting the winner of a close election race and you want to be quite certain that your prediction is correct, then you need a relatively large sample to obtain the high accuracy and low risk. On the other hand, if you are interested only in getting a rough idea of the universe figures, then you can tolerate lower accuracy, higher risk, or both. To achieve very high levels of accuracy and low levels of risk, one pays an exorbitant price in sample size. For example, assuming maximum variability in our problem (half non-Democrats) and a simple random sample, a ±1 percent accuracy level and a 1 percent risk level (i.e., the probability of the sample figure being within ±1 percent of the true population figure is 99 percent or the chances of it not being within ±1 percent are only 1 percent) would require a sample size of 16,587. If you loosen the accuracy and risk levels to ±3 percent and 5 percent respectively, then the appropriate sample size falls all the way to 1,067.

Our first intuitive explanation shows that the size of any sample is directly related to the amount of variability in the study variables and the desired level of accuracy and is inversely related to the tolerable level of risk. It does not, however, explicitly state a formula for computing the size of a sample nor does it present any reasons why we are able to interrelate variability, accuracy, risk, and sample size in a specified manner. The development of actual formulas for computing sample size is beyond the scope of this book.[1] Instead, a table listing approximate sample sizes for certain common situations is presented later in the chapter. Nonetheless, in order to get some idea how a central proposition of probability theory allows us to compute accuracy and risk for given sample sizes and amount of variability, let us look at another example.

Suppose that we somehow knew that the true population average for Democratic party identification in the United States was 50 percent (half Democrats, half non-Democrats). If we were to draw a thousand samples of 10, 20, 50, and 100 each, what would be the expected distribution of sample estimates of Democratic proportion? We can utilize a bit of probability theory to calculate these distributions. We wish to know the probability of getting exactly r number of Democrats in samples of 10, 20, 50, and 100 respectively drawn from a population where the actual proportion of Democrats is 50 percent. Taking just the samples of size 10 as an example, we want to determine the probability of getting 0 Democrats, 1 Democrat, 2 Democrats, and so forth. The formula for calculating these probabilities is

$$P(r) = \left(\frac{N(N-1)(N-2)\cdots(N-r+1)}{r(r-1)(r-2)\cdots(1)} \right)(p^r)(q^{N-r})$$

where

$P(r)$ = the probability of getting "r" Democrats
N = the size of the sample
r = the number of Democrats for which the probability is being calculated
p = the probability that an individual is a Democrat
q = the probability that an individual is not a Democrat

For example, in computing the probability of getting 2 Democrats in a sample of 10 drawn from a universe with a 50–50 split of Democrats and non-Democrats (i.e., the probability that an individual is a Democrat is .5 and the probability that he is not a Democrat is also .5), we get

$$P(r) = \left(\frac{(10)(9)}{(2)(1)} \right) \left(\frac{1}{2} \right)^2 \left(\frac{1}{2} \right)^8$$

$$= (45)(.2500)(.0039)$$

$$= .0439$$

For 1,000 samples, we would expect that (1000) (.0439) or 44 would have exactly two Democrats. Looking at Table 4.1, we see that the 17–20 percent entry in the Democratic proportion column (if there are 2 Democrats in a sample of 10, the percentage of Democrats is 20 percent) for the samples of size 10 contains the number 44.

---

[1] For these formulas, see Leslie Kish, *Survey Sampling*, New York, John Wiley, 1965.

TABLE 4.1 DISTRIBUTION OF 1000 SAMPLE ESTIMATES FOR FOUR SAMPLE SIZES WHERE TRUE POPULATION VALUE IS 50 PERCENT[a]

Sample estimate of Democratic proportion (percentage)	Sample size			
	10	20	50[b]	100[b]
0–4	1	0	0	0
5–8	—[c]	0	0	0
9–12	10	0	0	0
13–16	—	1	0	0
17–20	44	5	0	0
21–24	—	—	0	0
25–28	—	15	1	0
29–32	117	37	6	0
33–36	—	74	25	3
37–40	205	120	69	25
41–44	—	—	139	107
45–48	—	160	204	247
49–52	246	176	220	309
53–56	—	160	175	212
57–60	205	120	102	79
61–64	—	—	43	16
65–68	—	74	13	2
69–72	117	37	3	0
73–76	—	15	0	0
77–80	44	5	0	0
81–84	—	—	0	0
85–88	—	1	0	0
89–92	10	0	0	0
93–96	—	0	0	0
97–100	1	0	0	0
Total	1,000	1,000	1,000	1,000

[a] This example assumes a large population.
[b] If it were not for the collapsing of possible estimates into four-point groups, this distribution would also be symmetrical.
[c] A dash (—) indicates that it was arithmetically impossible for a sample estimate to be within a particular range.

Table 4.1 summarizes the estimates for all of these samples. First, note that no matter what the sample size, the estimates are not randomly distributed between 0 and 100 percent, but instead cluster at the true population value (50 percent). Second, as the sample size increases, the clustering at the middle increases; for a sample size of 10, 656 (or 65.6 percent) of the sample estimates are between 33 and 68 percent, while for the samples of 100, all 1,000 estimates are within this range. All of this leads up to an important proposition of probability theory: the *law of large numbers*. This law states that the distribution of sample means for *any* variable from *any* population always assumes the same form, provided the sample is relatively large (over 30); moreover, the sample estimates will approximate the true population value more frequently than any other value.[2] The basic form of this distribution is always the same, and its precise shape is determined by just two factors: the sample size and the amount of the variable's variability in the population. This means that once you know the sample size and the variability, you can calculate the odds that your single sample estimate is within a specified distance of the true population value. Returning to Table 4.1 for a sample size of 100 and the maximum possible variability for a dichotomous nominal variable (50–50 split), probability theory tells us that over 950 out of every 1,000 samples will be within ±10 percent of the true population figure since, as Table 4.1 indicates, over 950 of the sample estimates are between 40 percent and 60 percent. Thus we have computed the risk (less than 5 percent) for a given level of accuracy (±10 percent). If we narrowed the accuracy limits (say to ±5 percent), the risk of getting a sample estimate outside these limits increases to about 25 percent; thus, if we wished to increase the accuracy while maintaining the same risk level (or lessen the risk while keeping the same accuracy level), we must increase the sample size.

The purpose of this discussion was to eliminate some of the mystery surrounding sampling and not to explain in detail modern sampling theory. You should now be aware of two points:

1. The three factors that determine sample size are variability, accuracy, and risk.[3]

2. Because all sample estimates assume the same distribution, we are able to calculate accuracy and risk for any given sample size and level of variability.

TYPES OF PROBABILITY SAMPLES

Knowing the appropriate size does not tell us which members of the population should be included in the sample. How, then, do we select a sample? All of the above logic rests on the assumption that we can specify the probability of each population unit being included in the sample; if we cannot, then the probability theory underlying Table 4.1 is inapplicable.

---

[2] This statement is somewhat oversimplified. A more precise definition, the meaning of which will become clearer after the discussion of the normal distribution in Chapter 9, is, "If repeated random samples of size N are drawn from any population (of whatever form) having a mean μ and a variance σ^2, then as N becomes large the sampling distribution of sample means approaches normality, with mean μ and variance σ^2/N." This definition is taken from Hubert M. Blalock, Jr., *Social Statistics*, New York, McGraw-Hill, 1960, p. 138.

[3] When the population is small, then the sampling fraction (sample size/population size) also influences the sample size. This is a significant factor only when the sample is more than 20 percent of the total population and, even in these cases, the sampling fraction helps increase accuracy or lessen risk or both for a given sample size and variability.

This means that we must use chance procedures in selecting the sample. The only way to ensure that a person will be unbiased (i.e., rely entirely on chance) is not to give him any opportunity to make a mistake. The aphorism that "If anything can go wrong, it will" has a research analogue: "If you give bias any chance to occur, it will." We will now discuss three ways of choosing a sample: simple random, disproportional stratified, and multistage cluster.

Simple random sampling is the most straightforward selection method. A simple random sample is one where every member of the population has an equal chance of being selected. Although this might seem like an easy objective to achieve, several pitfalls stand between an investigator and a simple random sample.

First, in order for every member to have an equal selection probability, you must be aware of its existence. This means you need a list of all population members. Unfortunately, there are many populations for which there is no accurate and complete list. For example, there is no complete list of all persons in any large American community, although many partial lists exist (e.g., city and telephone directories, voter registration lists, and taxpayer rolls). If there is no complete list, you have three alternatives. First, you can utilize some partial list and accept the accompanying bias. This should only be done when the incomplete list comes close to perfection (90 percent or above), or when outside evidence indicates that the kinds of units not on the list are relatively the same, in terms of the study variables, as those on the list. Taking a common example, telephone directories meet neither of these requirements. In almost every American community, more than 10 percent of the adult population does not have a listed telephone number and the kinds of people not having phones generally differ sharply from those with phones, the former tending to be poorer, less educated, and so forth. Second, you can redefine your population in terms of an actual list. For example, the population might be changed from "all citizens from the St. Louis metropolitan area" to "all individuals having a listed number in the Greater St. Louis Telephone Directory." Although logically pure, this tactic generally leads one away from his original study objectives; for in the above example, the investigator is interested in all citizens—not just those with listed telephone numbers. Nevertheless, you should be alert to those cases where a redefinition of a population in order to have an accurate list does not seriously damage the study objectives. When no list exists, the third alternative is to undertake a multistage cluster sample, a process which will be discussed later.

If an accurate and complete list exists, the sample selection process is quite easy. One assigns a different number to each element in the list, secures a table of random digits,[4] randomly selects a starting point in the random digit table, and proceeding from that point on in any consistent

[4] For one such table, see Appendix 2.

direction (up, down, or sideways) through the table, selects each element whose number occurs until the desired sample size is achieved. For example, let us suppose that there are 5,000 elements in our list and that we need a sample of 200. We would then assign each element a unique number with the set of the assigned numbers in this case going from 0001 to 5000. Looking at our table of random digits, we see that it is composed of sets of two-digit numbers (e.g., 06 51 48 92). Since our population has 5,000 elements, each one has a unique four-digit number; we randomly pick a starting point (close your eyes and point) and note the four digits at that point. If the number is between 0001 and 5000 (e.g., 06 51), we then select for our sample the element having that number (e.g., 0651); if the number is less than 0001 (e.g., 00 00) or greater than 5000 (e.g., 96 45), we ignore it and move on to the next set of four digits. Since the digits in the table are randomly distributed, one can move in any direction without risking bias as long as we maintain the originally chosen direction. We continue this process until we have found 200 different numbers between 0001 and 5000. If the same number is chosen a second time, ignore it and move on. This is known as sampling without replacement; once an element is chosen, it cannot be selected again. Alternately, we could sample with replacement by allowing each element to be selected more than once. Actually the probability theory underlying sampling assumes sampling with replacement. The bias introduced by sampling without replacement is very small if the sample size is less than one-fifth the population size, as it almost always is.

Using random numbers, although often a bit cumbersome, is highly preferable to selecting every nth element in the list (e.g., for a population of 5,000 and a sample size of 200, choosing every 25th element). The latter procedure (called *systematic sampling*) is probabilistically valid only when the starting point is randomly selected and when the list is unbiased (i.e., an element's position on a list is solely a product of chance, or on a more relaxed basis, totally unrelated to the study variables). Although starting points can be randomly chosen, we can never be certain that the lists are free from bias. Even alphabetical lists that are seemingly randomly distributed often have a bias; Irish, for example, are disproportionately found in the "O" group. Again, our guiding maxim is that the only way to avoid bias is not to give it a chance to occur; hence, it is best to use random digits as the selection device.

In Chapter 2, we mentioned the problem of studying a phenomenon which occurs infrequently. In such instances, a simple random sample is apt to yield an insufficient number of cases for full analysis. Disproportional stratified sampling provides a means for ensuring a sufficient number of certain types of subjects while maintaining the capability of making inferences to the entire population.

In choosing a disproportional stratified sample, one first divides the population into several groups or strata according to their values on the relevant variable(s). In doing this, each population element must be in one and only one stratum. For each stratum, one decides how large a sample is needed and then proceeds to select a simple random sample of that size. Overall population estimates are calculated by combining the results from each stratum according to their proportion vis-à-vis the entire population.

For example, suppose you wish to select a sample from a large university student body in a study of attitudes toward college governing procedures. You expect race to be a significant explanatory variable, yet only 2 percent (or 200) of the 10,000 students are black. If you drew a simple random sample of 500 (let us assume practical reasons limit your sampling capability to this size), only about 8 to 12 blacks would be included—too few cases to permit detailed analysis. Applying disproportional stratified sampling, you divide the population into two strata: white and black. From the 9,800 whites, you select a simple random sample of 400; from the 200 blacks, a sample of 100. Now you can perform relatively complete analyses both between and within racial groups. Overall population estimates can be obtained by weighting the white figures 49 times as much as the black results, since the overall black-white ratio is 9,800:200 or 49:1.

Disproportional stratified sampling clearly requires prior knowledge of each stratum's proportion vis-à-vis the entire population in order to weight each stratum properly in making overall estimates; thus only certain common sociological variables (generally those collected by the Bureau of the Census, such as age, sex, race, income, and occupation) are used to form strata. Moreover, it is extremely helpful, although not absolutely necessary, to have a separate list for each stratum or, in other words, to know in advance which specific cases fall into which strata. In our university-sample example, obtaining a sample of 100 blacks without such a list would be extremely time-consuming, since you would need to make preliminary contacts with thousands of students in order to find the desired 100.

One can also construct a proportional stratified sample where the sample size for each stratum is equal to that stratum's proportion vis-à-vis the total population. Proportional stratified sampling can be slightly more efficient—lower sample size for the same accuracy and risk levels or greater accuracy and lower risk for the same sample size—than simple random sampling, since one or more sources of variation (the variable[s] determining the strata) has been controlled. The gains in efficiency, however, are generally less than a 10 percent lower sample size for equivalent accuracy and risk levels, so that unless the stratification process does not involve much time or expense, the price of ignoring it is not very high.

Quite frequently, one wishes to sample a geographically dispersed population for which no accurate and complete list exists. A geographically dispersed population raises cost problems if face-to-face interviews are to be employed. If the population is all adults in a state or nation and if the sample is randomly distributed, travel expenses of the interviewers will be extremely high; we would prefer a sampling process which would concentrate or cluster the sample into a limited number of small areas. The absence of an adequate list means that no direct sample can be chosen; instead, one must go through multiple stages of sampling in order to select the sample. Combining these two features, we get a multistage cluster sample.

Say, for example, we need a sample of 600 Oregon adults, yet we have no list and only 10 interviewers. Since we have no list containing the name of each adult, we must devise a means of conducting successive samples until we reach a stage where we do have such a list; moreover, since we do not have funds to send our 10 interviewers scurrying all over the state, we want the sample at the final stages to be clustered. For the first stage of our sample, we can randomly select certain counties since we do have a relatively accurate list of the number of adults in each county (see Table 4.2). Since we only have 10 interviewers, it makes sense to select 10 counties. In making the selections, however, we want each adult to have an equal chance of being chosen; to accomplish this goal, we must weight each county by its number of adults. We can do this by assigning each county as many unique random numbers as it has adults. Looking at Table 4.2, we see that Baker County, with an adult population of 10,515, has 10,515 random numbers (0000001 to 0010515); Benton County, with 22,089 adults, has 22,089 random numbers (0010515–0032604); and so forth. Randomly entering a table of random digits, we find the first seven-digit number between 0000001 and 1073456 and select the county which was assigned that number (e.g., if the first number was 0245311, we would select Hood River County); we continue this process until we have obtained 10 counties.

We now need to select a sample of 60 (600/10) from each county. Since we have already weighted the counties by population in the initial selection stage, we do not weight again by proportionally allocating the sample among the ten counties according to the relative population of each county. To do so would be to increase the chances of an individual from a large county being included in the sample and to decrease the chances of a small-county resident. Again, however, there is no adequate list of all adults in a given county. What we do have, in most counties, is a list of all dwelling units. Most frequently, this list is found in the form of a map in the county engineer's or the county planner's office. A dwelling unit is defined as a place where one family resides; thus for example, an apartment building has several dwelling units. Within each county each dwelling unit can then be assigned a unique number and, again using a table of random digits, 60 can be chosen in each county. If more clustering is desired, one can group the structures (e.g., by city blocks or census tracts), select 20 of these groups, and in the final stage choose 3 respondents from each group. Now that we have reached this stage, we can construct an accurate list of individuals by going to each of the 60 dwelling units and asking for

TABLE 4.2 ADULT POPULATION AND NUMBER ASSIGNMENTS FOR ALL OREGON COUNTIES

County	Adult population	Assigned numbers
Baker	10,515	0000001-0010515
Benton	22,089	0010516-0032604
Clackamas	67,145	0032605-0099749
Clatsop	17,660	0099750-0117409
Columbia	13,338	0117410-0130747
Coos	31,929	0130748-0162676
Crook	5,451	0162677-0168127
Curry	8,138	0168128-0176265
Deschutes	13,929	0176266-0190194
Douglas	38,884	0190195-0229078
Gilliam	1,832	0229079-0230910
Grant	4,558	0230911-0235468
Harney	3,992	0235469-0239460
Hood River	8,144	0239461-0247604
Jackson	45,339	0247605-0292943
Jefferson	3,864	0292944-0296807
Josephine	18,519	0296808-0315326
Klamath	28,058	0315327-0343384
Lake	4,288	0343385-0347672
Lane	93,988	0347673-0441660
Lincoln	15,273	0441661-0456933
Linn	33,907	0456934-0490840
Malheur	12,884	0490841-0503724
Marion	73,983	0503725-0577707
Morrow	2,889	0577708-0580596
Multnomah	335,123	0580597-0915719
Polk	15,755	0915720-0931474
Sherman	1,492	0931475-0932966
Tillamook	10,975	0932967-0943941
Umatilla	26,833	0943942-0970774
Union	10,999	0970775-0981773
Wallowa	4,311	0981774-0986084
Wasco	12,264	0986085-0998348
Washington	53,959	0998349-1052307
Wheeler	1,565	1052308-1053872
Yamhill	19,584	1053873-1073456

SOURCE: *County and City Data Book, 1962*, Washington, D.C., U.S. Bureau of the Census, 1962, p. 302.

the names of all adults who live there. From this list we can randomly select one adult to interview. In this final selection, we must carefully maintain our principle of equal-selection probabilities. We cannot, for example, simply select the person who comes to the door since door-answering is not a randomly distributed activity: women tend to answer more frequently than men. Instead, we construct our list of adults in some consistent fashion. One standard procedure is to order all men from the oldest to the youngest (21 or over), and then all women from oldest to youngest, and assign them a number corresponding to their order (i.e., the oldest male "1," the next oldest "2," etc.).[5] For example, the Smith household of Herman (41-year-old husband), Norma (39-year-old wife), Gramps (Herman's 68-year-old father), and Martha (Herman and Norma's 22-year-old daughter) would be listed and numbered in the following order: Gramps (1), Herman (2), Norma (3), and Martha (4). The sample elements are divided into 6 equal groups, 2 of these groups are split in half, and each of the 8 is assigned one of the selection tables in Table 4.3. This procedure comes as close as is practically possible to achieving the goal of equal-selection probabilities.

Cluster samples—whether singlestage or multistage—generally require a larger sample for given accuracy and risk levels than either simple, random or stratified samples because, when we cluster the cases (e.g., into 10 counties), we are not giving the sample as much opportunity to disperse itself among the entire population as we do with the other selection procedures. How much larger a cluster sample must be in order to achieve equivalent accuracy and risk levels depends on a comparison between clusters on the study variables. The greater homogeneity within clusters and the greater heterogeneity between clusters, the larger the difference between cluster and other sample sizes. This is so because in cases where the clusters differ widely while being internally homogeneous, the chances

[5] This technique is taken from Leslie Kish, "A Procedure for Objective Respondent Selection Within the Household," *Journal of the American Statistical Association,* 44 (September, 1949), 380–387.

TABLE 4.3 DECISION TABLES FOR SELECTING ADULTS IN A HOUSEHOLD SAMPLE

Relative frequency of use	Selection table number	If number of adults in household is					
		1	2	3	4	5	6 or more
		Select adult numbered					
1/6	I	1	1	1	1	1	1
1/12	II-A	1	1	1	1	2	2
1/12	II-B	1	1	1	2	2	2
1/6	III	1	1	2	2	3	3
1/6	IV	1	2	2	3	4	4
1/12	V-A	1	2	3	3	3	5
1/12	V-B	1	2	3	4	5	5
1/6	VI	1	2	3	4	5	6

SOURCE: Leslie Kish, "A Procedure for Objective Respondent Selection Within the Household," *Journal of the American Statistical Association,* 44 (September, 1949), 384, with the permission of the author and publisher.

of choosing an unrepresentative set of clusters would be high; to compensate for this, more clusters, more cases within each cluster, or some of each must be done. On the other hand, if clusters have approximately the same spread of values on the study variables, then the odds of selecting an unrepresentative set would be low and the difference between cluster-sample size and simple-random or stratified-sample size would be minor. In most instances of political research, variability within clusters is much lower than variability between clusters, since similar things (nations, states, people) empirically tend to be geographically grouped together; the United States is more similar to Canada than to Indonesia, Alabama resembles Mississippi more than it does Idaho, and you are more like your neighbor than the man across town. Despite this sampling inefficiency, cluster samples are frequently used because they are much less expensive in many applications. Because the subjects are concentrated in a limited number of areas, time spent in locating respondents is drastically reduced. Thus in deciding between cluster sampling and the other two methods, one must weigh the cost savings against the loss of sampling efficiency.

SAMPLE SIZE GUIDELINES

Table 4.4 gives approximate sample sizes for different accuracy and risk levels. Since most political distributions can be expressed in terms of percentages, the table expresses accuracy in those terms. If the dominant variable were income, then one might state accuracy in terms of plus-or-minus so many dollars. It also assumes maximum variability so that the sample sizes in Table 4.4 are conservative estimates, overstating the required sample size for given accuracy and risk levels in many studies. The

TABLE 4.4 SAMPLE SIZE FOR VARIOUS LEVELS OF RISK AND ACCURACY[a]

Desired accuracy	Risk of sample estimate being outside accuracy limits				
	1%	2%	5%	10%	20%
±1%	16,587	13,533	9,604	6,765	4,108
±2%	4,147	3,384	2,401	1,691	1,027
±3%	1,843	1,504	1,067	752	457
±4%	1,037	846	600	423	257
±5%	663	541	384	271	164
±6%	461	376	267	188	114
±7%	339	276	196	138	84
±8%	259	212	150	106	64
±9%	205	167	119	84	51
±10%	166	135	96	68	41
±15%	74	60	43	30	18
±20%	41	34	24	17	10

[a] See text for the assumptions underlying these sample sizes.

table also assumes simple random sampling; however since stratified sampling (proportional or disproportional) is quite similar to simple random selection and since it is generally slightly more efficient, these figures can be used as rough, conservative estimates for stratified samples. *They cannot be used for cluster samples.* Finally, the table is appropriate only for those instances where the population size is at least five times as large as the sample size.

In order to take some of the mystery out of the procedure for calculating sample size, let us briefly examine how the sample sizes in Table 4.4 are computed. As we saw earlier in this chapter, sample size varies directly with population variability and desired accuracy and inversely with desired risk. All we need do, then, is develop measures for each of these factors and construct a formula which expresses the relationship among them. We use a statistical measure of variation—the *standard deviation*—for population variability. (This measure is explained in Chapter 6.) In the current instance, where the population is split 50–50, the standard deviation equals .50. Various levels of risk are represented by normal curve Z-scores. The normal curve, a particular type of probability distribution, is covered in Chapter 9. All we need know now is that, for risk levels of 1, 2, 5, 10, and 20 percent, the corresponding Z-scores are 2.5758, 2.3267, 1.9600, 1.6450, and 1.2818. The measurement of accuracy is straightforward: ±1 percent is .01, ±2 percent is .02, ±10 percent is .10, and so forth. If the data were expressed in some form other than percentages, then the measurement of accuracy would change according to the type of unit used to measure the phenomenon being sampled. Population variability's measurement increases as the variation increases. Accuracy, however, has the peculiarity that lower numerical values (e.g., ±1 percent) indicate stricter accuracy requirements while higher numbers (e.g., ±15 percent) indicate those of less stringency. Similarly, risk is measured in a way that higher numbers indicate lower risk and vice versa. Taking the measurement mode into account, we must restate the relationship: Sample size varies directly with the measures of population variability and risk and inversely with the measure of accuracy. Expressing the one inverse relationship as a fraction and noting that the relationship is exponential (i.e., it is the square root of the sample size which varies with the other three factors), we can state that

$$\sqrt{\text{Sample size}} = (\text{Population variability})(\text{Risk})\left(\frac{1}{\text{Accuracy}}\right)$$

Then, for a situation where the desired accuracy is ±4 percent and the desired risk is 5 percent (a Z-score of 2.3267) and remembering that the population variability is .50, we see that

$$\sqrt{\text{Sample size}} = (.50)(2.3267)\left(\frac{1}{.04}\right)$$
$$= 29.0850$$

and that $\qquad$ Sample size $= (29.0850)^2 \cong 846$

The sample sizes in Table 4.4 imply that the desired data are collected from all of the elements. Since studies involving human beings limit the possibility of gathering all necessary information from every sample element, you should take this into account in determining how many elements to include in your initial contact list. For example, if you wanted a completed sample size of 1,000 and you expect that for a variety of reasons (e.g., refusal to respond or unable to locate) only 80 percent of the sample will actually be measured, then you should select an initial list of 1,250 in order to get a completed sample of 1,000 (i.e., [1,250] [.80] = 1,000). For predictions of expected completion rates, review studies gathering similar information from similar respondents by similar interviewing methods and supplement this with your own experience. You should attempt to get as high a completion rate as possible in order to ensure optimal representativeness. (When a person is no longer a member of the population being sampled [e.g., because he died or moved away], he should not be counted when computing the response rate.) If there are a high number of noncompletions, the nagging doubt that the noncompletions differ significantly from the completions always exists. Such a situation means that the results are biased, since certain kinds of subjects have been disproportionally excluded from the study.

EXERCISES

1 Using the U.S. Bureau of the Census tract statistics for any standard metropolitan statistical area (SMSA), draw a random sample of 20 tracts. Compute the mean sample scores for three variables (e.g., percentage with incomes greater than $10,000). An explanation of how to calculate the mean—which is nothing more than the everyday average—can be found in Chapter 6. How do the sample means compare with the mean scores for the entire SMSA? Repeat the above procedure nine more times, always remembering to return the preceding sample to the list of all tracts before drawing the next sample. How does the mean of the means for the ten samples compare with the average values for the entire SMSA?

2 You decide to draw a disproportional stratified sample. The population and sample sizes for the strata are: college graduates (30,000 and 300), high-school graduates (50,000 and 300), and nonhigh-school graduates (70,000 and 300). From the sample data, you discover that 60 percent of the college graduates, 40 percent of the high-school graduates, and 30 percent of the non-high-school graduates are Republicans. What is the best estimate of the Republican percentage for the entire population?

5 COLLECTING AND STORING DATA

Once the subjects have been selected, the next research step is to gather the required information concerning these subjects. In this section, we will discuss three major methods of collecting data: *surveying individuals, content analysis, and statistical records.* Surveying individuals involves asking some set of questions, either through a self-administered questionnaire, a telephone interview, or a face-to-face interview. Content analysis is the systematic measurement of communications. Statistical records refer to the use of information collected by some private or public agency, such as the Bureau of the Census. Since surveys are the dominant collection tool in political research, we will devote the most time to this technique. The following discussion concentrates on the kinds of situations where each of these techniques can be applied and does not give detailed guidelines for their application. For this latter type of information, consult the appropriate sources cited in the footnotes and text.

SURVEYING INDIVIDUALS
Whenever the subjects of a study are living human beings, surveys provide an important means of gathering information. This is especially true when the necessary data cannot be found in statistical records. Mass publics, special publics (e.g., college students), and political elites—all have been the focus of survey investigations.[1] When you need information about people, the most obvious tactic is to ask them. Whether you wish to know individuals' social characteristics (e.g., their religious affiliation), their

[1] For an excellent review of survey work in political science, see Herbert McClosky, "Survey Research in Political Science," in Charles Y. Glock (ed.), *Survey Research in the Social Sciences*, New York, Russell Sage Foundation, 1967, pp. 63–143. Some major examples of survey applications in political research are Gabriel A. Almond and Sidney Verba, *The Civic Culture*, Princeton, N.J., Princeton University Press, 1963; Angus Campbell et al., *The American Voter*, New York, John Wiley, 1960; and John C. Wahlke et al., *The Legislative System*, New York, John Wiley, 1962.

opinions (e.g., on aid-to-education), attitudes (e.g., liberalism), or beliefs (e.g., nature of man), their knowledge of political affairs (e.g., which party controls Congress), or their behavior (e.g., how often do they vote), surveys are an appropriate tool, and in some instances (e.g., ghetto residents' attitudes), the only tool. The remainder of this section will discuss, in order, the kinds of questions which can be asked, the means by which they can be asked, and some do's and don't's in questionnaire construction and interviewing procedures.

Survey researchers have developed a wide array of questions. Some are appropriate for a broad range of uses, while others are intended for quite specific purposes. Here we will review each major type of question, discuss its possible application, and give an example of its use.

Open-ended questions are ones where no structured alternatives are given; the corresponding academic form is the essay question. (Example: "What do you personally feel are the most important problems the government in Washington should try to take care of?")[2] The advantages of open-ended questions are that they do not force the respondents to fit preconceived categories, thereby avoiding the problem of structuring response categories in advance. They make it easier to obtain a richer response, because once the respondent begins answering, it is easier to draw him out. On the other hand, compared to structured or closed-ended questions (see below), open-ended questions take longer to ask, thereby limiting the amount of time that can be spent on other topics; they make more demands on the respondent's intellectual and vocal energies and therefore might increase the chances of interview break-offs; they can cause uncomfortable lags or gaps in the interview as the respondent hems and haws before answering and the interviewer sometimes subsequently pauses while recording the response verbatim; and finally, the answers are more difficult to categorize since all respondents will not as a rule use the same framework in answering the question. The upshot of this balance sheet is that open-ended questions are useful for gaining insights into individual feelings (including the words they use to express these feelings) without biasing answers by suggesting set responses; but because of their practical limitations, they should be employed sparingly.

Dichotomous questions give the respondent a simple yes-no, agree-disagree, true-false choice. (Example: "Now, in 1964 you remember that Mr. Goldwater ran on the Republican ticket against Mr. Johnson for the Democrats. Do you remember for sure whether or not you voted in that election?") Like all structured questions, they are easy to ask. Their primary weakness is that they limit the respondent to two possible answers. Thus, they should be employed only when the question deals with a natural

[2] This question was developed by the University of Michigan Survey Research Center and is used in many of its surveys. Unless otherwise noted, all questions used as examples in this section are taken from SRC surveys.

dichotomy (Example: The only two logical substantive responses to the above question are "I voted" and "I didn't vote."), or when the set of possible answers can be easily and unambiguously reduced to two choices (Example: "Is your annual income above or below $10,000?"). Even in cases like this you should realize that a dichotomous question throws away information. Instead of knowing an individual's income to the closest $1,000, for example, you only know whether it is above or below the designated cutting point. On many attitude or opinion questions, limiting the respondent to an "agree" or "disagree" response might be misleading. Not only does it keep you from knowing how much the respondent agrees or disagrees, but it also might force more sophisticated respondents to reject the oversimplified responses in favor of an ambiguous "it depends" alternative, when in fact they have a directional preference.

Multiple-choice questions—those with three or more structured alternatives—can be used when one desires specific answers but also wants to give the respondent a wider variety of choices. Most commonly, respondents are given between three and five alternatives; in most instances, a larger number of choices would only confuse the respondent (leading to a flurry of "would you repeat that?"s) and create artificial distinctions (Example: Is there any real difference between "agree very strongly" and "agree very very strongly?"). An example of a three-alternative question is: "If you had some trouble with the police—a traffic violation maybe or being accused of a minor offense—do you think that most likely you would be given a harder time than other people, would be treated about the same as anyone else, or would be treated a little better than most people?" The most common version of the five-choice case, known as a *Likert-type item,* is an opinion or attitude question which has the following alternatives: strongly agree, agree, undecided, disagree, and strongly disagree. Sometimes, in order to keep things as simple as possible, the multiple-choice question is divided into two parts—direction of opinion and intensity of opinion. The respondent is first asked whether he agrees or disagrees with a certain statement (Example: "Do you agree that the government ought to see to it that labor unions don't have much to say about how the government is run, or do you disagree?"), and after he has expressed a simple directional preference, he is asked about the intensity of his opinion (Example: "Do you [agree] [disagree] strongly, or not very strongly?").

Ranking-list questions are useful when you wish to determine the respondent's priorities for several objects or reasons. The respondent is given a printed list of all alternatives and then asked to rank some or all of them according to some criterion. For example, if you wanted to know why West Germans or Italians supported the idea of having a presidency that is largely honorific, you might ask:

Here is a list (hand list to respondent) of reasons which people have given as to why the presidency is needed. Which of these do you think is the most important?

1. A nation needs someone to symbolize it to foreign countries.
2. People get real pleasure out of following the activities of the president.
3. A nation, like a family, needs a respected figure at its head.
4. The president is needed to appoint the prime minister and to open parliament.
5. A nation needs someone at its head who stands above political conflict.

Which is next in importance?[3]

Since there is some evidence that people's choices are often affected by an answer's order within the list (e.g., items listed first often are oversupported), there should be as many lists as there are alternatives, with each alternative being in each location an equal number of times and with each list being used with the same frequency. Ranking-list questions can often be substituted for open-ended questions (Why do we need a president?) when you are reasonably certain of the kinds of responses which will be made; in these cases, the flexibility of open-ended items is not as essential and the more structured ranking list type is easier to administer.

Filter questions are employed to ascertain whether the respondent has sufficient knowledge or interest to give a meaningful response to a succeeding question. In many cases, respondents are reluctant to volunteer their ignorance or disinterest, so that unless they are directly given an "out," they will make some kind of substantive response. (Example: "The government in Washington should stay out of the question of whether white and black children go to the same school. Do you have an opinion on this or not?") If the answer is Yes, the respondent is asked his opinion; if the reply to the filter is No, then the interview proceeds to the next item. If there is suspicion that a relatively large proportion of the sample (10 to 20 percent or more) might not pass a filter question, then one should be used.

Probe questions are open-ended items tacked on to any type of question in order to find out why the respondent answered as he did. The typical form is simply to ask "Why do you feel that way?" Like any open-ended question, probes are useful for gaining a better insight into the background behind any attitude, belief, or opinion. They are particularly helpful in distinguishing between groups who support the same thing for different reasons, especially since there is often a strong temptation for the investigator to assign his pet rationale to a given kind of response. For example, you might prefer to believe that most people support integrationist policies because of a belief in the universal brotherhood of mankind when instead many are motivated by fear of further racial violence; a probe question is one way of finding out which inference is more correct.

There are four ways of asking the questions. You can mail the questionnaire, you can gather the respondents together into several large groups

---

[3] This question was taken from a National Opinion Research Center survey which served as the data base for Gabriel A. Almond and Sidney Verba, *op. cit.*

TABLE 5.1 EVALUATION OF FOUR SURVEY METHODS

Criteria	Survey method			
	Face-to-face	Group	Mail	Tele-phone
Cost	High	Low	Low	Moderate
Return rate	High	High	Low	Moderate
Control of physical interview situation	Moderate	High	Low	Moderate
Applicability to geographically dispersed sample	Moderate	Low	High	Moderate
Ease of using lengthy question-naire	High	High	Moderate	Low
Ease of asking open-ended questions	High	Moderate	Low	Low
Ability to reach all kinds of people	High	Moderate	Moderate	Low
Respondent's perceived ano-nymity	Low	Moderate	High	Moderate

and have them fill out the questionnaire in the same manner that students take tests, you can telephone them, or you can go out and personally interview each person. We will refer to these four methods as, respectively, *mail surveys, self-administered group surveys, telephone surveys,* and *face-to-face surveys.*

Table 5.1 summarizes the comparative advantages and disadvantages of the four ways of asking questions. Cost is generally the most important factor in deciding which method to use. Face-to-face surveys are much more expensive than the other three; each respondent must be individually sought out, this process takes a good deal of time, and time equals money. Telephone surveys of local areas are not too costly assuming we have access to several phones; but nonlocal telephone interviews incur long-distance charges, which causes a sharp increase in expenses. The other two methods are relatively inexpensive.

Face-to-face and group surveys normally yield 70 to 90 percent completed returns, telephone surveys between 50 and 80 percent, and mail surveys rarely have a return rate of over 50 percent. For reasons mentioned earlier, low return rates endanger the ability to make inferences about the entire population since it is difficult to ascertain whether non-interviewed respondents differ substantially from those interviewed. When the return rate gets below 50 percent, the suspicion that significant differences do exist becomes stronger.[4]

[4] For ways of improving the return rates of mail surveys, see Stanley D. Bachrack and Harry M. Scoble, "Mail Questionnaire Efficiency: Controlled Reduction of Nonresponse," *Public Opinion Quarterly,* 31 (Summer, 1967), 265–271; Charles S. Mayer and Robert W. Pratt, Jr., "A Note on Nonresponse in a Mail Survey," *Public Opinion Quarterly,* 30 (Winter, 1966–67), 637–646;

Mail surveys have little control over when or how the questionnaire is completed. Some respondents might answer the questions alone, others with help; some might do it while listening to television, others in a quiet room. Worse yet, there is no way of knowing how much these kinds of factors varied. Since reliability is directly correlated with the standardization of the questions *and* the conditions under which the questions are answered, mail surveys will tend to have greater reliability problems. Neither face-to-face nor telephone surveys fully standardize these interviewing conditions, but they do provide somewhat greater control over them as well as greater knowledge of what factors vary. (Example: the face-to-face interviewer can record whether others are present.) Group surveys do the most to control physical variability because they lump large sets of respondents together in similar physical settings (e.g., classrooms).

If the sample is spread out over a large geographical area, it is difficult, if not impossible to use group surveys; the problems associated with gathering people together into several central locations would be insurmountable. Face-to-face and telephone surveys are still possible, especially if some clustering is employed. Mail surveys are hardly affected by geographic dispersal, since it is just as easy to send a letter across town as it is across the nation.

If you are using a lengthy questionnaire—one that takes more than fifteen to twenty minutes to complete—then face-to-face or group surveys are your best bet. It is difficult to hold people on the telephone for long periods of time, and it is a bit foolhardy to think that a high percentage of people will devote a large amount of time to filling out a mail questionnaire. For similar reasons, it is difficult to use open-ended questions on telephone or mail surveys, since this type of item requires more intellectual effort and more time to complete. Moreover, since an open-ended question yields the best results when there is some type of conversational interchange, face-to-face interviews can utilize them better than group surveys.

Not all of the survey methods can reach every portion of the population with equal success. Telephone surveys quite clearly cannot be used for people who do not have telephones or listed numbers; in 1960, slightly more than one out of every five American adults lived in a residence without a telephone. Mail questionnaires assume a certain level of literacy and, if they are written in a single language, competency in reading that language. Although few Americans are complete illiterates, far more (10 percent and up) would not have the necessary reading and writing skills to answer most mail questionnaires. For these reasons, mail surveys are rarely used

---

and G. Allan Roeher, "Effective Techniques in Increasing Response to Mailed Questionnaires," *Public Opinion Quarterly*, 27 (Summer, 1963), 299–302. The do's and don't's of interviewing to be given below will contain hints for improving return rates in face-to-face and telephone surveys. *Public Opinion Quarterly* is an extremely helpful source for those doing survey research; in addition to reports of substantive findings, it provides summaries of poll results and analyses of methodological techniques.

for surveys of the general population but are confined instead to those groups known to have high literacy skills (e.g., professional groups). Group surveys, as has already been mentioned, are inapplicable to geographically dispersed samples. This leaves face-to-face interviews as the best means for reaching general populations since they alone have the flexibility to dig out the hard-to-reach cases.

Although the investigator can ascertain who said or wrote what on most surveys, different kinds of surveys make the respondents feel more or less anonymous. In mail surveys, the questioner is represented only by words on a page and it is easier for the respondent to think that he will not be personally identified with his answers. This is less the case in telephone and group surveys, where there is voice contact and even more absent in face-to-face interviews in which the interviewer and the respondent are engaged in more of a one-to-one relationship.

In deciding which survey method is best for your investigation, you must judge which criteria are most important to your survey. For example, if you have a long questionnaire with several open-ended questions and a sample of the general population, and if sufficient funds are available, then you should use a face-to-face survey. As a general rule, face-to-face surveys should be used whenever possible, group and telephone surveys substituted when funds are not plentiful and the inherent limitations of group or telephone surveys are minimized (Example: Can the sample be formed into groups? can most be reached by telephone?), and mail surveys used only as a last resort.

In the thirty or so years that survey methods have been employed in social research, its practitioners have made a great number of mistakes. Like a good many sinners they are anxious that later generations not repeat the transgressions of their elders. Consequently, they have developed a number of do's and don't's concerning questionnaire construction and interviewing procedures. Some of the more important ones are given below; others can be found in the books cited at the end of this section.

When constructing a questionnaire, don't construct ambiguous questions. There are several ways of violating this precept. First, your question might be imprecise. (Example: "Did you vote in the last election?" could mean the last local election, the last national election, or the last fraternity election.) Second, when asking the respondent to describe or evaluate something, your criteria might be too vague. (Example: Don't ask "Do you usually attend church services?"; instead, inquire "About how often do you attend church services? Daily? Once a week? Once a month? Less than once a month?") Third, your item might be asking two or more questions at the same time, thereby leading to ambiguous interpretations. (Example: "Do you approve or disapprove of President Trueheart's suggestion that the U.S. devote fewer tax dollars to military goods?" asks both about approval of an individual and a policy.)

Use words that all your respondents will understand. Simply because you have learned some fancy terms such as "totalitarian," "cultural," "paranoic," and "charismatic," don't think that the proverbial man-on-the-street knows them too. If the sample includes individuals from all walks of life, then the average eighth-grader should be able to comprehend your language. Moreover, don't use words that are subject to a wide variety of interpretations. Asking a man whether he is a liberal might, according to his perception of the term, refer to his politics, his financial habits, or his sex life.

Don't embarrass the respondent. Nobody, including survey respondents, likes to be put on the spot. Asking someone point-blank whether they failed to perform a "good" activity, when in fact they did not, is apt to yield inaccurate answers. In the United States, for example, voting is often considered a civic duty and, correspondingly, failure to vote a civic sin. Thus, in ascertaining voting behavior, make nonvoting a bit more respectable when asking the question. The Survey Research Center format is a good one:

In talking to people about the election we find that a lot of people weren't able to vote because they weren't registered or they were sick or they just didn't have time. How about you, did you vote this time or did something keep you from voting?

Keep bias out of the questions. Few people are likely to construct extremely biased questions (Example: "Should we stop wasting money on foreign aid?") unless they are attempting to predetermine the results. There are, however, more subtle ways of committing the sin of bias. First, we might not give each alternative equal weight. (Example: The question "Do you approve of increased federal aid to education?" is biased toward a "yes" answer since it does not give equal status to the negative alternative; the proper phraseology would be "Do you approve or disapprove . . . ?") Second, wherever possible you should avoid words having a strong emotional impact. Asking Americans whether they approve or disapprove of socialized medicine, for example, is apt to yield a larger number of "disapprove" responses than asking them about greater governmental aid for medical expenses, since the term "socialism" has a negative connotation for most Americans.

Avoid lengthy questions. Individual attention spans tend to be quite limited. If the question takes longer than fifteen seconds to ask or to read, then the chances that many people will forget certain parts of it are quite high. If you are going to be clear, you must be brief.

Plagiarize. Don't think you can write the great American questionnaire. Many survey organizations have spent a great deal of time and money developing questions for practically every kind of topic. Whenever possible you should employ these questions, both because they are probably better than anything you could come up with in a short period of time and because use of the same questions enhances comparability. In addition to finding questions in research reports,[5] a great many items relevant for

[5] For bibliographies of political research studies, see Chapter 2.

political investigations can be found in the codebooks published by the Inter-University Consortium for Political Research.[6] Another useful source is the *Gallup Opinion Index,* a monthly publication which lists questions and results of the preceding period's Gallup Polls. Utilizing these last two sources is especially appropriate when you are surveying the general population.

Don't be stilted. In telephone and face-to-face surveys, the questions are meant to be spoken, not read. Thus your objective is smooth conversation, not beautiful prose. If it sounds better to end the question with a preposition, then do so. (Example: Don't say "Do you think that there are significant distinctions between the issue positions of the Republican Party and the Democratic Party?"; instead, ask "Do you think there are any important differences in what the Republicans and Democrats stand for?")

Pay attention to question sequence. In order to achieve a successful interview, the questions cannot be ordered randomly. They must be organized so as to achieve a smooth overall effect. Although sequences will vary according to the specifics of a study, a typical pattern is:

1. A brief introduction, explaining who you are, what organization you represent, and the broad purpose of the study: "Hello, I'm Irving Interviewer, a student at Upper Middlebrow U., and we're doing a study of citizen's opinions on civic affairs."
2. If necessary, item(s) determining whether the individual belongs in the sample, such as when you must select one adult in a household.
3. A warm-up question which is interesting and easy to answer. For example, you might ask about their general opinion of the performance of some governmental unit, their view of the major problems of the day, or who they think will win an upcoming election.
4. The important questions of the study, ordered so that earlier questions will not prejudice the answers to later ones. For example, you shouldn't ask whether or not they consider crime to be an important problem before you use an open-ended item about what are the most important problems. To do so would be to risk biased answers to the open-ended question since you have already mentioned one problem (crime) but not others.
5. The standard demographic questions about age, education, income, and so forth.

When conducting a telephone or face-to-face interview, be neutral. Your job is to find out what the respondents think, not to enlighten them with your own opinions. Like an experienced confessor, you should not express shock at any answer. Many people are more interested in telling others what they think the others want to hear than they are in revealing their

---

[6] If your school is a member of the ICPR, then the codebooks will be located somewhere on campus; a good place to start looking is the political science department. A list of all codebooks, complete with prices, can be obtained from ICPR, P.O. Box 1248, Ann Arbor, Michigan 48106.

own feelings. Thus, if you give them any hint about what you consider to be the "correct" responses, these are the ones you will get. This is especially the case when the interviewer has a higher social or economic status than the respondent.

Be friendly. Some people think that in order to be objective, you must be a first-class sourpuss. You can, however, be friendly without losing your neutrality. After all, our task is to turn people on, not off.

Be persistent. In order that the study be a success, it is very important that as many people as possible answer the questionnaire and that all the questions on the interview schedule be completed. You must sell the respondent on the importance of his answering all the items. Only take "No" for an answer after it's been said at least twice.

Be consistent. As we have already seen in Chapter 3, reliability is critical in the measurement process. In order to maximize reliability in the interview, the questions must be put in the same way to every respondent. Question wording and question sequence should not be altered, even when it might seem to help a particular interview. It may indeed improve one interview, but it makes that interview much less comparable with all the others.

Like all complex activities, constructing questionnaires and interviewing respondents must be practiced before applied. You should always try out your questionnaire on a preliminary group in order to see if the items are interpreted in the way you want them understood. In these sessions, you should ask the test respondents their opinions on the questions and take their comments into account when constructing the final version. In addition, these pretests provide an opportunity for you to sharpen your interviewing skills.

If you decide to use the survey approach in your study, there are several books and manuals which you can consult. These sources will elaborate on the points made here and present additional information concerning planning and applying a survey instrument. A good introductory book which covers all aspects of the survey process is Charles H. Backstrom and Gerald D. Hursh, *Survey Research* (Evanston, Ill., Northwestern University Press, 1963). The best book on writing questions is S. L. Payne, *The Art of Asking Questions* (Princeton, N.J., Princeton University Press, 1951). There are several excellent works on interviewing; among the most helpful are Robert L. Kahn and Charles F. Cannell, *The Dynamics of Interviewing* (New York, John Wiley, 1957); and the Survey Research Center's *Interviewer's Manual*, rev. ed. (Ann Arbor, Mich., Survey Research Center, 1969).

CONTENT ANALYSIS

Every day a huge amount of information relevant in political research is printed or broadcasted. Content analysis—the systematic collection of these communications—is a set of procedures for mining this rich lode. It is especially appropriate when it is difficult or impossible to interview a study's subjects, either because they are rarely available for lengthy interview sessions or because they are dead, or when the research is directly concerned with the communications process. Communications amenable to content analysis include printed material in newspapers, magazines, books, government documents, private correspondence, and minutes to meetings; transcripts of radio and television broadcasts; scripts of motion pictures and plays; and pictorial material such as cartoons, photographs, comic strips, and movies.

Although content analysis has not been a major data-collection method in political research, it has been employed in several studies. In testing the hypothesis that U.S. senators having executive political experience (former governors, local officials, or federal executives) are more likely than those having a legislative background (former representatives or state legislators) to violate the Senate's norm against speaking too much in legislative sessions, one investigator used the number of speeches reported in the *Congressional Record* over a four-year period as his indicator of floor activity.[7] Robert C. North and his associates have content-analyzed a wide variety of intergovernment communications (diplomatic reports, messages between heads of states, and so forth) in order to test a set of hypotheses involving the behavior of nations during periods of international crises.[8] In his study of the psychological factors influencing national economic growth, David C. McClelland measured the achievement motivation in several nations by counting the number of times achievement values were stressed in children's readers.[9] In general, one can find out a great deal about a society's value system by content-analyzing textbooks. This is a particularly fruitful source when one wishes to compare changes in value emphasis over time. Other possible uses of content analysis in political research include studies of the values stressed in different nations' propaganda (e.g., do democratic nations emphasize equality more frequently than do communist countries?), analyses of the attention paid to political news by different media (e.g., do urban newspapers devote more space to national political news than do small town publications?), and investigations of the informational proximity of sets of nations (e.g., what proportion of Country A's news concerns Country B, and vice versa?)

The four major steps in any content analysis are specifying the population and unit of analysis, sampling (if a complete enumeration is not possible), developing categories, and coding the data. Here, we will discuss

[7] Donald R. Matthews, *U.S. Senators and Their World*, Chapel Hill, N.C., University of North Carolina Press, 1960, chap. 5.
[8] Robert C. North et al., *Content Analysis*, Evanston, Ill., Northwestern University Press, 1963.
[9] David C. McClelland, *The Achieving Society*, New York, Van Nostrand-Reinhold, 1961.

only the specification of the unit of analysis and the development of categories; population definition and sampling procedures are the same as with any study, and the coding and storing of data will be discussed in the last part of this chapter.

The three most common analysis units for any communication are *words,* *themes,* and *space/time.* A word is the simplest and smallest unit, but it is also the most tedious one to work with. If your variable is equality, you might construct a dictionary listing all words having a denotation or connotation of equality. For example, your list might include the following words: "parity," "evenness," "balance," "peer," "equality," "commensurate," "proportionate," "symmetric," and "equivalent." You then go through the passages and count the number of times "equality" words occur in each one, divide these results by the total number of words and the quotient is your equality measure. The sheer tedium of this collection process can sometimes be alleviated by employing computers at the counting stage of the analysis.[10] The chief advantage of using words as the unit of analysis is their definitional simplicity; the primary disadvantage is the amount of effort required to collect the data.

The next unit of analysis—themes—refers to any proposition (e.g., democracy is good) contained in the communication. Since themes can be found in clauses, sentences, paragraphs, illustrations, and entire stories, it is also necessary to specify which of these places (including all of them) will be searched when using theme as the unit of analysis. For example, you might count only the primary theme in each paragraph or you might include every theme, no matter how slight the reference to it. An example of the theme approach to content analysis is McClelland's study of achievement motivation. The biggest problem with this unit of analysis is coder-reliability. Two different people can conceivably arrive at quite different sets of themes after examining the same communication. Thus it is common practice that at least two individuals code each communication, that their measurements be compared, and that any differences be worked out.

Space/time refers to the amount of space (written communications) or time (broadcast communications) devoted to a certain topic. If you are studying the amount of news about Country A found in Country B's leading newspapers, you might use the number of column inches of newspaper space as your unit of analysis. Similarly, the number of seconds is an appropriate unit for broadcasts. In using space/time units, it is often helpful to weight the original measures by their location in the printed document or broadcast. For example, a story appearing on the front page of a newspaper might be weighted twice as much (i.e., the number of column inches would be multiplied by two) as a story buried among the classified ads.

---

[10] For the main computer approach to content analysis, see P. J. Stone *et al.,* *The General Inquirer,* Cambridge, Mass., M.I.T. Press, 1966.

This brief outline of some of the major units employed in content analysis gives only an imperfect glimpse of the research possibilities. Not only can any communication have several different units of analysis, it can also contain many variables. In order to give you some idea of the kinds of variables that can be measured through content analysis and the ways in which these variables can be categorized, here is a list of the types of categories frequently employed in content analysis.

"What is said" categories:

Subject Matter. What is the communication about?

Direction. How is the subject matter treated (e.g., favorable-unfavorable, strong-weak)?

Standard. What is the basis on which the classification by direction is made?

Values. What values, goals, or wants are revealed?

Methods. What means are used to achieve goals?

Traits. What are the characteristics used in description of people?

Actor. Who is represented as undertaking certain acts?

Authority. In whose name are statements made?

Origin. Where does the communication originate?

Target. To what persons or groups is the communication directed?

Location. Where does the action take place?

Conflict. What are the sources and levels of conflict?

Endings. Are conflicts resolved happily, ambiguously, or tragically?

Time. When does the action take place?

"How it is said" categories:

Form or Type of Communication. What is the medium of communication (newspaper, radio, television, speech, etc.)?

Form of Statement. What is the grammatical or syntactical form of the communication?

Device. What is the rhetorical or propagandistic method used?[11]

If you decide to employ content analysis, you should read more about the technique. The best elementary introduction is Robert W. Budd, Robert K. Thorp, and Lewis Donohew, *Content Analysis of Communications* (New York, Macmillan, 1967). For a recent analysis of content analysis methodology and its applications, see Ole Holsti, "Content Analysis," in Lindzey and Aronson (eds.), pp. 596–692.

STATISTICAL RECORDS

A large amount of quantitative information is collected by government, quasi-public, and private agencies. These data, however, are not found in

[11] This list is taken from Ole Holsti, "Content Analysis," in Lindzey and Aronson (eds.), *op. cit.*, p. 645. This list can also be helpful in developing categories for analyzing the responses to open-ended survey questions.

any single location; they must be ferreted out from a variety of publications. The following annotated bibliography covers some of the major sources in six arbitrarily defined areas: U.S. Census materials, American state and local data, American election returns, congressional materials, comparative-international data, and data archives. In allowing other agencies to do your data collection, you should not haphazardly pick the data fruit from their trees. In all cases, you should check the adequacy of the methods used by the collecting agency and examine its operational definitions in order to see if they accord with your interpretation of the study variables.

1. U.S. Census Materials. The major data collector in the United States is the Bureau of the Census. Although its primary efforts are devoted to the Decennial Census, the Bureau conducts censuses of agriculture, manufactures, minerals, transportation, foreign trade, construction, and governments. In order to give you some idea of the scope of variables provided by various Census publications, here is a selective list:

population density, population change in last decade, black population, population over 65, presidential vote, median school years completed, white-collar employment, median income, number of families with incomes less than $3,000 and greater than $10,000, number of welfare recipients, number of owner-occupied housing units, median rent, bank deposits, governmental revenue, governmental expenditures (by broad categories: education, highways, public welfare, health and hospitals, and police protection), number of manufacturing establishments by industry classification, and number, size, and value of farms.

In utilizing these data, you will find any one of three Census publications helpful, depending on your level of analysis. If your focus is regions, states, counties, or cities with a population of 25,000 or more, then you should use the County and City Data Book, issued every five years with the latest edition being the 1967 one. The Congressional District Data Book, which has been published for each Congress since the Eighty-Seventh (1961–1962), gives the data by congressional district. For each major metropolitan area, a separate report called Census Tract Statistics is published giving the data by census tract—an artificial geographical unit which is a small, permanently established area having an average population of 4,000 which is as homogeneous as possible in population and housing characteristics.

A special census which is quite relevant for political researchers is the Census of Governments, taken in years ending in 2 and 7 (e.g., 1962 and 1967). This undertaking collects, for all U.S. governmental units (including special districts), information on the number of elective offices, government employees, size of payroll, revenue (by type), public school enrollment, expenditures (by character and function), indebtedness, and assessed value of taxable property. The results of this census are published in several volumes, all of which have "Census of Governments" as part of their title.

2. American State and Local Data. The primary sources of information on American states and cities are the Census publications. Other sources include *The Book of the States*, published biennially by the Council of State Governments, which provides (for all fifty states) data on governmental structure, state legislators, governmental revenue and expenditures, indebtedness, intergovernmental aid, and utilization of state services; and the *Municipal Yearbook*, issued annually by the International City Managers' Association, which reports data on governmental matters for all cities with a population of 10,000 or more. This information is gathered through a questionnaire sent to the city officials, and the topics vary from year to year. For individual cities or states we can consult state manuals, city directories, and planning commission studies. A helpful guide to this rather fugitive body of literature is given in E. E. Schattschneider and Victor Jones, *Local Political Surveys* (New York, Holt, Rinehart and Winston, 1962).

3. American Election Returns. Strangely enough, in a country that calls itself the world's greatest democracy, there is no systematic collection of election data. Fortunately, for presidential contests, one can combine the resources of several works to yield a record of the presidential vote, by county, from 1836 to the present time. These publications are W. Dean Burnham, *Presidential Ballots, 1836–1892* (Baltimore, Md., Johns Hopkins University Press, 1955); Edgar Eugene Robinson, *The Presidential Vote, 1896–1932* (Stanford, Calif., Stanford University Press, 1934); and Richard M. Scammon, *America at the Polls: A Handbook of American Presidential Election Statistics, 1920–1964* (Pittsburgh, Pa., University of Pittsburgh Press, 1965). The county-by-county results for all elections for U.S. senators, U.S. representatives, and U.S. governors since 1952 are found in Richard M. Scammon, *America Votes*, vols. 1–2 (New York, Macmillan, 1956–1958), vols. 3–5 (Pittsburgh, Pa., University of Pittsburgh Press, 1959–1964), vols. 6–7 (Washington, *Congressional Quarterly*, 1966–1968); this series will continue to publish a volume for each biennial election period. Total returns for Congressional elections are given in the *Congressional Directory*, a semiannual government publication. For election results for other offices or by smaller civil divisions (e.g., wards), we must go to state manuals, local election offices, or newspapers. For a useful survey of state practices in publishing election returns, see William Riker, *The Study of Local Politics* (New York, Random House, 1959, pp. 114–117).

4. Congressional Materials. Since its founding in 1945, Congressional Quarterly, Inc. (CQ) has been the leader in collecting data on the U.S. Congress. In addition to reporting each legislator's vote on all record roll calls, CQ publications provide data on the history of individual bills, committee assignments, legislators' backgrounds, and certain election results.

The primary CQ publications are the annual *Congressional Quarterly Almanac* and the weekly *Congressional Quarterly Weekly Report*. A compilation of the highlights of the post-World War II Congresses is found in CQ's *Congress and the Nation, 1945–1964*. Biographical data for national legislators (e.g., birthplace, education, other political offices) is given in the *Biographical Directory of the American Congress, 1774–1961* and, for later periods, the *Congressional Directory*.

5. Comparative and International Data. The two best sources for comparative and international data are the United Nations' *Statistical Yearbook* and *The Europa Year Book* (London, Europa Publications). The U.N. *Statistical Yearbook*, issued annually since 1948, presents data on items such as population, employment, agricultural output, forestry, fishing, and mineral production, manufacturing production (by broad industry classification), energy output, transportation facilities and traffic, internal and foreign trade, communication facilities and traffic, consumption, wage and price levels, national accounts, health facilities, housing, education, and mass communications for most nations. *The Europa Year Book*, published annually in two volumes since 1960, gives country membership lists for over 100 international organizations and, for most of the world's nations, data on: area, population, employment, economic production, national accounts, foreign trade, tourism, transportation, mass communications, education, current holders of major governmental posts, diplomatic ties, voting results (by party for the last national election), names and leaders of the major political parties, religious membership figures, major newspapers and periodicals and their circulation, size and scope of broadcast networks, list of trade unions with membership figures, and major universities and their enrollments. All sets of comparative data, including these two, are plagued with a lack of information on certain variables for certain countries. Although almost every nation is included in each collection, there are very few variables for which data are reported for every nation.

Two collections of special interest to political investigators are Arthur S. Banks and Robert B. Textor (eds.), *A Cross-Polity Survey* (Cambridge, Mass., M.I.T. Press, 1963); and Bruce M. Russett *et al.*, *World Handbook of Political and Social Indicators* (New Haven, Conn., Yale University Press, 1964). In addition to presenting some standard population, economic, and social variables for 115 nations, *A Cross-Polity Survey* also presents measurements for a large number of political concepts and variables. A sample listing includes political modernization, ideological orientation, governmental stability, vertical power distribution, and role of police. The *World Handbook* covers 141 countries and includes socioeconomic variables, governmental expenditures, military personnel, voting results, and communications facilities and usage. Both works have excellent discussions of the problems of cross-national measurement, and these should be read before using any comparative data in your research studies.

Although it is not possible to give a discussion of other countries' individual statistical collections here, two excellent bibliographies are Joyce Ball (ed.), *Foreign Statistical Documents* (Stanford, Calif., Hoover Institute, 1967); and Phyllis G. Carter (ed.), *Statistical Bulletins, Annotated Bibliography of the General Statistical Bulletins of Major Political Subdivisions of the World* (Washington, U.S. Library of Congress, 1954).

6. Data Archives. The last decade has witnessed the development of a new mechanism for collecting and storing quantitative information: the social-science data archives. These archives obtain, organize, maintain, and disseminate data collected by individual scholars and survey research organizations and, in a few instances, sponsor new collection efforts. The three most prominent data archives are the Inter-University Consortium for Political Research (ICPR), the Roper Public Opinion Research Center, and the International Data Library and Reference Service (IDLRS).[12] ICPR —a partnership among more than 100 universities—has many major national surveys on American and European political behavior; they are also adding to archives election returns, legislative roll calls, and socioeconomic census data for the entire history of the United States. The Roper Center is the major repository for the Gallup Poll surveys, conducted both in the United States and in many other nations. The IDLRS concentrates on surveys from outside the United States, particularly from developing nations. In all cases, the archives store the data in machine-readable form in order to facilitate easy transfer and smooth analysis. "Machine-readable" means that the data are stored in such a manner that they can be read by a digital computer. The primary storage medium is the IBM card, which will be explained in the next section. Other storage media are magnetic tapes and computer disk packs.

The most important comparison to make about these three information-gathering methods is the degree of control and flexibility possessed by the investigator. With the survey instrument, you have the largest amount of power: You provide the stimuli (the questions) and you construct the categories, and every individual in the world is a possible subject. Content analysis provides less power: You still provide the categories, but the number of subjects is limited to those who write or say something which somebody happened to print or record. With statistical records all you have is a list of sources. Somebody else—a census bureau or other scholars— has done the rest and all you can do is shop among them. Information-gathering, however, has its price. If you wish to have a high degree of con-

---

[12] For more information about these and other data archives including how to obtain status reports about current holdings and dissemination costs, see Ralph L. Bisco, "Social Science Data Archives: A Review of Developments," *American Political Science Review*, 60 (March, 1966), 93–109. UNESCO now publishes a quarterly, *Social Science Information*, which monitors new developments in the availability of data.

trol over the collected information, then you must pay for it in time and money. It is much more time-consuming and expensive to conduct your own survey than it is to borrow data from others.

CODING THE DATA

If the information collected in a study exceeds one- or two-hundred scores —and in almost every situation it will—then you must have some systematic way of storing the data. Such a recording system should not only safeguard the data, but also put it in a form amenable to analysis by computers or unit-record equipment.[13] The one device that achieves both of these objectives is the IBM card.

Before discussing how the data are transformed into holes or punches on the card, let us take a close look at the card itself. The standard IBM card (Figure 5.1) has 80 vertical columns, numbered from 1 to 80 on the card. Each column has 12 possible single punch positions; 10 of these (0,1,2,3, 4,5,6,7,8,9) are printed on the card, while the other two possible punches are located immediately above the 0 punch, with the higher known as the & or 12 punch and the lower called the — or 11 punch. By using the punches singly or in combinations of two or three according to a specified code, each column can signify a digit, a letter, or a special character. Figure 5.1 shows all the possible characters with their corresponding punch code; for example, the digit 9 is represented by an punch in the 9 position, the letter C by punches in the & and 3 positions, and the character (by punches in the 12, 5, and 8 positions. All computers do not have the same set of characters; the ones given here apply to the IBM 360 series of computers.

The mechanical means for entering data on cards is a key-punch machine, a typewriter-like device where pressing the appropriate character on a keyboard causes the machine to place the corresponding punches in the card, and if desired, print the character on the card immediately above the column giving the punchcode. Instructions on the use of keypunches can be obtained from any computer center or from manuals published by the International Business Machine Corporation (IBM). Once the data have been punched, a special kind of keypunch—called a *verifier*—should be used to check the accuracy of the initial punching. The punched cards can be read by data-processing equipment which can produce duplicate sets (or decks) of cards, print the data on paper in any of several formats, transfer data from one set of columns to another, compute statistical coefficients, and transfer the data to other storage mediums such as magnetic tapes and disks.

[13] Computers and unit-record equipment are described in Appendix 1. For a more detailed account, see Kenneth Janda, *Data Processing*, 2nd ed., Evanston, Ill., Northwestern University Press, 1969.

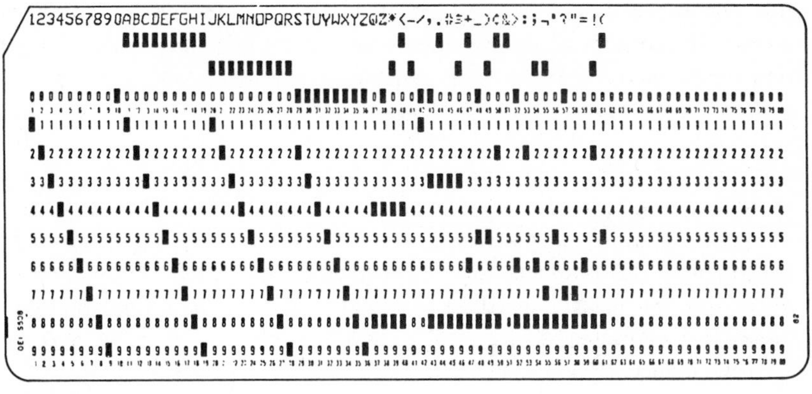

FIGURE 5-1 An IBM card

How do you organize your data so that it can be placed on IBM cards? The first step is to develop a numeric code for each variable. Although one could use letters instead of numbers as codes, the structuring of most data-processing equipment and *computer programs* (sets of instructions telling the computer which operations to perform) assume numeric codes. The function of the code is to assign a unique number for each possible value of the variable. For example, if the variable is sex, the three possible scores are male, female, and not ascertained; the code might be 1 for male, 2 for female, and 3 for not ascertained. If the variable is age and no respondent is over 99 years old, then the code might simply be the respondent's age (22 for a 22-year-old) with one other number (e.g., 00) being reserved for those cases where the age was not ascertained. In constructing codes, keep in mind the following useful hints.[14]

1. Wherever possible, use a coding scheme which corresponds to the actual values of the data. If the variable is a metric one, such as age or years of schooling, then the actual value of the variable is the best code. If the variable is measured at the ordinal level, then assign high numbers to high scores and low numbers to low scores. This lessens the chance of misunderstanding, eases the coding process, and enhances later computer analysis possibilities. With nominal data, of course, there is generally no natural coding scheme.

2. Wherever possible, telescope multidigit codes so that as many individual digits as possible can have a substantive meaning. For example, if the variable is a person's state of residence, it is unwise to arbitrarily assign any two-digit number to any state (e.g., to list the states alphabetically

[14] These hints are based, in part, on Janda, *op. cit.*, chap. 5. Another excellent source on coding is the *Manual for Coders*, Ann Arbor, Mich., Institute for Social Research, 1961.

and assign the code 01 to Alabama, 02 to Alaska, and so on). Group the states by region instead, assigning the first digit on the basis of region (e.g., 1 for New England and 2 for Middle Atlantic) and then giving a unique second digit to each state within the region (e.g., 11 for Connecticut, 12 for Maine, 21 for New Jersey). With this coding technique, later analyses involving regions can be made easily without regrouping the data.

3. Do not use a blank (no punch) as a substantive code; always assign a number to each possible score, even when the score is no answer or not ascertained. The rationale for this dictum is, first, that the lack of any punch can be misleading (Did you forget to code it or is that the proper code?) and, second, that most computer programs do not distinguish between a 0 punch and a blank.

4. Use consistent codes. If there is a set of opinion questions, all of which have the same set of categories (e.g., "agree," "disagree," "don't know," and "not ascertained"), then either use the same code for all agree responses (e.g., 1), all disagree responses (e.g., 5), etc., or, in cases where all the questions involve a single concept (e.g., liberalism), assign the same code to a pro-liberal response. Again, such an approach lessens confusion, eases coding, and takes many complications out of later analyses.

5. Do not hesitate to use as many codes as you need. Although, at the coding stage, it is tempting to give the same code to two or more slightly different scores on a variable (e.g., combine strong and weak Democrats into a single code), such parsimony can end up being false economy when it is necessary later to distinguish between the scores. If scores are not combined at the coding stage, it is always possible to do so later without much difficulty while still retaining the original codes; but if combined early, then a change of heart requires laborious recoding.

After we have developed a coding scheme for each variable, the next stage involves mapping the locations of the variables on the IBM card(s). First, you must determine how many columns will be needed to score the information for each study subject. For example, if you have 40 variables with one-digit codes, 25 variables with two-digit codes, and 10 variables with three-digit codes, you will need 120 columns ([40] [1] + [25] [2] + [10] [3] = 120) for each subject. Second, you must reserve columns for a unique identification number (ID) for each subject. If the number of subjects is under 100, you will need two columns for the ID; if it is more than 100 but less than 1,000, you will require three columns; and so on. Third, if the number of columns needed to store the variable codes and the ID exceeds 80, more than one card will be required for each study subject. It will then be necessary to reserve one column (for studies where there are less than ten cards per subject) or two columns (ten or more cards per respondent) to identify each card in the set of cards belonging to each study subject; this code is called a deck number. The ID together with the deck number (if necessary) gives each card a unique identification sequence so that lost or misplaced cards can be easily detected. The final step in this stage is to assign a specific column or columns for each variable, for the ID, and for the deck number (if required). If more than one card is needed for each subject, the ID should be repeated on each card in the same set of columns in order to obtain a unique identification for each card. Under no circumstances should more than one variable be assigned to the same set of columns. In the early days of data processing, analysis was sometimes simplified by condensing the data storage as much as possible, even to the extent of placing the codes for two or more variables in the same column. Today, this practice complicates analysis, since few computer programs are designed to handle such a format. The location assignments together with the codes for each variable constitute a *codebook.*

The final stage in the coding process is to translate the collected data into IBM card punches using the codebook as the dictionary. Suppose that from a sample of 1,100 persons we obtained measurements on 50 variables. The first step is to develop a code for each variable. In large part, the codes should be developed before the data are collected. For open-ended questions, however, it is necessary to examine the responses before constructing the final code and, for all types of items, it is frequently necessary to modify the code after the study has been executed. Although we will not develop codes for all 50 variables here, let us construct them for the following four: sex, political party identification, age, and respondent's state of birth. Our codes might be:

Sex: 1 = Male
                              2 = Female
                              3 = Not ascertained

Political party
    identification: 0 = Strong Democrat
                              1 = Not very strong Democrat
                              2 = Independent, leans toward Democrats
                              3 = Firm Independent
                              4 = Independent, leans toward Republicans
                              5 = Not very strong Republican
                              6 = Strong Republican
                              7 = Other party, minor party, refused to say
                              8 = Apolitical, don't know
                              9 = Not ascertained

Age: Actual age in years (e.g., 22 = 22-year-old)
                              00 = Not ascertained

State of birth: 01 = Connecticut   04 = New Hampshire
                              02 = Maine   05 = Rhode Island
                              03 = Massachusetts   06 = Vermont

11 = Delaware	49 = Texas
12 = New Jersey	51 = Kentucky
13 = New York	52 = Maryland
14 = Pennsylvania	53 = Oklahoma
21 = Illinois	54 = Tennessee
22 = Indiana	55 = District of
23 = Michigan	Columbia
24 = Ohio	56 = West Virginia
25 = Wisconsin	61 = Arizona
31 = Iowa	62 = Colorado
32 = Kansas	63 = Idaho
33 = Minnesota	64 = Montana
34 = Missouri	65 = Nevada
35 = Nebraska	66 = New Mexico
36 = North Dakota	67 = Utah
37 = South Dakota	68 = Wyoming
40 = Virginia	71 = California
41 = Alabama	72 = Oregon
42 = Arkansas	73 = Washington
43 = Florida	80 = Alaska
44 = Georgia	81 = Hawaii
45 = Louisiana	97 = Other (U.S. territory,
46 = Mississippi	foreign country)
47 = North Carolina	98 = Don't know
48 = South Carolina	99 = Not ascertained

One of these codes (state of birth) has the telescoping feature, and all attempt to provide a code for every contingency. Although the political party identification code partially violates the earlier advice about not combining slightly different categories (e.g., 7 combines minor party and refused to say), this practice is acceptable when you are highly confident that only an extremely small percentage of the respondents will choose either of these responses; if any doubt exists, you should have separate codes.

Assuming that codes have been developed for all 50 variables, we next must decide how many columns are needed for each study subject. Since, say, 15 variables have one-digit codes (e.g., sex) and the remaining 35 have two-digit codes (e.g., age), we will require 85 columns to store the codes for the variables. The ID code will take up four columns, since, with 1100 subjects, each must have a four-digit number for a unique ID. The combined column requirements for the variable codes and ID's (85 + 4 = 89) exceeds the one-card limit (80 columns), so we must reserve a column for the deck number.

Now we are ready to assign a column location to each variable, ID, and deck number. Our codebook might be:

IBM card location

Deck	Column(s)	Item	Codes
1	1–4	ID	0001 to 1,100
1	5	Deck number	1
1	6	Sex	See text
.	.	.	.
.	.	.	.
.	.	.	.
1	41	Political party ID	See text
.	.	.	.
.	.	.	.
.	.	.	.
1	79–80	Age	See text
2	1–4	ID	0001 to 1,100
2	5	Deck number	2
.	.	.	.
.	.	.	.
.	.	.	.
2	14–15	State of birth	See text

This study required a total of 95 columns: 85 for the variable codes (Deck 1, Columns 6–80; Deck 2, Columns 6–15), 4 on each card for the ID (Deck 1, Columns 1–4; Deck 2, Columns 1–4), and one on each card for the deck number (Deck 1, Column 5; Deck 2, Column 5).

The final step in the coding process is to translate the collected data into codes. Suppose that interviews with three of the subjects yielded the following responses: Subject A (ID = 0001): male, not very strong Democrat, 26-years-old, and born in Virginia; Subject B (ID = 0002): female, political party identification not ascertained, 49-years-old, and born in Missouri; Subject Z (ID = 1100): female, strong Republican, 64-years-old, and born in Kansas. The respective codes for these subjects would be: A(0001,1,26,40); B(0002,9,49,34); and Z(1100,2,6,64,32).

CONCLUDING COMMENTS

Chapters 3, 4, and 5 have all dealt with the measurement and collection of data for political research, and in addition to presenting the major tools for these tasks, it has been constantly emphasized that there are many errors to be made. The remainder of this book will consider statistical techniques for describing and analyzing the collected data. In performing the statistical operations, it is very easy to forget the fragility of the measurement and collection process and to mistakenly assign an almost sacred status to the data. There is, it seems, something about numbers that gives us a false sense of exactitude. You should always remember that the numbers you are manipulating are not abstract entities but representations of real phenomena; it is never simply 2 + 2, but 2 Democrats + 2 Republicans, with Democrats and Republicans each defined, measured, and collected in a specified way. The numbers are only as good as the means used to measure and collect them.

EXERCISES

1 Prepare a questionnaire for a survey of a general population. Your questionnaire should have a minimum of three questions in each of the following areas: opinions, attitudes, and beliefs; social characteristics; knowledge of political affairs; and past behavior. Give two versions of each question, and briefly explain why one version is better than the other.

2 Using the above questionnaire, interview at least three persons. If at all possible, the respondents should have diverse socioeconomic backgrounds. Write a short report on the questionnaire's efficacy (including suggestions for improvement) based on your interview experiences.

3 Briefly review three of the following content analysis studies. Pay particular attention to the data sources, the level of analysis, and the categorization of variables. The studies are Ibrahim Abu-Lughod, "International News in the Arabic Press: A Comparative Content Analysis," *Public Opinion Quarterly, 26* (Winter, 1962), 600–612; Leonard Broom and Shirley Reece, "Political and Racial Interest: A Study in Content Analysis," *Public Opinion Quarterly, 19* (Spring, 1955), 5–19; Daniel Lerner, Ithiel de Sola Pool, and Harold Lasswell, "Comparative Analysis of Political Ideologies: A Preliminary Statement," *Public Opinion Quarterly, 15* (Winter, 1951), 713–733; Milton Lodge, "Soviet Elite Participatory Attitudes in the Post-Stalin Period," *American Political Science Review, 62* (September, 1968), 827–839; Richard L. Merritt, "Public Opinion in Colonial America: Content Analyzing the Colonial Press," *Public Opinion Quarterly, 27* (Fall, 1963), 356–371; David L. Paletz and Robert Dunn, "Press Coverage of Civil Disorders: A Case Study of Winston-Salem, 1967," *Public Opinion Quarterly, 33* (Fall, 1969), 328–345; Ralph K. White, "Hitler, Roosevelt and the Nature of War Propaganda," *Journal of Abnormal and Social Psychology, 44* (April, 1949), 157–174; and Dina A. Zinnes, "A Comparison of Hostile Behavior of Decision-Makers in Simulated and Historical Data," *World Politics, 28* (April, 1966), 474–502.

4 Construct a codebook for the questionnaire prepared in the first exercise. The coding scheme should give the IBM card location and all codes for each question.

6 DESCRIBING ONE VARIABLE

The first task in data analysis is to describe each study variable. We should carefully examine each tree before attempting to explain the composition of the forest. A relatively complete description of any variable has three components: What is the distribution of scores (*frequency distribution*)? What is the typical or average score (*measure of central tendency*)? How much do the scores vary (*measure of dispersion or variation*)? In addition to providing a solid base for further analysis, frequency distributions and measures of central tendency and variation of and by themselves give a great deal of insight into the workings of phenomena. (Example: If a variable does not vary—if each subject has approximately the same score—there is little purpose in computing its covariation with another variable.) Because this is especially so when similar sets of scores are compared, many of the examples in this chapter involve calculating these measures for two or more variables. Finally, before going on, you should review the discussion in Chapter 3 of nominal, ordinal, and metric levels of measurement, since in most instances the particular statistic used depends on the measurement level.

FREQUENCY DISTRIBUTIONS

A frequency distribution is simply a list of the number of subjects in each category of a variable. Since there are usually a large number of possible categories or scores for metric variables, sets of categories are constructed and frequencies are tabulated for each set. Once the raw frequencies have been counted, percentages, graphical representations, and cumulative frequency distributions for ordinal or metric data can be used to improve our understanding of the variable's distribution. This section will first cover these methods for nominal and ordinal data and then discuss them for metric variables.

To construct a frequency distribution for a nominal or ordinal variable, list all the categories and count the number of subjects that fall into each category. Suppose that the variable is party identification and that the categories are: Strong Democrat, Weak Democrat, Independent Democrat, Independent, Independent Republican, Weak Republican, Strong Republican, and Other (other parties or apolitical, don't know, and not ascertained). Taking the set of subjects (in this case, five national samples for five presidential election years, each of which constitutes one set), we count how many are Strong Democrats, how many are Weak Democrats, and so on. The results of this counting process—the frequency distribution—can then be put in the form of a table, as in Table 6.1 which gives the five frequency distributions. Such a table should, at a minimum, give the name of the variable (e.g., party identification), the variable's categories (e.g., Strong Democrat), the number (or N) for each category (e.g., 392 Strong Democrats in 1952), the total number of subjects or the total N (e.g., 1799 in 1952), and the space-time location of the subjects (e.g., U.S. citizens in 1952). In addition, the table's title should indicate what statistical operation is being performed (e.g., determining frequency distribution), and if the data were originally collected by someone other than the investigator, the source should be footnoted (e.g., Inter-University Consortium for Political Research).

Giving raw frequencies and clearly listing the variable, categories, and

TABLE 6.1 FREQUENCY DISTRIBUTION OF PARTY IDENTIFICATION IN THE UNITED STATES: 1952–1968

Party identification	Year				
	1952	1956	1960	1964	1968
Strong Democrat	392	364	389	417	311
	(22%)	(21%)	(20%)	(27%)	(20%)
Weak Democrat	449	402	476	385	396
	(25%)	(23%)	(24%)	(25%)	(25%)
Independent Democrat	173	111	121	144	153
	(10%)	(6%)	(6%)	(9%)	(10%)
Independent	90	155	188	121	164
	(5%)	(9%)	(10%)	(8%)	(11%)
Independent Republican	128	146	128	88	135
	(7%)	(8%)	(7%)	(6%)	(9%)
Weak Republican	245	250	263	210	224
	(14%)	(14%)	(13%)	(13%)	(14%)
Strong Republican	241	262	299	171	149
	(13%)	(15%)	(15%)	(11%)	(10%)
Other, apolitical, don't know	81	72	90	35	25
	(4%)	(4%)	(5%)	(2%)	(2%)
Total	1799	1762	1954	1571	1557
	(100%)	(100%)	(100%)	(101%)[a]	(101%)[a]

[a] Because of rounding, percentage totals do not always equal 100 percent.
SOURCE: Inter-University Consortium for Political Research.

subjects gets us part of the way toward a ready interpretation of a variable's distribution, but it does not provide a fully unambiguous means for gauging the importance of an individual frequency or for making comparisons between frequencies for different variables. What proportion of the 1952 sample were Strong Democrats? Does the increase in the number of Strong Republicans from 262 in 1956 to 299 in 1960 indicate a real jump in Republican strength? To answer these kinds of questions, we must calculate the percentage of the total set of subjects found in each category. The percentages give us a method for determining any category's proportion to the whole and a consistent yardstick for making comparisons within and between sets of scores.

To calculate a percentage for any category, divide the number of subjects in the category by the total number of subjects and multiply the quotient by 100 or

$$\text{Category percentage} = \frac{(\text{Category } N)(100)}{\text{Total } N}$$

For example,

$$\text{1952 Strong Democrat percentage} = \frac{(392)(100)}{1{,}799} = 21.8\% = 22\%$$

The percentages for the party-identification frequency distributions are given in Table 6.1. Percentages should never be reported without also giving, at a minimum, the base or total N. Obviously 66.7 percent means one thing when it is 2 out of 3 subjects and quite another when it is 667 out of 1,000.

In determining the degree of precision (i.e., the number of significant digits)[1] to use in expressing the percentage (e.g., 21.7899, 21.790, 21.79, 21.8, or 22) you should always avoid imparting a false sense of accuracy. Two rules of thumb are helpful. First, the percentage should have a unique, substantive meaning when translated back into real numbers. In this case, where there are 1,799 individual persons and where only the numbers 0, 1, 2, ... 1,798, 1,799 (and not 1.5 or 1,128.47) have any meaningful interpretation,[2] it does not make sense to express the percentage in more than hundredths (e.g., no more precise than 21.79), since changing the thousandth's digit would not change the rounded whole number result (e.g., you get 392 when multiplying 1,799 by either 21.790 or 21.799). The second guideline is that the percentage should be only as exact as the measurement and collection process. In this case, where the data were gathered from a national sample and thereby subject to a sampling error of about ± 3 percent (assuming a 5 percent risk), it makes little sense to use more than whole percentages.

---

[1] A significant digit is any digit except a leading zero. Thus 1112.4 has 5 significant digits, 6.002 has 4, and 0002 has 1.

[2] Data which can have only certain values are called discrete; those which can potentially assume any value are termed continuous

After you have determined the precision for any number (e.g., whole percentage), you should calculate one more digit (e.g., 21.8 percent) and then round off the number to the nearest whole percentage (e.g., 22 percent). The rule for rounding is: Round up if the last digit is 6 or greater, round down if the last digit is 4 or less, and round to the nearest even number if the last digit is 5 (21.7 = 22, 21.2 = 21, 21.5 = 22, and 22.5 = 22).

Even after the percentages have been calculated, one roadblock to ready interpretation still remains. While it is easy to compare one percentage with another and that percentage with still another, it is difficult to visualize the variable's distribution as a whole. To get a holistic perspective we must construct a graph. With nominal and ordinal data the most useful type of graph for displaying frequency distributions is the *histogram* or *bar chart*.

A histogram of the distribution of party identification in 1968 is presented in Figure 6.1 The categories are represented on the horizontal axis, percentages on the vertical axis, and the height of each bar is proportional to the number of percentage units in each category. When the categories are derived from nominal variables, their ordering along the horizontal axis is immaterial. When they are ordinal or metric, for purposes of clarity, they should be ordered from the lowest to the highest.

Finally, let us return to Table 6.1 to see the kinds of substantive information which can be obtained from frequency distributions. Statements which can be derived from this table include:

1. The Democratic Party has been consistently stronger than the Republican Party between 1952 and 1968.

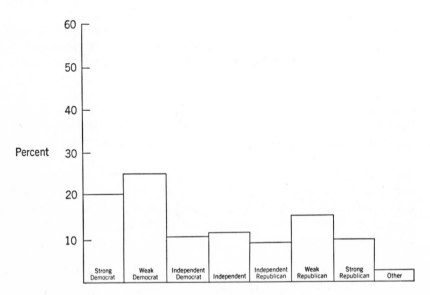

FIGURE 6-1 A histogram of party identification in the United States: 1968 (N = 1557)
SOURCE: Inter-university Consortium for Political Research.

2. A substantial majority of Americans identify to some extent with one of the two major parties.
3. The relative strength of party identification has remained quite constant during the 1952–1968 period. (One cannot state, on the basis of Table 6.1, that individuals' party identification has stayed largely the same during this period. It could be that there are wide shifts between the four-year intervals and that only the *net* figures remain relatively the same.)

In general, it is very good practice to list the major implications of each frequency distribution. Such a procedure not only helps you answer the questions you had initially in mind, but it also prevents you from carelessly overlooking new and interesting implications.

More than nominal or ordinal data, metric variables require frequency distributions in order to understand anything about them. Witness the following differences between the winning and losing vote percentages (i.e., a measure of competitiveness, with low numbers indicating close races and high numbers low competition) in the 110 U.S. senatorial elections held between 1950 and 1954: 53.0, 25.6, 100.0, 18.4, 6.6, 5.2, 52.6, 100.0, 23.4, 8.2, 6.6, 10.2, 10.6, 9.2, 75.4, 7.0, 7.2, 16.0, 18.8, 5.2, 37.4, 35.2, 15.0, 9.6, 52.6, 3.6, 100.0, 27.8, 8.0, 56.0, 7.4, 7.2, 0.2, 3.0, 34.4, 23.4, 2.6, 100.0, 8.4, 9.0, 100.0, 5.6, 25.4, 5.0, 3.0, 1.6, 14.2, 100.0, 8.0, 2.2, 42.6, 3.4, 12.0, 2.2, 20.8, 48.0, 9.2, 3.6, 9.6, 56.0, 100.0, 8.6, 44.6, 100.0, 12.8, 7.2, 8.6, 3.2, 2.6, 3.0, 27.2, 75.0, 100.0, 2.6, 13.8, 100.0, 25.6, 7.2, 4.6, 14.8, 9.0, 100.0, 17.2, 1.6, 1.8, 14.4, 91.2, 0.8, 22.2, 20.4, 0.2, 14.6, 31.8, 12.2, 0.4, 18.6, 16.4, 14.6, 40.0, 70.2, 100.0, 9.6, 3.0, 7.8, 15.6, 21.8, 16.2, 20.4, 100.0, 0.2. The human mind cannot cope with such a long series of numbers; they must be summarized.

It is evident that we cannot have a separate category for each possible value if we hope to simplify this set of numbers. In this instance, where the numbers represent percentages expressed to the tenths of 1 percent, there are 1,001 possible values (0.0, 0.1, . . . 99.9, 100.0); for other metric variables (e.g., income), there might be a near-infinity of possible scores. We must group the scores into a smaller number of categories, called *class intervals*. The following guidelines should be used in constructing class intervals:

1. There should be enough intervals to give an adequate notion of the shape of the distribution without having so many that a brief examination of the frequency distribution cannot encompass its major aspects. Ordinarily, this means that the number of intervals should be between about six and twenty. In our example (see Table 6.2), ten intervals are used.
2. The intervals should have the same width (in this case 10 percent) in order to enable comparisons between frequencies. Otherwise, it would be like comparing the shooting averages of basketball players who used different-sized baskets. In a few instances, it will be necessary to have a larger open-ended category as the last interval. For example, a frequency

distribution of family income might have one or two scores in the millions. If the common interval width were $2,000 or $3,000, it would clearly be impractical to have hundreds of intervals (almost all of which would have no cases) simply to include the few high incomes. In these cases, the common practice is to make the last or highest interval "x or higher" (e.g., $15,000 or higher).

3. The interval width should be small enough so that it makes sense to consider each case falling within it as effectively identical. Here we confront one of the seeming paradoxes of data analysis: In order to gain understanding, we must sacrifice information. By grouping the data in this example, we lose the precise identity of individual scores: 2.6 and 8.4 are both entries in the 0.0–10.0 interval. In order to justify this grouping and to guarantee that the price being paid for summarization is not too high, we must, in this example, be willing to assume that a percentage difference of 2.6 percent and one of 8.4 percent are effectively the same (e.g., both highly competitive). If we cannot make such an assumption, if we thought, for example, that an election with a 2.6 percent difference was distinctly more competitive than one with an 8.4 percent gap, then we would need smaller interval widths (say, 5 percent).

4. The class intervals should be exhaustive and mutually exclusive. For each score there should be one and only one interval. To achieve this objective, the interval limits must be expressed to at least the same degree of precision as the scores. In this example, the intervals cannot be 0–10, 11–20, and so on, since there are scores (e.g., 10.2) between 10 and 11.

TABLE 6.2 FREQUENCY DISTRIBUTIONS OF DIFFERENCES BETWEEN WINNING AND LOSING CANDIDATES' VOTE PERCENTAGES IN U.S. SENATORIAL ELECTIONS: 1950–1954 AND 1962–1966

Percentage difference	1950–1954		1962–1966	
	N	%	N	%
0.0–10.0	48	43.6	47	43.1
10.1–20.0	20	18.2	22	20.2
20.1–30.0	12	10.9	19	17.4
30.1–40.0	5	4.6	12	11.0
40.1–50.0	3	2.7	1	0.9
50.1–60.0	5	4.6	2	1.8
60.1–70.0	0	0.0	1	0.9
70.1–80.0	3	2.7	0	0.0
80.1–90.0	0	0.0	0	0.0
90.1–100.0	14	12.7	5	4.6
Total	110	100.0	109	99.9[a]

[a] Because of rounding, percentage totals do not always equal 100 percent.
SOURCE: Adapted from data in *Politics in America, 1945–1966*, 2nd ed., Washington, Congressional Quarterly, 1967, pp. 107–109 and 113–115, with the permission of the publisher.

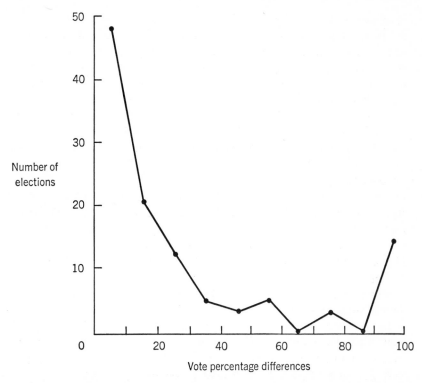

FIGURE 6-2 A frequency polygon of differences between winning and losing vote percentages in U.S. senatorial elections: 1950-1954
SOURCE: Adapted from data in *Politics in America*, 2nd ed., Washington, Congressional Quarterly, 1967, pp. 107-109, with the permission of the publisher.

Once the intervals have been constructed, one simply counts the number of cases falling into each interval and the resulting tabulation constitutes the frequency distribution. Two distributions—one for senatorial elections in the 1950–1954 period and one for senatorial contests in the 1962–1966 period—are presented in Table 6.2. Note that the tabular presentation is the same as for nominal and ordinal variables and that it is again useful to compute percentages.

Although metric frequency distributions can be graphically displayed on histograms, a more appropriate graph is the *frequency polygon*. Figure 6.2 presents a frequency polygon for the senatorial vote-percentage differences during the 1950–1954 period. The vertical axis represents the number of elections (it could also, if you wished, represent the percentage of elections) and the horizontal axis the set of intervals, going from the lowest (0.0–10.0) to the highest (90.1–100.0). For each interval, place a dot directly above the interval midpoint, with the height of the dot determined by the number of cases (or, if the vertical scale is percentage units, the percentage of cases) in the interval. For example, since there are 48 elections where the percentage difference is between 0.0 and 10.0, the dot is placed 48 units above that interval's midpoint. The midpoints are then joined by straight lines to form the overall polygon, which in turn pictorializes the shape of the distribution. You cannot, however, make any inferences about the number of cases at any point on the line between the dots. The fact that the line is at about the 16-level on the vertical axis when it is directly above the 20 percent mark on the horizontal axis does not mean that there are 16 elections with a 20 percent difference. It is important to realize this aspect of frequency polygons because there are other graphs where such inferences are valid.

Again, let us sample the kinds of conclusions which can be drawn based on a frequency distribution. In this example, we are interested in the changes, if any, in competition (as measured by the difference between the winning and losing percentage) for senatorial elections between 1950 and 1954 and between 1962 and 1966. What have we learned? First, if one postulates a 10 percent difference or less (i.e., a 55–45 percent split or closer) as a highly competitive election, slightly less than half of the races earn this label. Second, there has not been any change in the proportion of close contests between the two periods; in both instances the figure is about 43 percent. Third, there has been a noticeable decline in the proportion of unanimous and near-unanimous elections (the 90.1–100.0 interval) from 12.7 percent in the 1950–1954 period to 4.6 percent in the 1962–1966 period.

In some investigations, we are interested not only in the number of cases in each interval, but, for ordinal and metric variables, we also want to know how many cases are above or below each cutting point. Taking the vote-difference example, how many elections are decided by more than 10 percent? by more than 30 percent? by less than 20 percent? A cumulative frequency distribution is a way to arrange data so as to answer these questions. As Table 6.3 indicates, frequency distributions can be cumulated either down (how many cases are equal to or greater than each interval) or up (how many cases are equal to or less than each interval). For example, looking at the left side of Table 6.3, we see that 21 (or 19.3 percent) of the elections had a percentage vote difference of 30.1 percent or more; examining the right side, we can note that 69 (or 63.3 percent) of the elections had differences of 20.0 percent or less. Since the first (cumulating down) or last (cumulating up) interval contains the totals, there is no need for a separate totals entry.

By constructing a frequency polygon for a cumulative frequency distribution (called an *ogive*), we can get a graphic representation. If you are interested in both the up-and-down cumulative frequency distributions, both can be placed on the same graph as in Figure 6.3. In an ogive, the cutting points of the intervals are placed on the horizontal axis and, as was the case with the frequency polygon, the frequencies (e.g., number of elections)

TABLE 6.3 CUMULATIVE FREQUENCY DISTRIBUTION (UP AND DOWN) OF DIFFERENCES BETWEEN WINNING AND LOSING VOTE PERCENTAGES IN U.S. SENATORIAL ELECTIONS: 1962–1966

Differences equal to or greater than	Cumulating down	Differences equal to or less than	Cumulating up
0.0	109 (100.0%)	10.0	47 (43.1%)
10.1	62 (56.7%)	20.0	69 (63.3%)
20.1	40 (36.7%)	30.0	88 (80.7%)
30.1	21 (19.3%)	40.0	100 (91.7%)
40.1	9 (8.3%)	50.0	101 (92.7%)
50.1	8 (7.3%)	60.0	103 (94.5%)
60.1	6 (5.5%)	70.0	104 (95.4%)
70.1	5 (4.6%)	80.0	104 (95.4%)
80.1	5 (4.6%)	90.0	104 (95.4%)
90.1	5 (4.6%)	100.0	109 (100.0%)

SOURCE: Adapted from data in *Politics in America,* 2nd ed., Washington, Congressional Quarterly, 1967, pp. 113–115, with the permission of the publisher.

on the vertical axis. (The proportion of cases, expressed in percentages, could also be placed on the vertical axis.) The cumulated frequencies are represented as dots immediately above the cutting points, and to form the ogive, connect the dots with straight lines. Again, no inferences can be drawn from points between the dots.

MEASURES OF CENTRAL TENDENCY
A frequency distribution exhausts the summarizing techniques for nominal data; once we have tabulated the number of cases in each category, computed the percentages, and graphed the results, we have essentially completed the statistical description. For ordinal and metric variables, however, we can calculate certain measures of central tendency in order to determine the typical or average value in a distribution. In the next section, we will see how measures of dispersion can also be employed to describe the distribution of metric variables. In effect, these two kinds of measures give us specific numerical figures for summarizing the main characteristics of a variable's distribution: what value does the distribution center around and to what extent is the distribution concentrated or dispersed? Although there are many possible ways of defining a typical score, only two central tendency measures are normally used in political research: the *median* and the *mean.*

If we are to have a central tendency measure for ordinal data, it must be one that does not require addition, subtraction, multiplication, or division to calculate it since ordinal data lack the constant intervals that these arithmetic operations assume. Its computation must be based, instead, simply on order or position. Since, positionally, the most typical score is the

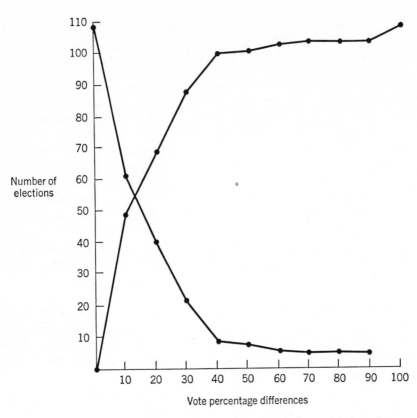

Number of elections

Vote percentage differences

FIGURE 6-3 Ogive (up and down) of differences between winning and losing vote percentages in U.S. senatorial elections: 1962-1966

SOURCE: Adapted from data in *Politics in America*, 2nd ed., Washington, Congressional Quarterly, 1967, pp. 113-115, with the permission of the publisher.

one that falls in the middle of the distribution, we will consider this to be our measure of central tendency for ordinal variables. This middle score, called the median, is specifically defined as the score of that case which has the same number of cases above it (i.e., higher scores) as below it (i.e., lower scores). When the total number of cases (N) is odd, the median is the score of the middle case. When the total number of cases is even, any number between the two middle cases can be considered the median although, by convention, the median, under these circumstances, is computed by adding the two middle cases and dividing by two. For example, for the set of five (i.e., N is odd) scores:

$$1, 4, 5, 8, 9$$

the median is the score of the middle case or 5. For the set of six (i.e., N is even) scores:

$$2, 6, 8, 10, 14, 16$$

the median is somewhere between the two middle scores (8 and 10) and, by our convention, is equal to $(8 + 10)/2$ or 9.

Medians can also be used with metric variables. When the data are un-grouped, the calculation procedures are the same as above. When the data are grouped into intervals, the median is defined as the midpoint of the interval which contains the middle case. Reexamining the 1962–66 election data in Table 6.2, we see that with an N of 109, the middle case would be the 55th one. Cumulating the frequencies (see Table 6.3), we find that this case occurs in the 10.1–20.0 interval. The median, then, is the midpoint of this interval or $(20.0–10.1)/2 = 15.05$, which when rounded to the origi-nal precision of the data is 15.0. This calculation procedure assumes that all the values in the middle interval are evenly distributed around the mid-point. Since this assumption is rarely fully met, the median value is nor-mally slightly different from the median which would have been obtained from calculations based on the ungrouped data. For example, the value of the median calculated from the ungrouped version of the same election data is 14.7.

Since metric data can be added, subtracted, multiplied, and divided, we can utilize these operations in calculating a measure of central tendency for metric variables. We can take the precise score for each case, sum them up, and divide by the total number of cases. The result—called the mean—corresponds to the everyday meaning of average. For example, the mean of the scores (1.2, 5.8, 9.1, 4.5) is:

$$\frac{1.2 + 5.8 + 9.1 + 4.5}{4} = \frac{19.6}{4} = 4.9$$

If the mean is for a set of sample scores, its symbol is $\overline{X}$; if it represents the entire population, its symbol is μ (the Greek letter mu).

To calculate means from grouped data, such as the 1962–1966 election data in Table 6.2, one multiplies the midpoint of each interval by the num-ber of cases in that interval and divides the sum by the total number of cases. In this example, the mean based on the grouped data is

$$\frac{5.0(47) + 15.0(22) + \cdots + 95.0(5)}{109} = \frac{2155}{109} = 19.8$$

This calculation procedure assumes that the mean of the scores in each interval is equal to the midpoint of that interval. When the number of inter-vals is relatively large (10 or more), any difference between the means cal-culated from grouped and ungrouped data because of the midpoint assump-tion is ordinarily quite small. (In the present example, the mean from the ungrouped data is 19.9.) When there are only a few intervals, however, the differences often become much greater. In any event, the best procedure is to calculate the mean (and, for that matter, the median) from the un-grouped data wherever possible in order to ensure the highest possible accuracy.

Since both the median and the mean can be used as measures of central tendency for metric variables, which one should be employed as the main indicator? With one exception, the mean is the preferable measure since it takes into account the precise score of each case; it thereby incorporates more information than the median, which only reflects a score's relative position. The one exception to this generalization is a metric variable having a disproportionate number of extreme scores at one end (but not both ends) of the distribution. Because the mean utilizes the precise score in these instances, it is pulled away from the center of the distribution by the overwhelming effect of a few extreme scores; the median, on the other hand, is not so affected by extreme scores since only a score's relative position—not its absolute value—determines the median's value. For example, the median for the scores (1, 3, 6, 10, 1,000) is 6 while the mean for the same set is 204. If one reported the average value of this set to be 204, the normal person—unaware of the scores of each case—would naturally expect that many of the scores were close to 204. Yet because of the influence of one extreme score, not one score in the entire set is even close to the supposed typical value. For such distributions both the median and the mean should be reported, and for purposes of interpretation, more reliance should be placed on the median as the measure of central tendency.

In order to get some understanding of the substantive value of computing measures of central tendency, let us return to the senatorial election data in Table 6.2. First, using the grouped data-calculation procedures, let us compute various means. For the 1950–1954 set, the mean is 27.1 percent; for the 1962–1966 data, it is 19.8 percent. Relying solely on the mean as our measure of central tendency, we would conclude that since the mean difference between winning and losing percentages had decreased from 27.1 percent in the first period to 19.8 percent in the second period, there had been a substantial increase in competition, although the mean race still was not too competitive (i.e., a 19.8 difference indicates that the mean winning percentage was 59.9 percent). Second, noting that each distribution after gradually sloping downward has a bulge in the last interval (90.1–100.0), we decide to compute the medians in order to see the effect of these extreme values. Again using the grouped-data procedures, we find that the median for each set is 15.0. Thus according to the medians, there has been no change in competition between the two periods. Combining both measures of central tendency with a reexamination of the frequency distribution, we note that the reduction in the value of the mean reflects fewer cases in the 90.1–100.0 interval (from 14 to 5), not more elections in the 0.0–10.0 interval (the number of cases is virtually the same: 48 and 47). Positionally, as the median indicates, the number of cases above and below the 20.0 percent mark has remained approximately the same. Overall, we would conclude that between the early 1950s and the mid-1960s, there has been a decrease in the number of highly noncompetitive senatorial elections, but that the proportion of highly competitive elections has remained the same. If we were carrying the analysis further, we might next want to see what kinds of elections (e.g., which states? what years?) account for this moderate change.

MEASURES OF VARIABILITY

There is one more piece of information which can be extracted from a set of metric scores: the amount of variation or the extent to which the scores change from one case to the next. To help understand why we need to know how much a variable varies, let us look at a few examples. Suppose you want to cross a wide unbridged stream, but being unable to swim, you are naturally wary about the stream's depth. Not being familiar with the area you ask a passing native "How deep is this river?" He tells you that the average (i.e., mean) depth is about three feet. Do you (a six-footer) have enough information to predict a safe crossing? No. In addition to the mean depth, you also need to know the variability of the depth. If there is no variability and the river is three feet deep at every point, you can wade across. But if the variability is high—the depth varies between one and ten feet—then you best secure some water wings.

Turning to a political setting, suppose someone tells you that the mean Democratic vote percentage for a state's ten congressional districts over the past two decades is 54 percent. Can you automatically conclude that many of the state's districts are competitive, since the mean vote is only 4 percent above the win-lose point in the typical two-party race? No again. It could be that the vote percentage is extremely variable: About half the districts have very high Democratic percentages (85–100 percent) and the other half have very low percentages (0–15 percent). Or there might be almost no variability: in each and every election the Democratic candidate polls between 53 percent and 55 percent of the vote. In either event, none of the districts could be termed competitive.

In addition to these two examples, two earlier points concerning the importance of variability deserve repeating. First, the size of a sample is highly dependent on the variability of the study variables among the population: The higher the variability, the greater the sample size for given levels of accuracy and risk. Second, one cannot examine the covariability or relationship between two variables unless both of them vary.

In this section, we will discuss five measures of variation: *range, mean deviation, standard deviation, variance,* and the *coefficient of variability.*

The simplest way to get an initial impression of the amount of dispersion in a set of scores is to calculate the difference between the highest and lowest score. This difference is the range. For the data from the 1950–1954 senatorial elections the lowest score is 0.2 and the highest is 100.0; the range, then, equals

$$100.0 - 0.2 = 99.8$$

The principal advantage of the range is that it is easy to calculate and gives us a quick idea of the amount of variability. Its chief disadvantage is that it is based on only two scores and consequently does not reflect the amount of variability in the rest of the data. Conceivably, every other score in the 1950–1954 series might be the same, in which case the wide range (99.8) is misleading.

The mean deviation makes use of every score in determining the amount of variability. To calculate it, we take the difference between each individual score and the mean; disregarding the signs of the differences (e.g., 52 minus 42 and 42 minus 52 are both treated as an absolute difference of 10), we sum and divide them by the total number of cases. (If we did not ignore the signs, the resulting sum would, by definition, always equal zero. If this is not immediately clear, you should review the concept of the mean.) This procedure gives us the mean amount by which each score differs (or deviates) from the mean of the total distribution. In formula terms,[3]

$$\text{Mean deviation} = \frac{\sum_{i=1}^{N} |X_i - \mu|}{N}$$

where X represents any metric variable

μ = the mean of X
N = the total number of X scores (normally, the total number of cases)
X_i = each individual X score
$|\ |$ = the absolute difference, ignoring signs

and $\sum_{i=1}^{N}$ means that each of the scores from the ith (in this instance, the first) to the Nth (if the total number of scores or N is 110, then the Nth score is the 110th or last one) is summated.

For example, to compute the mean deviation for the scores (4, 10, 12, 28, 36), we first calculate the mean:

$$\mu = \frac{4 + 10 + 12 + 28 + 36}{5} = \frac{90}{5} = 18$$

Next, we obtain the absolute difference between each score and the mean, sum the differences, and divide by the total number of scores:

$$\text{Mean deviation} = \frac{|4 - 18| + |10 - 18| + |12 - 18| + |28 - 18| + |36 - 18|}{5}$$

$$= \frac{14 + 8 + 6 + 10 + 18}{5} = \frac{56}{5}$$

$$= 11.2 = \text{(rounded to original precision) } 11$$

Thus, the mean difference between any individual score and the overall

[3] Some students are initially put off by mathematical formulas. Such formulas are nothing more than a form of shorthand or compact codes and, with a little time and effort, can be readily deciphered. Because they are condensed descriptions however, they must be read slowly and carefully.

mean is 11. To calculate the mean deviation from grouped data, one simply assumes that each case's score is the midpoint of its interval.

The chief advantages of the mean deviation as a measure of variation are its inclusion of every score and its straightforward interpretation. Unfortunately, these good qualities are not enough in most applications to outweigh the mean deviation's not-so-obvious mathematical limitations. Using absolute differences severely limits further arithmetic manipulations. The mean deviation, in short, is a mathematical dead end. Conversely, the standard deviation, which we will discuss next, can be readily plugged into certain aspects of probability theory that are of great assistance in interpreting research results. One of these connections will be presented in Chapter 9. In sum, the mean deviation should be used only when no further analysis is planned *and* when an easily understood measure is needed for some statistically unsophisticated audience.

The standard deviation is the most frequently used measure of variation. Although its computation (and hence its definition) is quite similar to the mean deviation's, the two measures differ in one respect. In calculating the mean deviation, we solved the signs problem by ignoring them and taking the absolute difference. The standard deviation uses a more respectable mathematical trick for making the signs the same: squaring the differences. For example, $(-5)^2$ and $(+5)^2$ both equal 25. Now, if there is any variation, the sum of the squared differences will be greater than zero. Because its calculation involves squaring instead of taking absolute differences, the standard deviation, as mentioned earlier, can easily be employed in further analysis.

The complete calculation procedure, with the accompanying rationale, for the standard deviation has the following steps. First, as before, compute the difference between each score and the mean; this ensures that every score is considered. Second, square each difference and sum the squares of the differences; this makes all the signs the same. Third, divide by the total number of scores in order to keep the final result relative to the total number of cases. (If the data come from a sample, divide by the total number of scores minus one. The reason for this slight adjustment is that the sample data, for mathematical reasons too involved to consider here, underestimates the amount of variability in the population. Since, with relatively large samples, subtracting one from the total has a very small impact on the final result, even this qualification can usually be ignored. With sample data, the standard deviation is frequently represented by the letter s.) Finally, take the square root of the quotient computed in the third step in order to compensate for the squaring in the second step and to enable use of the measure in certain parts of probability theory. In formula terms,

$$\text{Standard deviation } (\sigma) = \sqrt{\frac{\sum_{i=1}^{N}(X_i - \mu)^2}{N}}$$

Using the same set of scores (4, 10, 12, 28, 36) having a mean of 18,

$$= \sqrt{\frac{(4-18)^2 + (10-18)^2 + (12-18)^2 + (28-18)^2 + (36-18)^2}{5}}$$

$$= \sqrt{\frac{(-14)^2 + (-8)^2 + (-6)^2 + (10)^2 + (18)^2}{5}}$$

$$= \sqrt{\frac{196 + 64 + 36 + 100 + 324}{5}}$$

$$= \sqrt{\frac{720}{5}} = \sqrt{144} = 12$$

The higher the standard deviation, the greater the variation.

A simpler calculating procedure when there is a large number of scores is provided by the formula

$$\sigma = \frac{1}{N}\sqrt{N\sum_{i=1}^{N} X_i^2 - (\sum_{i=1}^{N} X_i)^2}$$

which is the mathematical equivalent of the earlier equation. In using these formulas, be careful not to confuse ΣX_i^2 and $(\Sigma X_i)^2$. ΣX_i^2 means square each X score then sum the squares; the parentheses around the term $(\Sigma X_i)^2$ mean that you should *first* add up the individual X scores and *then* square the sum of the entire set. Returning to our scores (4, 10, 12, 28, 36),

$$\sum_{i=1}^{N} X_i^2 = 4^2 + 10^2 + 12^2 + 28^2 + 36^2 = 2,340$$

and

$$(\sum_{i=1}^{N} X_i)^2 = (4 + 10 + 12 + 28 + 36)^2 = (90)^2 = 8,100$$

In computing standard deviations from grouped data, you again assume that each score is equal to the midpoint of its interval.

The variance is the square of the standard deviation or, if you prefer, the standard deviation is the square root of the variance. Thus, the basic formula for the variance is

$$\text{Variance } (\sigma^2) = \frac{\sum_{i=1}^{N} (X_i - \mu)^2}{N}$$

Although, for the statistical techniques discussed in this book, the standard deviation will be used almost exclusively, several more advanced methods, including the analysis of variance and the analysis of covariance, utilize the variance measure.

Standard deviations and variances can also be calculated for nominal or ordinal variables having only two values. Almost any nominal or ordinal variable can be transformed into a dichotomy by conceiving of it as the presence or absence of an attribute. For example, a person is either a male or a nonmale, a nation is either democratic or nondemocratic, and an organization is either hierarchical or nonhierarchical. Such dichotomies can be treated as a special kind of metric variable, called a *dummy variable*, where an attribute's absence is scored 0 and its occurrence 1. These numbers can be considered legitimate metric scores and therefore can be added, subtracted, multiplied, and divided. For example, let us compute the standard deviation of Democratic party identification in a population of five individuals. Supposing that the first three subjects are Democrats and the remaining two are non-Democrats, we have the following set of scores: 1, 1, 1, 0, 0. Summing them and dividing by the total number of scores (5) gives us a mean of 3/5 or .6. Computing the difference between each individual score and the mean, squaring each difference, summing the squares and dividing by the total number of cases gives us the variance:

$$\sigma^2 = \frac{(.6 - 1)^2 + (.6 - 1)^2 + (.6 - 1)^2 + (.6 - 0)^2 + (.6 - 0)^2}{5}$$

$$= \frac{(-.4)^2 + (-.4)^2 + (-.4)^2 + (.6)^2 + (.6)^2}{5}$$

$$= \frac{.16 + .16 + .16 + .36 + .36}{5}$$

$$= \frac{1.20}{5}$$

$$= .24$$

Taking the square root of the variance (.24) yields a standard deviation of .49.

A simpler formula for computing the variance and standard deviation of dummy variables is:

$$\sigma^2 = pq$$

$$\sigma = \sqrt{pq}$$

where p = the proportion possessing the attribute
and q = the proportion not possessing the attribute

In the current example, where $p = .60$ and $q = .40$, $\sigma^2 = (.60)(.40) = .24$. It was this method of computing variation, incidentally, which was used in measuring variation for the sampling error table in Chapter 4.

If we wish to compare the amount of dispersion between two or more variables, we cannot make our decision solely on which one has the highest standard deviation. All other things being equal, variables with high scores will have greater standard deviations than variables with lower values. To see why this is so, let us look at a single score (4) for Variable A, which has a mean of 2, and one score (8) from Variable B, which has a mean of 4. In each instance, the selected score is twice as large as the mean, but in calculating the standard deviation for Variable B, the square of the difference (8–4) will be 4^2 or 16. The fact that Variable B has, on the average, higher scores (i.e., its mean is higher) causes greater absolute differences (e.g., 8–4 as opposed to 4–2), even when the relative or proportional differences might be the same (as they were in this example); greater absolute differences, in turn, cause a higher standard deviation.

In order to control for the size of the scores, we must divide the standard deviation by the mean in order to arrive at a comparable measure of variability. Thus, the formula for the coefficient of variability (V) is

$$V = \frac{\text{Standard deviation}}{\text{Mean}}$$

With this equation, we can compare the homogeneity of any two or more variables.

In order to indicate how measures of variability can be used to interpret political phenomena, let us look at the coefficients of variability for the 1950–1954 and 1962–1966 competition percentages for the senatorial elections (see Table 6.2). Using the grouped data-computation procedures, the coefficient of variability for the 1950–1954 scores is 1.13 and for the 1962–1966 data V equals 1.06. The relative amount of variability of competition in senatorial elections between the two periods has decreased only slightly. Other instances where comparisons of variability might prove valuable are the income distributions of different states or countries, the vote distribution (by party) among geographical units, and the distribution of opinions (using dummy variables) among ethnic groups. More generally, whenever one is involved in determining the amount of cleavage/consensus, the coefficient of variability can be a useful indicator.

CONCLUDING COMMENTS
In this chapter, we have seen how individual variables can be described so that we can better understand their characteristics and the phenomena they represent. We have used frequency distributions, percentages, and various graphs to gain an overall perspective, and then employed measures of central tendency and variation to provide precise summarizing figures. All of these techniques improve our insight into the workings of individual phenomena and enable us to make some preliminary comparisons between variables. Now that we have seen how one describes a tree, let us go on to techniques designed to help us interpret the structure of the forest.

EXERCISES
1 Construct a histogram for the following frequency distribution of religious affiliation: Roman Catholics, 324; Protestants, 465; Jews, 112; Other Religion, 13; and No Religious Affiliation, 77.
2 Here are the ages of all 100 U.S. senators as of the beginning of the 91st Congress (1969–1970): 56, 69, 45, 38, 61, 59, 63, 72, 54, 66, 61, 53, 61, 58, 59, 64, 76, 54, 71, 55, 44, 61, 44, 69, 72, 49, 40, 49, 46, 52, 45, 48, 42, 67, 78, 50, 54, 71, 40, 46, 36, 49, 56, 45, 52, 40, 64, 67, 39, 67, 65, 57, 63, 64, 59, 56, 53, 68, 49, 64, 73, 53, 42, 64, 72, 72, 60, 71, 79, 52, 38, 47, 46, 36, 42, 68, 61, 50, 46, 66, 46, 68, 61, 43, 65, 43, 57, 70, 76, 62, 54, 48, 56, 63, 50, 66, 52, 53, 53, 56. For this set of data, specify the

class intervals, construct a frequency distribution, compute the percentage of cases in each interval, and construct a frequency polygon.

3 Using the above data on senatorial ages, construct two cumulative frequency distributions (one cumulating up, the other cumulating down) and the two corresponding ogives.

4 Again using the senatorial age data, compute the median, the mean, the range, the mean deviation, the standard deviation, the variance, and the coefficient of variation. Write a short paragraph summarizing your description of this variable.

7 DESCRIBING TWO-VARIABLE RELATIONSHIPS

Although the proper collection, valid and reliable measurement, and precise description of individual variables are extremely important in the conduct of political research, the real payoffs begin to come when we examine the relationships between two or more variables. For most of us, the key question is to what extent can x explain y? To what extent, for example, is democracy dependent on a high literacy rate? How much does a man's educational background affect the direction of his vote? Is a legislator's voting record a direct function of his party affiliation?

As was noted in Chapter 2, in order to move toward answering these kinds of causal questions, we need three types of evidence: temporal order (the cause or independent variable must precede the effect or dependent variable), common variation (the two variables must change together in some consistent manner), and the elimination of other possible causes. Evidence of proper temporal order is built into the original study design. One does not posit a hypothesis where the dependent variable occurred prior to the independent variable. One method of analyzing other possible causes— randomization—was presented in Chapter 2. Other techniques for dealing with this problem will be covered in Chapter 8, but this chapter will concentrate on the second type of evidence: common variation. It will present methods for describing the amount of common variation between one independent variable and one dependent variable. (Chapter 8 will deal with the more complex case of two or more independent variables.)

A description of common variation has two main aspects: degree and form. The degree of the relationship involves the amount of *covariation* or *correlation* between two variables. If two variables are highly related, then they will vary together and will have a high degree of association. Conversely, if two variables are only minimally related, then they will not vary in common, and there will be a low degree of association. Thus we first need *measures of association*, or as they are also called, *correlation coefficients*.

In addition to wanting to know the degree of the relationship, we also wish to know its form. For nominal factors, which values of one variable are associated with which values of the other variable? For higher levels of measurement, do the variables tend to move up and down together (i.e., a direct relationship) or go in opposite directions (i.e., an inverse relationship)? Finally for metric measurements, we can determine whether the factors vary in a constant fashion or whether the relationship differs for particular ranges of values.

Because the different levels of measurement generally require different measures of association, we will discuss, in turn, relationships between two nominal variables, two ordinal variables, two metric variables, and relationships involving either two dummy variables or one dummy variable and one metric variable.

NOMINAL RELATIONSHIPS

The first step in describing the association between any two variables is to arrange the data in order to get a preliminary notion of the relationship; we wish to look at the data before we leap into the calculations. The best way to gain an initial impression of the relationship between two nominal variables is to construct a *contingency table,* also known as a *cross-tabulation.*

In the example to be used in this section, we are interested in seeing if there was any change in the relationship between an individual's race and his party identification in the American South between 1961 (when the two national parties' civil-rights positions were difficult to distinguish) and 1964 (when many of Senator Goldwater's presidential campaign statements were apparently directed at gaining the support of white segregationist Southerners). The extent of the change in the relationship will give us some idea about the stability of party identification.

In order to construct a contingency table for this relationship, we begin with the frequency distributions for each of the two variables. In this case, the independent variable is race, the dependent variable is party identification, and the frequency distribution for the 1961 sample is as follows:

Race	N	Party identification	N
Black	451	Democrat	837
White	604	Republican	218
Total	1,055	Total	1,055

Next, we must discover how many of each race identified with each party. To do this, we take each value of the independent variable and construct a separate frequency distribution of the dependent variable for that subset. In this example, we first find the frequency distribution of party identification for blacks and then do the same for whites. The end result for the 1961 sample is given in Table 7.1; the 1964 cross-tabluation of race and party identification is presented in Table 7.2. In order to help interpret the tables, it is normal practice to calculate percentages (e.g., the percentage of blacks who are Democrats) for each table or cell entry. It is especially important to obtain percentages when either or both of the variables have categories with widely unequal numbers.

The next stage in the analysis is to examine the tables in order to get a preliminary notion of the relationship. We are first interested in the association between race and party identification for each of the two years. The 1961 results (Table 7.1) show almost no relationship between the two variables; members of both races identify with the two parties in approximately the same proportions (81–19 percent for the blacks, 78–22 percent for the whites). The 1964 findings (Table 7.2), on the other hand, reveal a moderate relationship; blacks identify with the Democratic Party more often (95–5 percent) than do whites (78–22 percent). Comparing the two years, we find that the relationship between race and party identification among American Southerners has increased. This increase has been entirely the result of a change in party identification among blacks, for in both 1961 and 1964 whites had exactly the same party identification split (78–22 percent).

In the preliminary examination of the results, we were forced to use such terms as "almost no" and "moderate" to qualify the noun "relationship." One function of measures of association is to make these qualifications more precise; if we confine our analysis to a verbal description of the results, we run the risk that one man's moderate relationship might be another man's strong association. Moreover, when we are comparing twenty or thirty tables and not simply two, it is difficult to make comparisons unless we have a constant yardstick.

There is a variety of measures of association for nominal relationships. Some are only applicable to 2×2 *contingency tables*—relationships where both variables have only two possible values—while others can be applied regardless of the number of categories. Here we will discuss only one:

TABLE 7.1 PARTY IDENTIFICATION OF AMERICAN SOUTHERNERS BY RACE, 1961

Race	Party identification		Total
	Democrat	Republican	
Black	365 (81%)	86 (19%)	451 (100%)
White	472 (78%)	132 (22%)	604 (100%)
Total	837 (79%)	218 (21%)	1,055 (100%)

SOURCE: From *Negroes and the New Southern Politics* by Donald R. Matthews and James W. Prothro, © 1966, by Harcourt Brace Jovanovich, Inc. and reproduced with their permission. Adapted from Table 13-1, p. 373.

TABLE 7.2   PARTY IDENTIFICATION OF AMERICAN SOUTHERNERS BY RACE, 1964

Race	Party identification		Total
	Democrat	Republican	
Black	154 (95%)	8 (5%)	162 (100%)
White	202 (78%)	58 (22%)	260 (100%)
Total	356 (84%)	66 (16%)	422 (100%)

SOURCE: From *Negroes and the New Southern Politics* by Donald R. Matthews and James W. Prothro, © 1966, by Harcourt Brace Jovanovich, Inc. and reproduced with their permission. Adapted from Table 13-1, p. 373.

Goodman and Kruskal's tau. (The naming of most statistical coefficients, including this one, is simply the reverse of the baby-naming process; the first name refers to the parents and the second name is bestowed by the creator[s].) The principal reason for concentrating on this measure of association is that it can be applied regardless of the number of categories, and it has a readily understandable interpretation.

One way to look at the degree of relationship between two variables is to ask how much knowing the independent variable helps us predict the dependent variable. If the two variables are perfectly related, then knowing one will enable us to predict the other with unerring accuracy; if the two variables have absolutely no relationship, then knowing one will be of no help in predicting the other; and in the most normal situation—the two variables are partially related—then knowing one will improve our ability to predict the other. Tau tells us precisely how much our predictive value has been increased.

For any two-variable relationship, there are actually two taus: one for predicting Variable I from Variable II and the other for predicting Variable II from Variable I. These are generally referred to as *tau-alpha* and *tau-beta*. Although it is important to note that the two taus will not generally be identical for any given table, the logic behind them and the procedure for calculating them are essentially the same. In addition, we are normally interested only in calculating the ability of the independent variable to predict the dependent variable. This section ignores the distinction and refers only to a nonqualified tau.

The first step in calculating tau is to discover how many mistakes we would make in predicting party identification when we know nothing except its frequency distribution. This figure will give us a baseline against which to judge any possible predictive improvements provided by the independent variable. Looking at Table 7.1, we see that there are 837 Democrats and 218 Republicans. Let us assume that this group will walk through a door, and as each one comes through we will predict (i.e., guess) his party identification. Since all we know are the marginal totals (837 and 218), our strategy will be to guess "Democrat" 837 times and "Republican" 218 times.[1] How many mistakes would we expect to make? We would guess Democrat 837 times, but on the average, 218 of the 1,055 individuals are not Democrats; therefore, our average number of mistakes in guessing Democrat would be 837 (218/1,055) or 172.9 errors. Similarly, we would predict Republican 218 times when, in fact, 837 of the 1,055 respondents are not Republicans; in this case, our average number of errors would be 218 (837/1,055) or 172.9. Adding these two numbers (172.9 + 172.9), we get the total number of errors (355.8) we would make in predicting party identification with no knowledge of the independent variable.

The next step is to calculate how many mistakes we would make when we know each individual's race. Returning to our door analogy, 451 blacks will walk through the door, and for each we will predict his party identification. Since, for the blacks, there are 365 Democrats and 86 Republicans, we will guess Democrat 365 times and Republican 86 times. The procedure for calculating the expected number of errors is the same as before. Of the 365 times that we predict Democrat, we would be wrong 86/451 percent of the time; hence we would make 365 (86/451) or 69.6 errors. For our 86 Republican predictions, we would be incorrect 86 (365/451) or 69.6 times. Next, we determine the number of assignment errors we would make in predicting the party identification of the whites. Guessing Democrat 472 times and Republican 132 times, we would make 472 (132/604) and 132 (472/604) errors respectively; this works out to 103.2 errors for each party. Our total number of errors, based on knowing the independent variable (race), are 69.6 + 69.6 + 103.2 + 103.2 = 345.6.

Now we are ready to calculate tau; it is simply the proportion by which knowledge of the independent variable enables us to reduce our number of predictive errors. In formula terms,

$$\text{Goodman-Kruskal Tau} = \frac{\text{Number of errors not knowing independent variable} - \text{Number of errors knowing independent variable}}{\text{Number of errors not knowing independent variable}}$$

Or, in this case,

$$\text{Tau} = \frac{355.8 - 345.6}{355.8} = \frac{10.2}{355.8} = .029$$

Knowing the respondent's race, then, has enabled us to reduce our predictive error by 2.9 percent. (The value of tau is always positive; thus it does not indicate the direction of the relationship. This information must be

[1] Another strategy would be to predict the largest category (in this case, Democrat) every time. There is another measure of association, called *lambda*, based on this approach. The principal difficulty with lambda is that it is insensitive to small degrees of association; unless the two variables are moderately related, lambda will tend to equal zero. In political science, where strong relationships are the exception and not the rule, this lack of sensitivity to weaker relationships is a serious defect.

obtained from an inspection of the contingency table.) If the relationship were a perfect one (e.g., if all blacks were Democrats and all whites Republicans or if all whites were Democrats and all blacks Republicans), tau would be 1.00 and our predictive error would have been reduced 100 percent; on the other hand, if there were no relationship (e.g., blacks and whites identified with the two parties in exactly the same proportions), tau would be zero and the proportional reduction in error would have been zero percent.

For the 1964 data, tau equals .054; in this case, knowledge of race reduces the predictive error by 5.4 percent. (The student should perform the calculations for the data in Table 7.2 in order to clarify his understanding of the computational procedure.) On the basis of these two taus, we can conclude first, that race was only slightly related to party identification among American Southerners in both 1961 and 1964, and second, that there was a small increase in the relationship between the two years.

In general, the procedure for computing tau for any size table is as follows: Assuming that the independent variable is always the row variable, you take each column total, multiply it by the total number of cases minus that column total, and divide by the total number of cases. The summation of these calculations is the expected number of errors not knowing the independent variable. For each row (i.e., value of the independent variable), you take each entry within that row, multiply it by the row total minus the entry number, and divide by the row total. The summation for all rows constitutes the expected number of errors knowing the independent variable. Referring to the summation of the first procedure as X and the second as Y, tau equals

$$\frac{X - Y}{X}$$

To illustrate this procedure, let us calculate tau for the data in Table 7.3. In this analysis, we are examining whether countries with different colonial

TABLE 7.3 CONSTITUTIONAL STATUS OF REGIME BY FORMER COLONIAL RULER FOR 47 NATIONS

Former colonial ruler	Constitutional status of current (1960) regime			
	Constitutional	Authoritarian	Totalitarian	Total
Britain	15 (71%)	6 (29%)	0 (0%)	21 (100%)
France	5 (45%)	5 (45%)	1 (9%)	11 (99%)
Spain	11 (73%)	3 (20%)	1 (7%)	15 (100%)
Total	31	14	2	47

SOURCE: Inter-University Consortium for Political Research. The data were originally compiled by Arthur S. Banks and Robert B. Textor, *A Cross-Polity Survey*, Cambridge, Mass., M.I.T. Press, 1963.

rulers tend to have different constitutional statuses after they attain independence. The number of errors not knowing the independent variables is

$$\frac{(31)(16)}{47} + \frac{(14)(33)}{47} + \frac{(2)(45)}{47} = 10.6 + 9.8 + 1.9 = 22.3$$

For each of the three rows, the number of errors knowing the independent variable is

$$\text{Britain} = \frac{(15)(6)}{21} + \frac{(6)(15)}{21} + \frac{(0)(21)}{21} = 4.3 + 4.3 + 0.0 = 8.6$$

$$\text{France} = \frac{(5)(6)}{11} + \frac{(5)(6)}{11} + \frac{(1)(10)}{11} = 2.7 + 2.7 + 0.9 = 6.3$$

$$\text{Spain} = \frac{(11)(4)}{15} + \frac{(3)(12)}{15} + \frac{(1)(14)}{15} = 2.9 + 2.4 + 0.9 = 6.2$$

Summing up the errors of the three rows, the total number of errors knowing the independent variable is 8.6 + 6.3 + 6.2 or 21.1. Now we are ready to employ the final formula. Tau equals

$$\frac{22.3 - 21.1}{22.3} = \frac{1.2}{22.3} = .054$$

Thus, knowing which country was the former colonial ruler enables one to reduce his errors in predicting current constitutional status by 5.4 percent.

Goodman and Kruskal's tau has several properties which, on the whole, argue for its frequent usage. First, its possible values always range from 0 to 1, a characteristic considered desirable for measures of association because it simplifies understanding. Second, tau can be used regardless of the number of rows or columns. Third, unlike most other nominal measures of association, tau has a ready interpretation—the proportional reduction in prediction errors provided by the independent variable. Fourth, the use of tau does not require any assumptions about the nature or distribution of the data.

One final note of warning: In constructing contingency tables, you often have some flexibility in deciding the number of categories for a particular variable. In the first example, we could have specified four party categories (Strong Democrat, Weak Democrat, Weak Republican, and Strong Republican) instead of two. Frequently such changes in the number of categories will have a marked impact on the size of the correlation coefficient. In order to guard against misleading conclusions in cases like this, one should compute the coefficient for each possible set of categories.

ORDINAL RELATIONSHIPS
There are two methods for arranging ordinal data: a *rank ordering* and a contingency table. Rank orders are generally used when there are few scores having the same value (i.e., when the number of ties is low). To construct a rank ordering, one lists each case together with its rankings on the

two ordinal scales; listing the cases in the order of their ranking on one of the two scales facilitates understanding and computing the relationships (see Table 7.4). When the ordinal scale has only a few values and the number of tied scores is consequently quite high, then a contingency table provides the best picture of the relationship. This section will first discuss a measure of association (*Kendall's tau*) for ordinal data with no ties and then present a measure (*Goodman and Kruskal's gamma*) for ordinal relationships having a large number of ties.

Table 7.4 gives the rankings of 48 states (Alaska and Hawaii are excluded) for two variables: interparty competition and per capita state welfare payments. We are interested in seeing if the amount of party competition has any relationship to the states' welfare-payment policy; we might expect (i.e., hypothesize) that the closer the parity between the two parties, the greater the need for each to appeal to certain groups (e.g., the poor) and hence the larger the state welfare payments.

If the two variables are closely related, then their rankings should be similar; either a high ranking on one variable would be associated with a high ranking on the other variable (i.e., a positive relationship or a *positive pair*) or a high ranking on one would be associated with a low ranking on the other (i.e., a negative relationship or a *negative pair*). If the variables are unrelated there will be no consistent ordering, and the number of positive and negative pairs will be the same. What Kendall's tau gives us is a measure of the difference between the number of positive pairs of rankings and the number of negative pairs, standardized for the total possible number of pairs.

The first step in computing Kendall's tau is to count the number of positive and negative pairs; the summation of this operation will give us a statistic S which is equal to the number of positive pairs minus the number of negative pairs. (If there are more negative pairs than positive pairs, S will be a negative number.) Taking the first pair in Table 7.4 (Colorado-Massachusetts), we find that the rankings are ordered the same way; in each instance, Colorado has a higher ranking than does Massachusetts. (In this context, "higher" does not mean numerically greater. Clearly, the number assigned to Colorado [i.e., 1] is lower than the one given to Massachusetts in both variables. Instead, higher means having more of the variable; for example, Colorado has more interparty competition than does Massachusetts.) This, then, is a positive pair and we add a +1 to S. The second pair (Colorado-Nevada) is also positive, so we add another +1 to S.

At this point, we can see that unless we find a shortcut, the computation of S is going to be quite burdensome. It is here that the reasons for ranking one of the two variables from highest to lowest (or vice versa) become clear. In Table 7.4, we know that the party competition rankings run consecutively from 1 to 48. Thus, we need only examine the welfare payment-rankings in order to calculate S. For example, since Colorado is first on the welfare scale, the other 47 states must be positively paired with it; thus we add

+47 to S. Taking the next case (Massachusetts) with its welfare rank of 4, 44 of the remaining 46 states (we have already considered the Colorado-Massachusetts pair) have higher welfare scores (i.e., they are positively

TABLE 7.4 RANK ORDER OF 48 STATES BY INTERPARTY COMPETITION AND PER CAPITA STATE WELFARE PAYMENT, 1961

State	Interparty competition rank	Per capita state welfare payment rank
Colorado	1	1
Massachusetts	2	4
Nevada	3	22
Montana	4	16
Minnesota	5	8
Utah	6	25
Delaware	7	26
Connecticut	8	11
Washington	9	2
Pennsylvania	10	20
California	11	5
Nebraska	12	34
Illinois	13	10
Idaho	14	32
Michigan	15	12
Rhode Island	16	9
New Jersey	17	28
Indiana	18	38
Oregon	19	13
Ohio	20	14
Missouri	21	17
Wyoming	22	30
New York	23	7
Wisconsin	24	15
New Mexico	25	27
Maryland	26	45
West Virginia	27	39
New Hampshire	28	23
Arizona	29	37
Iowa	30	18
Kansas	31	21
Maine	32	24
Kentucky	33	43
South Dakota	34	31
North Dakota	35	19
Oklahoma	36	3
Vermont	37	29
Tennessee	38	46
North Carolina	39	44
Virginia	40	48
Florida	41	41
Arkansas	42	33
Alabama	43	35

Table 7.4, Continued

State	Interparty competition rank	Per capita state welfare payment rank
Texas	44	42
Mississippi	45	40
Louisiana	46	6
Georgia	47	36
South Carolina	48	47

SOURCE: From *Politics in the American States*, by Herbert Jacob and Kenneth N. Vines, eds., Table 1, page 65, and Table 6, pp. 392–393. Copyright © 1965, by Little, Brown and Company, (Inc.). Reprinted by permission of the publisher and author.

paired), and two states have lower welfare rankings (i.e., they are negatively paired); thus we add a net score of 42 (44–2) to S. Table 7.5 gives the outline and the results of the procedure for calculating S.

S gives us the number by which the positive pairs do or do not exceed the negative pairs; in this example, S is +472. In order to obtain a constant measuring stick, we must divide by the total number of possible pairs, which equals $N(N-1)/2$ where N is the total number of cases. By doing this, we obtain a measure of association which can range from −1 (perfect negative relationship) through 0 (no relationship) to +1 (perfect positive relationship). For 48 cases, the number of possible pairs is 48(47)/2 or 1,128. Now we are ready to calculate Kendall's tau, with the formula being

$$\text{Kendall's tau} = \frac{S}{N(N-1)/2}$$

Substituting the values, we get

$$\text{tau} = \frac{+472}{1,128} = +.418$$

Thus we see that there is a positive relationship between a state's degree of interparty competition and its per capita welfare payments; on the whole, the closer the competition, the higher the payments. Specifically, the amount by which the number of positive pairs exceeds the number of negative pairs is 41.8 percent of the total number of possible pairs.

Kendall's tau can also be used when there are ties. In order to calculate tau in these cases, any comparison involving a tied pair is not included in the computation of S, and the denominator of the formula for tau is adjusted to compensate for the tied pairs. The formula for Kendall's tau, adjusted for ties, is

$$\frac{S}{\sqrt{[N(N-1)-T_1]/2}\,\sqrt{[N(N-1)-T_2]/2}}$$

where T_1 equals the number of tied pairs in the first variable and T_2 is the number of tied pairs in the second variable. This formula is only applicable

TABLE 7.5 COMPUTATION OF S FOR KENDALL'S TAU

State	Number of positive pairs	Number of negative pairs	Net contri- bution to S
Colorado	47	0	+47
Massachusetts	44	2	+42
Nevada	26	19	+7
Montana	31	13	+18
Minnesota	38	5	+33
Utah	23	19	+4
Delaware	22	19	+3
Connecticut	33	7	+26
Washington	39	0	+39
Pennsylvania	25	13	+12
California	36	1	+35
Nebraska	14	22	−8
Illinois	31	4	+27
Idaho	15	19	−4
Michigan	29	4	+25
Rhode Island	29	3	+26
New Jersey	16	15	+1
Indiana	10	20	−10
Oregon	26	3	+23
Ohio	25	3	+22
Missouri	23	4	+19
Wyoming	15	11	+4
New York	23	2	+21
Wisconsin	22	2	+20
New Mexico	16	7	+9
Maryland	3	19	−16
West Virginia	9	12	−3
New Hampshire	15	5	+10
Arizona	8	11	−3
Iowa	16	2	+14
Kansas	14	3	−11
Maine	13	3	+10
Kentucky	4	11	−7
South Dakota	10	4	+6
North Dakota	11	2	+9
Oklahoma	12	0	+12
Vermont	10	1	+9
Tennessee	2	8	−6
North Carolina	2	7	−5
Virginia	0	8	−8
Florida	2	5	−3
Arkansas	5	1	+4
Alabama	4	1	+3
Texas	1	3	−2
Mississippi	1	2	−1
Louisiana	0	2	−2
Georgia	0	1	−1
South Carolina	0	0	0
Total	800	328	+472

when each variable has the same number of ranks. Another version of Kendall's tau, known as *tau-c*, must be employed when the number of ranks is different for each variable. In these situations, the formula is

$$\text{Tau-c} = \frac{S}{\frac{1}{2}N^2[(m-1)/m]}$$

where *m* equals the number of ranks for the variable having the fewer ranks.

Reviewing the properties of Kendall's tau, we see that it can range from −1 through 0 to +1, thereby measuring both the strength and the direction of the relationship; that it has a ready interpretation involving the proportion by which pairs ordered in one direction exceed pairs ordered in the opposite direction; and that the calculating procedure, although somewhat tedious, is straightforward.

Ordinal scales having few or no ties are rather uncommon. More often, political scientists deal with ordinal scales having a few ordered categories (generally three to six). In these cases, the number of ties is extremely high and it is easier to utilize a different measure of association.

Table 7.6 presents (in contingency-table format) a typical ordinal relationship where the number of categories (or ranks) is low. We are interested in the extent to which an individual's political efficacy (the feeling that individual actions actually affect the course of public policy) influences the level of his political participation; political efficacy has five categories, ranging from very high to very low, while political participation's four categories go from very high to low. In order to maintain consistency, the table orders both variables in the same direction (high to low).

As was the case with Goodman and Kruskal's tau, the calculations and interpretation of gamma are based on probabilistic logic. If the two vari-

TABLE 7.6 POLITICAL PARTICIPATION LEVEL BY SENSE OF POLITICAL EFFICACY FOR THE UNITED STATES, 1956

Sense of political efficacy	Participation level				
	Very high	High	Moderate	Low	Total
Very high	96	82	8	10	196
High	195	225	20	61	501
Moderate	120	226	23	92	461
Low	69	137	17	120	343
Very low	34	102	16	110	262
Total	514	772	84	393	1763

SOURCE: Adapted from V. O. Key, Jr., *Public Opinion and American Democracy*, New York, Alfred A. Knopf, 1961, p. 193, Table 8.10, with the permission of the publisher; the data were originally collected by the University of Michigan Survey Research Center.

ables are perfectly and positively related, then the chances of randomly drawing a positive pair (pairs ordered in the same direction on the two variables) from among all nontied pairs should be 100 percent; if the two factors have a perfect negative association, then the probability of randomly drawing a negative pair (pairs ordered in the opposite direction on the two variables) from among all nontied pairs should be 100 percent; and if the two variables are totally unrelated, then the probability of randomly selecting a positive pair should be equal to the probability of randomly choosing a negative pair.

In order to calculate the chances of drawing positive and negative pairs, we must first count up the total number of positive pairs (S) and the total number of negative pairs (D). To compute the number of positive pairs, we begin with the cell entry in the upper leftmost corner of the table (very high on political efficacy and participation). Each of the 96 individuals in this cell is positively paired with each individual in cells below and to the right (e.g., high on political efficacy, low on participation). Thus we should multiply 96 by the sum of the frequencies in all cells below and to the right of it or

$$96(225 + 20 + 61 + 226 + 23 + 92 + 137 + 17 + 120 + 102 + 16 + 110)$$
$$= 96(1{,}149) = 110{,}304$$

Similarly, for every other cell that has cells both below and to the right of it, we multiply that cell by the sum of the cells below and to the right. In this example,

$$S = 96(1{,}149) + 82(459) + 8(383) + 195(843) + 225(378) + 20(322)$$
$$+ 120(502) + 226(263) + 23(230) + 69(228) + 137(126) + 17(110)$$
$$= 566{,}713$$

The total number of negative pairs (D) is computed in an analogous manner. Beginning with the upper rightmost corner cell entry (very high on efficacy, low on participation), we can see that every case in cells both below and to the left (e.g., moderate on political efficacy, high on participation) is negatively paired with each of the 10 individuals in the top right cell. Thus we multiply 10 by the sum of the frequencies in all cells both below and to the left of it, or

$$10(20 + 225 + 195 + 23 + 226 + 120 + 17 + 137 + 69 + 16 + 102 + 34)$$
$$= 10(1{,}184) = 11{,}840$$

For the remaining 11 cells which have entries both below and to the left, we also multiply that cell by the sum of the cells below and to the left. For this example, then

$$D = 10(1{,}184) + 8(1{,}108) + 82(418) + 61(744) + 20(688) + 225(223)$$
$$+ 92(375) + 23(342) + 226(103) + 120(152) + 17(136) + 137(34)$$
$$= 255{,}153$$

Ignoring the cases having at least one tie, gamma equals the number of positive pairs minus the number of negative pairs over the total number of positive and negative pairs. In formula terms,

$$\text{Gamma} = \frac{S - D}{S + D}$$

For this example,

$$\text{Gamma} = \frac{566,713 - 255,153 = 311,560}{566,713 + 255,153 = 821,866} = +.379$$

Gamma can be interpreted as the difference between the probabilities of obtaining positive and negative pairs, ignoring all ties. In this instance, the probability of randomly selecting a positive pair (again, ignoring ties) is .689 (566,713/821,866), the chances of randomly choosing a negative pair is .310, and the resulting difference in probabilities (gamma) is .379. We can conclude, then, that a sense of political efficacy is positively associated with level of political participation.

It is worthwhile to remember that the tied pairs have been ignored in the computation of gamma. The coefficient, then, is not based on all the cases, but instead covers only the ordered instances. In order to measure the number of tied cases which have been omitted, we add the squares of each of the row and column totals and subtract the sum of the squares of all the cell entries. In this example, the number of tied pairs (T)

$$\begin{aligned} &= (196^2 + 501^2 + 461^2 + 343^2 + 262^2 + 514^2 + 772^2 + 84^2 + 393^2) \\ &\quad - (96^2 + 82^2 + 8^2 + 10^2 + 195^2 + \cdots + 110^2) \\ &= 1,709,916 - 245,479 \\ &= 1,464,437 \end{aligned}$$

Summarizing the properties of gamma, first, it can range from -1 (a high value on one scale is always associated with a low value on the other scale) through 0 (no association) to $+1$ (a high value on one scale is invariably associated with a high value on the other scale); second, it has a probabilistic interpretation involving the comparative likelihood of randomly selecting positive and negative pairs; and third, the coefficient does not take into account the number of tied pairs.

METRIC RELATIONSHIPS

In the analysis of nominal and ordinal relationships, the limitations of the data have forced us to concentrate almost exclusively on the degree of the association. With metric data, not only can we measure the degree of the relationship, but because the data can be mapped in two-dimensional space, we also can gain a rather precise notion of the form of the relationship.

Table 7.7 presents two metric measurements—the adult literacy rate and the mean voting turnout in national elections—for twenty-two countries. Our substantive question is, "To what extent and how does a nation's

TABLE 7.7   ADULT LITERACY RATES AND VOTING TURNOUT FOR SELECTED WESTERN HEMISPHERE COUNTRIES

Country	Adult literacy rate	Mean voting turnout rate
Argentina	86.4%	61.8%
Bolivia	32.1	51.4
Brazil	49.4	34.4
British Guiana	74.0	52.1
Canada	97.5	74.2
Chile	80.1	37.4
Colombia	62.0	40.2
Costa Rica	79.4	57.6
Dominican Republic	59.9	63.6
Ecuador	55.7	28.4
El Salvador	39.4	29.3
Guatemala	29.4	27.5
Honduras	44.0	36.5
Jamaica	77.0	70.6
Mexico	50.0	34.6
Nicaragua	38.4	92.7
Panama	65.7	56.2
Paraguay	65.8	29.1
Peru	47.5	39.2
United States	98.0	64.4
Uruguay	80.9	58.3
Venezuela	52.2	83.8

SOURCE: Bruce M. Russett et al., World Handbook of Political and Social Indicators, New Haven, Conn., Yale University Press, 1964, pp. 294–298, Table B.2, with the permission of the publisher.

literacy rate relate to its voting turnout?'' In order to gain an improved perspective, we first construct a scattergram, which is a graphical representation of the relationship. To do this, we draw two lines (or axes) perpendicular to each other. The vertical or Y axis is used for the dependent variable (e.g., voting turnout) and the horizontal axis represents the independent variable (e.g., literacy rate). For each case (in this example, country), we plot the appropriate point representing its values on the two variables. For example, Argentina has a turnout rate of 61.8 percent and a literacy rate of 86.4 percent; to pinpoint its place in the scattergram, we go up the vertical axis 61.8 units and across the horizontal axis 86.4 units. After doing this for each country, we get a scattergram like the one in Figure 7.1. (For the present, ignore the upward-sloping line in Figure 7.1.)

The scattergram, of and by itself, can tell us several things about a relationship. First, it can indicate whether there is any consistent pattern. From Figure 7.1, we can see that there is a positive association between literacy rates and voting turnout; as one goes up, the other also tends to rise. Second, the scattergram can help reveal the shape of the pattern. For the two variables in Figure 7.1, the relationship appears to be relatively constant or, in more technical terms, linear. A linear relationship is one where the dependent variable increases or decreases at a constant rate per unit change in the independent variable. For other sets of variables, the relationship might be nonlinear—the dependent variable increases or decreases at an increasing or decreasing rate per unit change in the independent variable. Third, the scattergram helps identify instances which do not fit the typical pattern (generally referred to as *deviant cases*). In Figure 7.1 for example, two countries—Nicaragua and Venezuela, in the top left center of the scattergram—have high voting turnouts despite low-to-average literacy rates. One might then examine the conditions in these two nations to see what other factor(s) might account for these high voting rates.

After examining the scattergram, we are ready to compute certain statistical coefficients which will give us a more precise description of the form of the relationship and a better idea of the degree of the association. For a linear relationship, we need an equation for the best line describing the data and a measure of association to tell us how well the line describes the

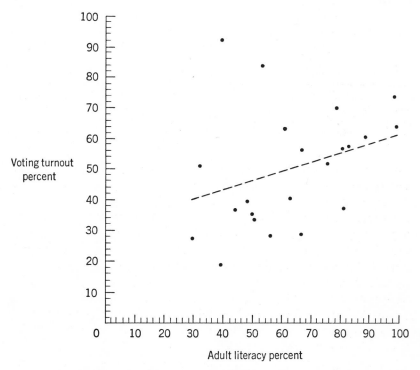

FIGURE 7-1 Scattergram and regression line for voting turnout (Y) and adult literacy rate (X)

SOURCE: Adapted from data in Bruce M. Russett *et al.*, *World Handbook of Political and Social Indicators*, New Haven, Connecticut, Yale University Press, pp. 294-298, Table B.2, with the permission of the publisher.

data. The line is known as the *regression line,* and the measure of associa-tion is called *Pearson's r* or the *product-moment correlation.* We will cover only procedures for computing linear coefficients; if the relationship is non-linear, then more advanced procedures must be employed.

The general equation for a line is $Y = a + bX$, where Y and X are vari-ables (voting turnout and literacy rate in this example), a is a constant rep-resenting the point at which the line crosses the Y axis, and b is a constant giving the slope of the line. Our task is to find a and b for the best line (the line that on the average comes closest to the entire set of points) for describing the relationship between voting turnout (Y) and literacy rate (X). To do this, we first compute five intermediate totals: $\sum X$, $\sum Y$, $\sum XY$, $\sum X^2$, and $\sum Y^2$. Table 7.8 lists the results of these calculations. Next, we take these sums and compute three new figures, all of which represent deviations from various means. (Since we want the best line, we are interested in minimiz-ing these deviations.) These deviation totals and their formulas are

$$\sum x^2 = \sum X^2 - \frac{(\sum X)^2}{N}$$

$$\sum y^2 = \sum Y^2 - \frac{(\sum Y)^2}{N}$$

$$\sum xy = \sum XY - \frac{(\sum X)(\sum Y)}{N}$$

For our example,

$$\sum x^2 = 93,205.2 - \frac{(1,364.8)^2}{22} = 8,538.0$$

$$\sum y^2 = 64,881.2 - \frac{(1,123.3)^2}{22} = 7,526.5$$

$$\sum xy = 72,397.8 - \frac{(1,364.8)(1,123.3)}{22} = 2,712.4$$

We are now ready to compute a and b. The equations are

$$b = \frac{\sum xy}{\sum x^2} \qquad\qquad a = \frac{\sum Y - b\sum X}{N}$$

For our data we obtain

$$b = \frac{2,712.4}{8,538.0} = .32$$

$$a = \frac{1,123.3 - (.32)(1,364.8)}{22} = 31.2$$

The equation for the regression line is then

$$Y \text{ (estimated)} = 31.2 + .32X$$

The graphical version of the line is presented in Figure 7.1. The line is not extended beyond the minimum and maximum literacy values since it is based solely on this set of figures. One would be engaging in sheer guess-work if, on the basis of this analysis, he estimated that for a totally illiterate

TABLE 7.8 INTERMEDIATE REGRESSION AND CORRELATION COMPUTATIONS

Country	X	Y	XY	X^2	Y^2
Argentina	86.4	61.8	5339.5	7465.0	3819.2
Bolivia	32.1	51.4	1649.9	1030.4	2642.0
Brazil	49.4	34.4	1699.4	2440.4	1183.4
British Guiana	74.0	52.1	3855.4	5476.0	2714.4
Canada	97.5	74.2	7234.5	9506.2	5505.6
Chile	80.1	37.4	2995.7	6416.0	1398.8
Colombia	62.0	40.2	2492.4	3844.0	1616.0
Costa Rica	79.4	57.6	4573.4	6304.4	3317.8
Dominican Republic	59.9	63.6	3809.6	3588.0	4045.0
Ecuador	55.7	28.4	1581.9	3102.5	806.6
El Salvador	39.4	29.3	1154.5	1552.4	858.5
Guatemala	29.4	27.5	808.5	864.4	756.2
Honduras	44.0	36.5	1606.0	1936.0	1332.3
Jamaica	77.0	70.6	5436.2	5929.0	4984.4
Mexico	50.0	34.6	1730.0	2500.0	1197.2
Nicaragua	38.4	92.7	3559.7	1474.6	8593.3
Panama	65.7	56.2	3692.3	4316.5	3158.4
Paraguay	65.8	29.1	1914.8	4329.6	846.8
Peru	47.5	39.2	1862.0	2256.2	1536.6
United States	98.0	64.4	6311.2	9604.0	4147.4
Uruguay	80.9	58.3	4716.5	6544.8	3398.9
Venezuela	52.2	83.8	4374.4	2724.8	7022.4
$\sum =$	1364.8	1123.3	72397.8	93205.2	64881.2

society the mean voting turnout would be 31.2 percent. Since there are no literacy rates below 25 percent in the cases studied, there is no statistical evidence on which to base voting turnout estimates for nations with extremely low literacy rates.

For this example, the regression equation indicates that, on the average, for every increase of 1 percent in the literacy rate, the mean voting turnout rises by .32 percent. Thus, there is a positive relationship between the two variables, but voting turnout is only mildly sensitive to increases in the literacy rate. If literacy had a sharper impact on voting, the line would go up at a much steeper angle (i.e., the slope—b—would be higher); if literacy rates had no influence, the regression line would be parallel to the horizontal axis (i.e., the slope would be zero).

Although the regression equation gives us the form of the relationship, it does not give us any direct information about the strength of the association. In order to discover how good a job the line does (i.e., how strong the linear relationship is), we must compute Pearson's r—a measure of association. Using the same deviation totals employed to calculate a and b, the formula for r is

$$r = \frac{(\sum xy)}{\sqrt{\sum x^2 \, \sum y^2}}$$

Examining the logic behind this formula helps us understand what Pearson's r represents for any set of data. The formula is a ratio of the common variation of the two variables (Σxy) to the square root of the product of their separate variation. (Σx^2 and Σy^2 are, respectively, the variances of X and Y.) If the two variables are perfectly related, then they will always vary together and the resulting ratio will be 1.0. If the two variables have no relationship with each other, then they will have no common variation; consequently, the numerator will be zero and the ratio will also be zero. Like Kendall's tau and Goodman-Kruskal's gamma, r can range from −1 (perfect negative relationship) through 0 (no relationship) to +1 (perfect positive relationship). It should again be emphasized that the adjective "linear" is implicit in this entire discussion. Pearson's r measures the amount of linear relationship and not the amount of total relationship. Two variables can be perfectly related in a nonlinear manner and Pearson's r might nonetheless equal zero.

For our data,

$$r = \frac{(2,712.4)}{\sqrt{(7,526.5)(8,538.0)}} = .34$$

The easiest way to interpret r is to square it; this new measure, known as the *coefficient of determination* or r^2, is the percentage held in common of the total variation of the two variables. For our case, $r^2 = (.34)^2 = .11$. Thus, 11 percent of the variation among literacy rates and voting turnout percentages for the twenty-two Western-Hemisphere countries is common variation. Stating this somewhat differently, 11 percent of the variation in the dependent variable (voting turnout) can be explained by (i.e., is statistically held in common with) the independent variable (literacy rates). Eighty-nine percent of the variation still remains unexplained, or in plainer terms, one best find some additional independent variables because there is a lot of explaining left to do.

In examining the relationship between any two metric variables, we do several things. First, we get an initial picture of the data by constructing a scattergram. Second, based on an examination of the distribution of the points in the scattergram, we devise a model for describing the relationship. In this example (and in most scientific work), that model is a linear one. In many cases, however, a linear model will be quite inappropriate and other models (e.g., some kind of curve) must be used. (More will be said about nonlinear relationship in Chapter 8.) Third, we calculate the best line for the relationship. Fourth, we measure how well the line describes the relationship.

DUMMY RELATIONSHIPS

Just as metric techniques for describing an individual variable (e.g., standard deviation) can be applied to a dummy variable (a dichotomous variable

TABLE 7.9 VOTING IN THE 1952 AND 1956 PRESIDENTIAL ELECTIONS, BY SEX, FOR U.S. CITIZENS

Sex	Voter turnout		
	Voted	Did not vote	Total
Male	1,190 (79.0%)	316 (21.0%)	1,506 (100.0%)
Female	1,254 (68.2%)	584 (31.8%)	1,838 (100.0%)
Total	2,444 (73.1%)	900 (26.9%)	3,344 (100.0%)

SOURCE: Adapted from Angus Campbell et al., *The American Voter*, New York, John Wiley, 1960, p. 495, Table 17–11, with the permission of the publisher.

where an attribute's presence is scored 1 and its absence 0), so also can the metric measure of association (*r*) be used to describe the common variation between two dummy variables or between one dummy variable and one metric variable. In each of these two instances, *r* masquerades under a different name; for the two-dummy-variable case, it is called the *phi coefficient* (ϕ), and for the mixed dummy-metric situation, it is termed the *point biserial coefficient* (r_{pb}). Although the computational procedure given above for *r* can be used to calculate ϕ and r_{pb}, it is easier in each case to employ a different (although mathematically equivalent) formula

For the relationship between two dummy variables (*X* and *Y*),

$$\phi = \frac{p_{xy} - p_x p_y}{\sqrt{p_x q_x p_y q_y}}$$

where p_x = proportion of cases where the X attribute is present (X = 1)
p_y = proportion of cases where the Y attribute is present (Y = 1)
q_x = proportion of cases where the X attribute is absent (X = 0)
q_y = proportion of cases where the Y attribute is absent (Y = 0)
p_{xy} = proportion of cases where both the X attribute and the Y attribute are present (X = 1 and Y = 1).

To illustrate this formula, let us calculate ϕ for the relationship between sex (*X*) and voting turnout (*Y*) in the combined 1952–1956 case (see Table 7.9). In considering sex as a dummy variable, we will treat being a male as the presence of the attribute (*X* = 1) and not being a male (i.e., being a female) as the absence of the attribute (*X* = 0). (This scoring procedure is an arbitrary exercise in male prejudice since males are certainly no sexier than females. Technically, it would be more consistent to term the variable *maleness*.) Having voted is scored as 1 and not having voted as 0. The proportions, then, are

$$p_x = \frac{\text{number of males}}{\text{total number of cases}} = \frac{1,506}{3,344} = .450$$

$$p_y = \frac{\text{number who voted}}{\text{total number of cases}} = \frac{2,444}{3,344} = .731$$

$$q_x = \frac{\text{number of non-males}}{\text{total number of cases}} = \frac{1,838}{3,344} = .550$$

$$q_y = \frac{\text{number of non-voters}}{\text{total number of cases}} = \frac{900}{3,344} = .269$$

$$p_{xy} = \frac{\text{number of males who voted}}{\text{total number of cases}} = \frac{1,190}{3,344} = .356$$

Inserting these quantities into the formula for ϕ we get

$$\phi = \frac{.356 - (.450)(.731)}{\sqrt{(.450)(.550)(.731)(.269)}}$$

$$= \frac{.356 - .329}{\sqrt{.049}}$$

$$= \frac{.027}{.221}$$

$$= .12$$

The formula for computing the point biserial coefficient is

$$r_{pb} = \frac{\mu_{Y(X=1)} - \mu_Y}{\sigma_Y} \sqrt{\frac{p_x}{q_x}}$$

where
  $X =$ the dummy variable
  $Y =$ the metric variable
  $\mu_{Y(X=1)} =$ the mean of the Y scores for those cases where the X attribute is present ($X = 1$)
  $\mu_Y =$ the mean of Y
  $\sigma_Y =$ the standard deviation of Y
  $p_x =$ the proportion of cases where the X attribute is present ($X = 1$)
  $q_x =$ the proportion of cases where the X attribute is absent ($X = 0$)

For an example of the calculation of r_{pb}, let us assume that the national adult literacy rates in Table 7.8 compose a dummy variable, with a literacy rate of 50.1 percent or above defined as the presence of the literacy attribute ($X = 1$) and a rate of 50.0 percent or below defined as the absence of the literacy attribute ($X = 0$). The Y variable, voting turnout, will be kept in its original metric status. Then,

$$\mu_{Y(X=1)} = (61.8 + 52.1 + 74.2 + 37.4 + 40.2 + 57.6 + 63.6$$
$$+ 28.4 + 70.6 + 56.2 + 29.1 + 64.4 + 58.3$$
$$+ 83.8)/14 = 777.7/14 = 55.6$$

$$\mu_Y = \frac{1123.3}{22} = 51.1$$

$$\sigma_Y = \sqrt{7526.5} = 86.8$$

$$p_x = \frac{14}{22} = .64$$

$$q_x = \frac{8}{22} = .36$$

Employing the formula for r_{pb},

$$r_{pb} = \frac{55.6 - 51.1}{86.8} \sqrt{\frac{.64}{.36}}$$

$$= \frac{4.5}{86.8} \sqrt{1.78}$$
$$= (.052)(1.33)$$
$$= .07$$

The interpretation of ϕ is, in two respects, different from that of r. First, ϕ can potentially equal ±1.0 only when the two variables have the same proportional split between their respective categories (i.e., when $p_x = p_y$); unless the proportions are equal, the maximum value is less than 1. The reason why this is so can be seen by reexamining the data in Table 7.9. A perfect positive relationship ($\phi = +1.0$) would mean that all males were voters and all females nonvoters, while a perfect negative relationship would only hold when all males were nonvoters and all females voters. Given the row and column totals (and these must be accepted as a given), both of these situations are impossible. There are 2,444 voters, 1,506 males, and 1,838 females. Since the total number of voters exceeds the total number of males or females, some of both sexes must be voters. The maximum possible relationship (ignoring sign) would occur if all females were voters and only 606 males (2,444 voters minus 1,838 females) were voters. The corresponding ϕ for this situation is $-.64$. Although ϕ can be placed on a 0 to 1 continuum by dividing the obtained ϕ by the maximum possible ϕ for the table in point, such a course of action is seldom recommended, since it is difficult to know how to interpret the new coefficient (known as ϕ/ϕ max or phi-over-phi-max). For example, a ϕ/ϕ max of ±1.0 does not reflect a perfect relationship and, depending on the proportional splits, can stand for a wide variety of relationships. The fact of the matter is that in cases where the proportions are unequal the world has given us a situation where it is impossible to achieve a perfect relationship. We are better off simply recognizing this fact than artificially manipulating some measure of association in order to give the appearance of perfection.

The second difference in interpretation between ϕ and r is that the linear qualifier does not apply to ϕ. With r, as has already been mentioned, a zero coefficient only means that there is no linear relationship between the two variables. With ϕ, a zero result means that there is no relationship whatsoever between the two variables (i.e., they are statistically independent).

The point biserial coefficient is subject to the linear qualifier and, like ϕ, it cannot always attain the typical perfect value of ±1. Both ϕ^2 and r_{pb}^2 are equivalent to r^2, the coefficient of determination. Thus, in our two examples, a ϕ of $+.12$ indicates that there is a mild positive relationship between being a male and voting turnout, and a ϕ^2 or $(.12)^2$ or $.01$ means that 1 percent of the variation between sex and voting turnout is held in common. Similarly, an r_{pb} of $+.07$ means that there is a slight positive relationship between a nation's being literate (i.e., a literacy rate of 50.1 percent or above) and its voting turnout and an r_{pb}^2 of $(0.7)^2$ or $.0049$ indicates that only a trace (0.49 percent) of the variation between the two variables is held in common.

Finally, although no examples will be presented here, dummy variables can also be used in regression equations. In general, because a wider and more powerful range of analytic techniques can be applied to metric data, it is better to treat dichotomous variables as metric (i.e., dummy) measurements rather than as nominal data.

CONCLUDING COMMENTS

Correlation does not equal causation. Throughout this chapter, we have been careful not to use "cause" (or its synonyms) to describe a high correlation between two variables; instead we have relied on terms like "associate" or "relate" which do not have any causal implications. The reason for this semantic caution is simple. The existence of a correlation between two variables does not necessarily mean that one variable causes the other. As we saw in Chapter 2, several kinds of relationships can result in a high correlation. In addition to cause-and-effect, for example, two variables may be strongly correlated because there is a third variable which influences both of them or because they have a mutual effect on each other. A high correlation between number of books owned and political participation, with the common background factor being a high level of education, is an example of the first case; a strong association between political efficacy and participation, with greater efficacy causing higher participation which in turn increases efficacy, might be an illustration of mutual effect. We need further analytic techniques, some of which will be covered in the next chapter, to help us differentiate between causal and spurious relationships.

All of this is not to say that the attainment of a high correlation is meaningless. If one does not obtain a strong correlation (and he is relatively certain that he has measured the variables well), then with a high degree of confidence he can conclude that the variables are not related. Moreover, a high correlation between two variables means that something is going on; it is a signal, in short, to keep on looking.

Correlation does not equal significance. Just as we have not mentioned cause in our presentation of measures of association, so too we have studiously avoided any discussion of whether the variables we have been correlating were drawn from a general population or from a sample. Unless this distinction is made clear, misinterpretations can result. If the variables refer to all cases in the population (e.g., the ordinal correlation between interparty competition and welfare payments for American states), then there is no problem; the correlation coefficient is based on every case and there is no question about whether the association is merely a chance result. For samples, however, there is a possibility that the correlation which exists in the sample does not exist in the population from which the sample was drawn; chance factors, and not some actual kind of relationship, might have produced a nonzero measure of association. In technical terms, the correlation might not be a significant one. In order to estimate the risk of inferring that the correlation found for the sample also exists among the general population, we need to apply additional techniques, called tests of significance. These will be covered in Chapter 9.

Not all measures of association are alike. There is an important difference between the nominal, ordinal, and dummy correlation coefficients and the metric measure of association. Neither Kendall's tau nor Goodman-Kruskal's tau nor ϕ requires any major assumptions. As long as the variables meet the appropriate level of measurement criteria, these measures of association can be used. Moreover, if they equal zero, one can properly conclude that there is no relationship between the two variables. In a few instances, gamma can equal zero when there is, in fact, a slight relationship between the two variables. For Pearson's r and r_{pb}, not only must the data meet the metric criteria, but the relationship must approximate a linear form. If they equal zero, one cannot infer that there is no relationship between the two variables; one can only say that there is no linear relationship.

Not all variables are measured at the same level. What coefficient do you use if the independent variable is measured at one level (e.g., ordinal) and the dependent variable at another level (e.g., metric)? The conservative strategy is to use the coefficient appropriate to the variable measured at the lower level. (Example: In the ordinal-metric case, use Kendall's tau or Goodman and Kruskal's gamma.) This solution requires no assumptions, since data measured at one level can always be reduced to a lower level: Metric data can be considered as ordinal or ranked data, and this level, in turn, can be changed into nominal data. Such a policy, however, does have its price; whenever one reduces a variable's measurement level, he discards information. For example, changing a variable from metric to ordinal means that you now know only its relative rankings whereas before you knew both the rankings and the absolute size of the differences. Accordingly, you should be alert to those instances when it may make more sense to assume that a variable is measured at a higher level. This is most often possible in the ordinal-metric case. If you think that the differences between ranks are roughly similar (i.e., that the intervals between each score are approximately equal) or if there are a large number of different ranks (the more ranks you have, the easier it is to make the equal interval assumption), then it might very well make sense to treat the ordinal variable as metric data. This is an especially appropriate assumption to make if you wish to utilize some of the more powerful statistical techniques (e.g., regression equations) which are unavailable at the ordinal level.

How strong is strong? How strong should a measure of association be before you can shout "Eureka"? It depends. That is not a very satisfying answer, but it is the only legitimate one. Clearly, a correlation of .99 for any of the types of coefficients covered in this chapter has strong substantive implications. Just as clearly, a coefficient of .01 means that not much is happening between the two variables. But what about the wide area in between? What about a Goodman and Kruskal tau of .15, a gamma of .21, an *r* of .42? The precise technical interpretations for each of these coefficients (e.g., proportionate reduction in error) have been given, but although these provide helpful guidelines, they by no means allow us to make automatic judgments about the importance of findings for furthering our knowledge of politics. Given the complexity of man's political and social behavior and our vast ignorance of its interrelationship, perhaps we should all keep in mind the aphorism that in the land of the blind, the one-eyed man is king. Very frequently, even a correlation coefficient of .03 or .04 can give sight to one eye.

EXERCISES

1 Consider the following cross-tabulation between two nominal variables where the row and column totals are given, but where the individual cell entries are missing:

| | | Dependent variable | | | |
		A	B	C	Total
Independent variable	D	?	?	?	60
	E	?	?	?	60
	F	?	?	?	60
Total		60	60	60	180

Without changing the row and column totals, construct four different tables: one where Goodman and Kruskal's tau (G-K tau) equals 1.0, one where G-K tau is somewhere between 0.6 and 0.8, one where G-K tau is somewhere between 0.2 and 0.4, and one where G-K tau equals 0.0.

2 Consider the following sets of rankings for ten cases (A through J) on two variables: A (1, ?); B (2, ?); C (3, ?); D (4, ?); E (5, ?); F (6, ?); G (7, ?); H (8, ?); I (9, ?); J (10, ?). For the first variable, the ranks are given; for the second variable, they are unknown. Supply five different sets of ranks for the second variable: one where Kendall's tau equals +1.0, one where it equals −1.0, one where it equals 0.0, one where it is somewhere between +0.6 and +0.8, and one where it is somewhere between −0.2 and −0.4.

3 Using the cross-tabulation given in Exercise 1, construct five different tables: one where gamma equals +1.0, one where it equals −1.0, one where it equals 0.0, one where it is somewhere between −0.6 and −0.8, and one where it is somewhere between +0.2 and +0.4.

4 Using the data on adult literacy rates and mean voting turnout in Table 7.7, change some or all of the scores so that the Pearsonian *r* increases to somewhere between +0.8 and +1.0; for the adjusted data, construct a scattergram and compute the regression line. Next, change the scores so that *r* is somewhere between −.05 and +.05; again, construct the scattergram and compute the regression line for this relationship. Finally, adjust the scores so that *r* is somewhere between −0.6 and −0.8 and, as before, provide the scattergram and regression line.

5 Consider the following cross-tabulation between two dummy variables where the row and column totals are given, but where the individual cell entries are missing:

		Dependent variable		
		0	1	Total
Independent	0	?	?	100
variable	1	?	?	100
Total		100	100	200

Without changing the row and column totals, construct five different tables: one where ϕ equals +1.0, one where ϕ equals −1.0, one where ϕ equals 0.0, one where ϕ is somewhere between +0.6 and +0.8, and one where ϕ is somewhere between −0.2 and −0.4.

6 For each of the adjusted sets of scores in Exercise 4, divide the literacy rate variable into two sets of scores, one set equal to or above 50.1 percent and the other 50.0 percent or below. Compute the point biserial coefficient for each set of scores.

8 DESCRIBING MULTIVARIATE RELATIONSHIPS

Once you have measured the association between an independent and a dependent variable, the analysis task is still incomplete. Although your study design has supposedly solved any time-order ambiguities and the correlation coefficient provides evidence that there is or is not common variation, other independent variables which might alter or even eliminate the original relationship between the two variables are lurking in the wings. If the study was one of the very few in political research which could employ randomization (see Chapter 2), you have already statistically eliminated the possibility of contaminating factors. Even in this instance, however, if your study hypothesis involved more than one independent variable, you will need to make use of the techniques presented in this chapter. Because we strongly suspect that the political world is quite complex or, in statistical terms, multivariate, we are almost positive that there are very few simple two-variable relationships which are not meaningfully affected by additional variables. As we saw in Chapter 2, there might be intervening factors between the independent and dependent variables, there might be additional or conditional causes, or the original relationship might be spurious. In order to see which if any of these situations might be applicable, we need techniques for describing the relationship among three or more variables.

In planning our study, we took care to collect measurements of additional independent variables which might relate in one way or another to the dependent variable. Now our analytic task is to see whether and how they relate. In order to do this, we must first understand what is meant by controlling or holding a variable constant.

THE CONCEPT OF CONTROL

If we are to understand how a third variable affects the relationship between a single independent variable and a single dependent variable, we must be able to hold the effects of the third variable constant or relatively constant and then reexamine the original relationship. We wish, in other words, to see what happens to the original relationship after any possible effects of the third variable have been eliminated. (Throughout this chapter, we will concentrate on the impact of a single additional variable on the original relationship. Utilizing four and five variables makes the calculations more complex, but does not change the logic of the procedure.)

How then can we control, eliminate, or hold constant a third variable? There are two possible solutions. First, for all levels of measurement, we can group the third variable into two or more categories or intervals and recompute the correlation coefficient for each category or interval of the control. For example, suppose that in examining an original relationship between education and party identification we want to hold sex constant. We would then divide the subjects into two groups—male and female—and compute two correlation coefficients: one for the males and one for the females. Within each of the two groups, the effects of sex have been held constant (i.e., not allowed to vary) because every group member has the same sex; in the one group all are males, and in the other group all are females.

The principal difficulty with this method of controlling—called *physical control*—arises when the total number of cases is relatively low, and it is consequently likely that one or more of the control variable categories will have only a few cases. Clearly a correlation coefficient based on five or ten cases is not a very trustworthy guide to interpretation. This problem becomes especially acute when one wishes to control simultaneously for two or more variables. For example, retaining the original relationship between education and party identification, suppose you wish to control for sex (2 categories), region (5 categories), and income (6 categories). You would then have to divide the set of cases into 60 ($2 \times 5 \times 6$) groups and separately compute correlation coefficients for each group. Even if you began with a relatively large number of subjects, say 1,200, there would be an average of only 20 (1,200/60) in each group and one might easily expect that some groups (e.g., rich Southern females) might have very few cases.

Despite this inherent limitation, physical control is the dominant control method used in political research because it is the only one which can be applied to nominal and ordinal data,[1] and more important, because it yields a wider amount of information about the impact of additional variables.

The second way of controlling for the effects of a third variable is *partial correlation*. This technique (used only with metric data) employs a mathematical strategy which cancels out any variation in the dependent variable that could be explained (i.e., held in common) by the joint relationship, first, between the independent variable and the third or control variable,

---

[1] In a limited number of instances, another control method involving mathematical manipulation rather than physical control can be applied to ordinal data. Given these conditions, however, it is usually better to assume that the ordinal data are metric and apply the metric technique of partial correlation.

and second, between the control variable and the dependent variable. This line of reasoning is best understood by examining the following diagram,

where IV represents the original independent variable, DV the original dependent variable, and CV the control variable. IV can explain the variation in DV in one of two ways: directly, as signified by the direct arrow from IV to DV, and indirectly through CV, as indicated by the arrow from IV to CV and the arrow from CV to DV. (Although in this example the control variable [CV] is in an intervening position, other arrangements such as the control variable being a mutual cause of the independent and dependent variables are also possible. These distinctions will be elaborated in the section on partial correlation.) If we wish to measure only the direct impact of IV on DV and control any influence IV might have on DV by acting through CV, we need a statistical procedure which will cancel out any influence due to the IV $\rightarrow$ CV $\rightarrow$ DV route. This is precisely what partial correlation does.

This procedure can be extended to any number of control variables. For example, if there were three control variables (CV_1, CV_2, CV_3), the diagram would be

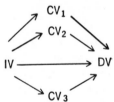

and the partial correlation procedure will cancel out any influence that IV has on DV due to the IV $\rightarrow$ CV_1 $\rightarrow$ DV, IV $\rightarrow$ CV_2 $\rightarrow$ DV, and IV $\rightarrow$ CV_3 $\rightarrow$ DV paths and only measure the association due to the direct path. In order to distinguish this more complex type of partial correlation from the simpler one-control-variable case, we modify the term partial correlation with the number of control variables being applied. Hence, the one-control-variable case is called a first-order partial correlation, and the three-control-variable situation a third-order partial correlation. By extension, the original metric correlation between two variables (Pearsonian *r*) is referred to as a simple or zero-order correlation.

The principal advantage of partial correlation is that one is not forced to have a large number of cases in order to introduce several simultaneous controls. The chief disadvantage arises out of the fact that the partial correlation coefficient summarizes the controlled relationship between the independent variable and the dependent variable over all values of the control variable, whereas the physical control procedure gives a separate correlation coefficient for each category of the control variable. Thus, if the controlled relationship is not the same for all values of the control variable (e.g., if the relationship is strong for high values of the control variable and weak for low values), the partial correlation coefficient, like any summary measure, hides this distinction. Thus even when one has metric variables, it is sometimes desirable to use the physical control technique when one suspects that the independent and dependent variables are related in different ways for different values of the control variable.

USING PHYSICAL CONTROLS

In this section, we will examine what can happen to a relationship when you institute a physical control. For our examples, we will use hypothetical data in order to highlight the possible outcomes as clearly as possible. The dependent variable will be party identification (Democrat or Republican), the independent variable religion (Catholic, Jewish, or Protestant), the control variable education (low, medium, or high), and there are a total of 450 subjects. Using only a three-part division of education exemplifies the "almost constant" characteristic of many controls. Although, of course, some people in the high-education group have more education than others in the same category, we treat them as effectively equal in order to have a sufficient number of cases in each control group.

In controlling for education, we begin with the original cross-tabulation (or contingency table) relating party identification and religion; next we divide the 450 subjects into three groups depending on their level of education (low, medium, or high), and for each group cross-tabulate party identification and religion. Finally, in order to gauge the implications of the results, we calculate the appropriate measure of association for each one of the control groups and compare them with the correlation coefficient for the original relationship.

Since the two original variables are nominal, we will use Goodman and Kruskal's tau as the measure of association in this exposition. The procedure for using physical controls in examining ordinal, metric, or dummy variables is the same, except that different correlation coefficients (Kendall's tau or Goodman and Kruskal's gamma for ordinal data, Pearsonian *r* and its variants for metric and dummy data) would be employed.

When you control, three things can happen to the original relationship: It can stay the same, it can vanish, or it can change without vanishing. The following four examples cover these situations respectively.

The original relationship between religion and party identification is given in Table 8.1A. Catholics and Jews identify with the Democratic Party much more frequently (67 versus 33 percent) than do Protestants and this difference is reflected in the Goodman and Kruskal's tau (G-K tau) of .11. When we control for education, we still find precisely the same relationship at each of the three levels of education (see Tables 8.1B, 8.1C, and 8.1D): 67 percent of the Catholics and Jews and 33 percent of the Protestants

TABLE 8.1 ORIGINAL RELATIONSHIP STAYS THE SAME[a]

Religion	Party identification		
	Democrat	Republican	Total
A. Original relationship (G-K tau = .11)			
Catholic	120 (67%)	60 (33%)	180 (100%)
Jewish	40 (67%)	20 (33%)	60 (100%)
Protestant	70 (33%)	140 (67%)	210 (100%)
Total	230 (51%)	220 (49%)	450 (100%)
B. Controlled relationship: Low-education group (G-K tau = .11)			
Catholic	40 (67%)	20 (33%)	60 (100%)
Jewish	10 (67%)	5 (33%)	15 (100%)
Protestant	15 (33%)	30 (67%)	45 (100%)
Total	65 (54%)	55 (46%)	120 (100%)
C. Controlled relationship: Medium-education group (G-K tau = .11)			
Catholic	50 (67%)	25 (33%)	75 (100%)
Jewish	20 (67%)	10 (33%)	30 (100%)
Protestant	35 (33%)	70 (67%)	105 (100%)
Total	105 (50%)	105 (50%)	210 (100%)
D. Controlled relationship: High-education group (G-K tau = .11)			
Catholic	30 (67%)	15 (33%)	45 (100%)
Jewish	10 (67%)	5 (33%)	15 (100%)
Protestant	20 (33%)	40 (67%)	60 (100%)
Total	60 (50%)	60 (50%)	120 (100%)
E. Dependent Variable by Control Variable (G-K tau $\cong$ .00)			
Low education	65 (54%)	55 (46%)	120 (100%)
Medium education	105 (50%)	105 (50%)	210 (100%)
High education	60 (50%)	60 (50%)	120 (100%)
Total	230 (51%)	220 (49%)	450 (100%)

[a] All data are hypothetical.

possess a Democratic party identification and the G-K taus are all .11. (Because G-K tau does not reflect the direction of the relationship, one cannot assume that equal taus means identical relationships. One must also examine the proportions within the table to see how the tau was obtained. G-K tau's capability to reach the same value for different kinds (but not different strengths) of relationships can be seen in Tables 8.4B and 8.4D.) Finally, in order to check whether education has any independent relationship with party identification (i.e., to see if education is an alternative cause), we cross-tabulate education with party identification (see Table 8.1E); in this example, there is no relationship (G-K tau = .00) and education is eliminated as a possible cause.

In summary, if after controlling, the original relationship remains the same (or virtually the same) and the control variable is not correlated with the dependent variable, the inference that the independent variable is the sole cause of the dependent variable is more credible. (The inference would not be completely credible until every possible factor was controlled, which is to say that the inference can never be completely proved.) If the original relationship remains the same (or virtually the same) and the control variable is correlated with the dependent variable, then it can be inferred that the independent variable is a cause of the dependent variable and the control variable is an alternative cause.

Table 8.2A displays the same original relationship between religion and party identification as was seen in Table 8.1A, but when we control for education this time, the original relationship evaporates. Within each educational grouping in Tables 8.2B through 8.2D, Catholics, Jews, and Protestants all identify with the two parties in approximately the same proportions. Among the low-education group the universal split is 67 percent Democrat and 33 percent Republican; in the medium-education category, about 30

TABLE 8.2 ORIGINAL RELATIONSHIP VANISHES[a]

Religion	Party identification		
	Democrat	Republican	Total
A. Original relationship (G-K tau = .11)			
Catholic	120 (67%)	60 (33%)	180 (100%)
Jewish	40 (67%)	20 (33%)	60 (100%)
Protestant	70 (33%)	140 (67%)	210 (100%)
Total	230 (51%)	220 (49%)	450 (100%)
B. Controlled relationship: Low-education group (G-K tau = .00)			
Catholic	70 (67%)	35 (33%)	105 (100%)
Jewish	8 (67%)	4 (33%)	12 (100%)
Protestant	2 (67%)	1 (33%)	3 (100%)
Total	80 (67%)	40 (33%)	120 (100%)
C. Controlled relationship: Medium-education group (G-K tau $\cong$ .00)			
Catholic	2 (25%)	6 (75%)	8 (100%)
Jewish	1 (33%)	2 (67%)	3 (100%)
Protestant	62 (31%)	137 (69%)	199 (100%)
Total	65 (31%)	145 (69%)	210 (100%)
D. Controlled relationship: High-education group (G-K tau $\cong$ .00)			
Catholic	48 (72%)	19 (28%)	67 (100%)
Jewish	31 (69%)	14 (31%)	45 (100%)
Protestant	6 (75%)	2 (25%)	8 (100%)
Total	85 (71%)	35 (29%)	120 (100%)

[a] All data are hypothetical.

percent identify with the Democrats and about 70 percent with the Republicans; and, for the highly educated the division is about 70 percent Democrat, 30 percent Republican. In each table G-K tau is zero, indicating that there is no relationship between religion and party identification once one controls for education.

What, then, do we conclude? There are three possible situations that could produce these results. First, the original relationship might be spurious, with the original correlation between religion and party identification being entirely due to the fact that education is mutually related to both variables. A classic example of an obviously spurious relationship is the high correlation between the number of umbrellas sold in a given year and the total amount of flood damages in the same period. Clearly, the umbrellas did not cause the flooding (or vice versa), but a third factor—total rainfall—caused both. Second, the control variable might be an intervening variable, and thus the independent variable influences the dependent variable solely through its acting on the control (intervening) variable; if this were the case, we would not expect the original independent variable to have any independent effect on the dependent variable. Level of education, for example, might be an intervening factor between father's occupational status (independent variable) being positively correlated with son's occupational status (dependent variable). If a father has a high occupational status, his son is more likely to get more education, and the higher level of education will give him a better chance to achieve a high occupational status. If we controlled for level of education, we might then expect the original correlation to reduce to zero. Third, if the original independent variable were some composite index or scale, the control variable might be precisely that component of the broader independent variable which causes the dependent variable. For example, if the independent variable were social class (an index composed of education, occupation, and income), the dependent variable were party identification, and the two highly correlated, one might control for education to see whether it was the sole component of social class which caused party identification. If, after instituting the education control, the original relationship disappeared, one would reasonably infer that it was the educational aspect of social class, and not social class as a whole which was influencing party identification.

Unfortunately, there is no statistical technique for distinguishing among these three alternative explanations; all three result in the controlled correlation going to zero (or almost zero). One must simply decide, on substantive grounds, which interpretation makes the most sense. Usually, this is not too difficult. If one is to accept the component interpretation, then the control variable must be a logical part of the broader independent variable. In order for the intervening explanation to be applicable, one must be willing to show a specific temporal ordering: the independent variable precedes the intervening (control) variable, which in turn precedes the dependent variable. If this time sequence does not make sense or if the control variable cannot be viewed as a component of the original independent variable, then one is left with the conclusion that the relationship is spurious.

Starting again with the same original relationship between religion and party identification (see Table 8.3A), the education control is applied, and the relationship changes for each category of the education variable. Among the low-education group (see Table 8.3B), the relationship becomes stronger: Approximately 80 percent of the Catholics and Jews identify with the Democratic Party and about the same proportion of Protestants affiliate with the Republicans. This increase in the split—between Catholics and Jews on the one hand and Protestants on the other—is reflected in a higher G-K tau of .36. For the medium-education category (see Table 8.3C), the relationship stays about the same as the uncontrolled original, with a G-K tau of .10. In the high-education category (see Table 8.3D), the relationship between religion and party identification disappears: each religious group splits 60 percent Democratic, 40 percent Republican, and the G-K tau of .00 reflects this identical division.

TABLE 8.3 CONDITIONAL RELATIONSHIP (TYPE I)[a]

| | Party identification | | |
Religion	Democrat	Republican	Total
A. Original relationship (G-K tau = .11)			
Catholic	120 (67%)	60 (33%)	180 (100%)
Jewish	40 (67%)	20 (33%)	60 (100%)
Protestant	70 (33%)	140 (67%)	210 (100%)
Total	230 (51%)	220 (49%)	450 (100%)
B. Controlled relationship: Low-education group (G-K tau = .36)			
Catholic	50 (83%)	10 (17%)	60 (100%)
Jewish	12 (80%)	3 (20%)	15 (100%)
Protestant	10 (22%)	35 (78%)	45 (100%)
Total	72 (60%)	48 (40%)	120 (100%)
C. Controlled relationship: Medium-education group (G-K tau = .10)			
Catholic	34 (57%)	26 (43%)	60 (100%)
Jewish	19 (63%)	11 (37%)	30 (100%)
Protestant	33 (28%)	87 (72%)	120 (100%)
Total	86 (41%)	124 (59%)	210 (100%)
D. Controlled relationship: High-education group (G-K tau = .00)			
Catholic	36 (60%)	24 (40%)	60 (100%)
Jewish	9 (60%)	6 (40%)	15 (100%)
Protestant	27 (60%)	18 (40%)	45 (100%)
Total	72 (60%)	48 (40%)	120 (100%)

[a] All data are hypothetical.

These results indicate that the control variable—education—is a conditional factor. When education is low, there is a fairly strong relationship (G-K tau = .36) between religion and party identification; for the moderate education group, there is a weaker relationship (G-K tau = .10); and among the highly educated, there is no relationship (G-K tau = .00). Such a set of results is quite plausible. Going a bit beyond the data, we might argue that religion's impact on party identification is effective only among those people whose low education did not allow them to see beyond their childhood association, and who consequently did not retest the partisan attachments received early in life. This interpretation assumes that, in the absence of any other influence, most Catholics and Jews would be Democrats and most Protestants would be Republicans. The higher the educational level, however, the higher the probability that some additional factor(s) would have an opportunity to influence party identification, and accordingly, the lower the correlation between religion and party identification. We could buttress this type of explanation by also controlling for other measures of the amount of different experience: geographic mobility, occupational mobility, and so forth. If this explanation is to make sense, these variables should also have the same conditional impact as the education factor.

Conditional relationships such as this one are very common in political research. Recalling again our grand hypothesis that the political world is a complex one, we would naturally expect (i.e., deduce) that there would be many conditional factors associated with any two-variable relationship. Identifying these conditional variables—one of the major purposes of this type of analysis—is thus an extremely important part of developing our knowledge of politics.

Sometimes after analyzing the data, we find that there is a zero or near-zero correlation between the independent variable and the dependent variable. Although we are tempted to conclude from this that there is no relationship between the two variables, such an inference is imprecise. All we can say is that there is no *overall* nonrandom relationship—no relationship, in other words, which extends throughout all the cases or scores. It could be that the overall table is hiding two or more relationships which cancel out each other when combined and thereby result in a *net* correlation of zero. Whether the zero relationship is true for all control-variable groupings of the two original variables can be determined only by instituting a physical control.

An example of such a situation is given in Table 8.4. In the uncontrolled cross-tabulation, as Table 8.4A shows, there is no relationship between religion and party identification: All religious groups split evenly in their identification with the two parties and the G-K tau is .00. But when you control for education, two non-zero relationships spring up. Among the low-education group (see Table 8.4B), Catholics and Jews are Democrats more frequently than are Protestants (67 to 33 percent) and, in the high-education category (see Table 8.4D), the relationship is exactly reversed:

TABLE 8.4 CONDITIONAL RELATIONSHIP (TYPE II)[a]

Religion	Party identification		
	Democrat	Republican	Total
A. Original relationship (G-K tau = .00)			
Catholic	90 (50%)	90 (50%)	180 (100%)
Jewish	105 (50%)	105 (50%)	210 (100%)
Protestant	30 (50%)	30 (50%)	60 (100%)
Total	225 (50%)	225 (50%)	450 (100%)
B. Controlled relationship: Low-education group (G-K tau = .09)			
Catholic	50 (67%)	25 (33%)	75 (100%)
Jewish	10 (67%)	5 (33%)	15 (100%)
Protestant	10 (33%)	20 (67%)	30 (100%)
Total	70 (58%)	50 (42%)	120 (100%)
C. Controlled relationship: Medium-education group (G-K tau = .00)			
Catholic	15 (50%)	15 (50%)	30 (100%)
Jewish	75 (50%)	75 (50%)	150 (100%)
Protestant	15 (50%)	15 (50%)	30 (100%)
Total	105 (50%)	105 (50%)	210 (100%)
D. Controlled relationship: High-education group (G-K tau = .09)			
Catholic	25 (33%)	50 (67%)	75 (100%)
Jewish	5 (33%)	10 (67%)	15 (100%)
Protestant	20 (67%)	10 (33%)	30 (100%)
Total	50 (42%)	70 (58%)	120 (100%)

[a] All data are hypothetical.

Protestants identify with the Democratic Party more often than Catholics or Jews (67 to 33 percent). In the medium-education group (see Table 8.4C), there is no relationship between religion and party identification. Thus within an overall no-relationship situation, we have two conditional relationships: one for the low-education group and one for the high-education category. The lesson to be drawn from this example is that one should institute controls on both random and nonrandom two-variable relationships in order to identify possible conditional factors.

The following items should be kept in mind when using physical controls. First, the above examples present relatively pure illustrations of what happens when you control for a third variable. You should not expect that every time a control is instituted, the relationship will either stay the same, vanish, or conditions will be clearly specified. More often than not, you will get a combination of these effects, and close, careful analysis is needed to interpret the results. Statistical techniques of and by themselves do not give answers; instead, they arrange the data in such a way that it is easier for you to arrive at some kind of tentative conclusion. There is no substitute for hard thinking.

Second, if a control variable can be categorized in several ways and if you think that the method of categorization might materially affect the results, then you should use as many of the different category schemes as possible. For example, let us assume that the control variable is income, and (trying to keep things uncomplicated) you divide it into three intervals: low (zero to $4,999), medium ($5,000 to $14,999), and high ($15,000 and above). If there were a difference in the original two-variable relationship between lower-middle ($5,000 to $9,999) and upper-middle ($10,000 to $14,999) income groups, the tripartite categorization would not reveal it.

Third, the search for understanding does not end with a single control variable. Additional controls should be tried and, when the number of cases is sufficiently large, simultaneous controls should be instituted. In the religion and party-identification case, for example, one might wish to control for both education and the degree of religious loyalty at the same time.

PARTIAL CORRELATION

The logic underlying the use of partial correlation with metric variables was outlined earlier in this chapter. In short, we said that partial correlation involves the use of a mathematical device which cancels out any influence that the independent variable might have on the dependent variable through their mutual relationship with the control variable, and only measures the direct influence (if any) that the independent variable has on the dependent variable. Now let us express this logic in terms of a formula and then translate it back into words:

$$\text{First-order partial} \atop \text{correlation coefficient} \quad (r_{YX_1 \cdot X_2}) = \frac{r_{YX_1} - (r_{YX_2} r_{X_2 X_1})}{\sqrt{1 - r_{YX_2}^2} \sqrt{1 - r_{X_2 X_1}^2}}$$

where Y = the dependent variable
   X_1 = the independent variable
   $\cdot$ = controlling for
   X_2 = the control variable
   $r_{YX_1 \cdot X_2}$ = the correlation between the independent variable and the dependent variable controlling for the control variable
   r_{YX_1} = Pearsonian r (or ϕ or r_{pb}) between the dependent variable and the independent variable
   r_{YX_2} = Pearsonian r (or ϕ or r_{pb}) between the dependent variable and the control variable
and $r_{X_2 X_1}$ = Pearsonian r (or ϕ or r_{pb}) between the independent variable and the control variable.

The first term in the numerator (r_{YX_1}) is the total correlation between the independent variable and the dependent variable; from it, we subtract the influence resulting from these two variables' joint relationship with the control variable ($r_{YX_2} r_{X_2 X_1}$). After subtracting for the influence of the control variable, the original independent variable no longer has a chance to explain all the variation in the dependent variable. Thus, only that variation unexplained by the control variable is left and we must standardize for this fact. This is accomplished by the formula's denominator, which taken as a whole is a measure of the amount of variation left unexplained by the control variable.

The properties of the partial correlation coefficient are similar to Pearsonian r's. First and most important to remember, it measures the *linear* relationship between variables. Thus a zero coefficient does not necessarily mean that there is no relationship between two variables; it only indicates that there is no linear relationship. (If all the simple correlation coefficients are ϕ, then the linear qualification does not apply and a zero coefficient would indicate no relationship.) Second, the partial can range from -1 (perfect negative linear relationship) through 0 (no linear relationship) to $+1$ (perfect positive linear relationship). Third, in order to interpret the partial correlation coefficient, it is squared. This squared coefficient— analogous to the coefficient of determination—represents the percentage of the dependent variable's variation left unexplained (i.e., not held in common with) by the control variable which is explained (i.e., held in common with) by the independent variable. In other words, after the control variable's explanatory influence is put aside, what proportion of the remaining variation can be explained by the independent variable?

The formulas for higher-order, partial correlation coefficients—situations where there are two or more control variables—are similar to the equation for the first-order coefficient. For each order, the terms are composed of the correlation coefficients of the next lower order. In the first-order case, we used zero-order coefficients. To compute a second-order partial, we use first-order partials in the formula:

$$\text{Second-order partial correlation coefficient} \quad (r_{YX_1 \cdot X_2 X_3}) = \frac{r_{YX_1 \cdot X_2} - (r_{YX_3 \cdot X_2} r_{X_1 X_3 \cdot X_2})}{\sqrt{1 - r_{YX_3 \cdot X_2}^2} \sqrt{1 - r_{X_1 X_3 \cdot X_2}^2}}$$

X_3 represents the second control variable and the other symbols are the same as in the first-order formula. Similarly, to compute a third-order ,partial, we use second-order partials in the equation

$$\text{Third-order partial correlation coefficient} \quad (r_{YX_1 \cdot X_2 X_3 X_4}) = \frac{r_{YX_1 \cdot X_2 X_3} - (r_{YX_4 \cdot X_2 X_3} r_{X_1 X_4 \cdot X_2 X_3})}{\sqrt{1 - r_{YX_4 \cdot X_2 X_3}^2} \sqrt{1 - r_{X_1 X_4 \cdot X_2 X_3}^2}}$$

In this formula, X_4 represents the third control variable and the other symbols are the same as before.

In interpreting the substantive implications of partial correlation coefficients, it is useful to set forth the more common possible causal arrangements among the variables, draw out the correlational implications of each one, and compare the hypothesized correlations with the ones actually obtained. Here, we will consider only the one-control variable case, although the general mode of analysis can be extended with some modifications to situations involving more control or independent variables or both.[2]

Designating the dependent variable as Y, the independent variable as X_1, and the control variable as X_2, four common causal arrangements are

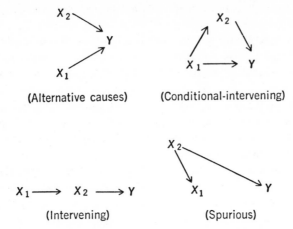

(Alternative causes)   (Conditional-intervening)

(Intervening)   (Spurious)

In the alternative cause situation, we would expect that there would be non-zero simple correlations between Y and X_2 ($r_{YX_2} \neq 0$) and between Y and X_1 ($r_{YX_1} \neq 0$), but that there would be no or almost no correlation between X_1 and X_2 when controlling for Y($r_{X_1X_2 \cdot Y} \cong 0$) since, given the posited causal arrangement, any common variation between X_1 and X_2 would be solely due to their mutual relationship with Y; hence, once the influence of Y has been eliminated, the correlation between X_1 and X_2 should vanish. Thus, if $r_{YX_1} \neq 0$, $r_{YX_2} \neq 0$, and $r_{X_1X_2 \cdot Y} \cong 0$, the most reasonable inference is that the independent and control variables are alternative causes of the dependent variable.

In the second causal arrangement, the independent variable (X_1) influences the dependent variable both directly and through the conditional-intervening control variable. (Note that in this case we are assuming both that Y occurs after X_1 and X_2 and that X_2 occurs after X_1. The correlations

---

[2] This way of examining causal relationships is called causal modeling; for a detailed treatment of this analytic approach, see Hubert M. Blalock, Jr., *Causal Inferences in Nonexperimental Research*, Chapel Hill, N.C., University of North Carolina Press, 1964. Two examples of the application of causal modeling are Charles F. Cnudde and Donald J. McCrone, "The Linkage Between Constituency Attitudes and Congressional Voting Behavior: A Causal Model," *American Political Science Review*, 60 (March, 1966), 66–72; and Raymond Tanter, "Toward a Theory of Political Development," *Midwest Journal of Political Science*, 11 (May, 1967), 145–172. This form of analysis makes two assumptions. First, it assumes that any variable not included in the analysis would not influence the essential pattern of the results. Second, it assumes that the variables' temporal sequence is at least partially established. In the present examples, we will assume that the dependent variable (Y) is last in the temporal order.

do *not* test these assumptions.) We would expect, first, that the simple correlations between all possible variable-pairs would be non-zero ($r_{YX_1} \neq 0$, $r_{YX_2} \neq 0$, and $r_{X_1 X_2} \neq 0$); second, we would predict that the partial correlation between the independent variable and the dependent variable, holding constant the control variable, would not reduce to zero since X_1 supposedly has an impact on Y independent of its relationship with X_2, but we would expect that this partial correlation would be less than the original simple correlation between X_1 and Y since some of X_1's influence on Y operates through the conditional-intervening status of X_2. In formal terms, we would predict that $r_{YX_1 \cdot X_2} \neq 0$ and that $r_{YX_1 \cdot X_2} < r_{YX_1}$. Even if we establish that these predicted correlations are present, adequately interpreting the causal relationships solely on the basis of this correlational exercise is almost impossible. In order to improve one's understanding, one must attempt to find out which values of X_2 increase X_1's causal impact on Y. In order to answer this question, it is necessary to use physical controls since the partial correlation coefficient (as mentioned earlier) summarizes the conditional-intervening effect for all values of the control variable and does not specify the impact for any subset of the scores. Thus wherever it appears likely that the control variable has a conditional impact on the original relationship, both partial correlation and physical control should be employed in order to gain the best possible understanding.

In discussing physical controls, we saw that the intervening and spurious cases both yielded the same statistical results. The same holds true when partial correlation is used as the method of control. In either causal situation, we would expect to find non-zero simple correlations between each X variable and the Y variable ($r_{YX_1} \neq 0$ and $r_{YX_2} \neq 0$), but we would also predict that the partial correlation between X_1 and Y would approximate zero ($r_{YX_1 \cdot X_2} \cong 0$) since, in the spurious case, the relationship between X_1 and Y is entirely due to their mutual association with X_2, and in the intervening situation, X_1 influences Y only through X_2. Thus, in distinguishing which one of these two arrangements provides the best interpretation, we must use the same extra-statistical reasoning presented in the section on physical controls.

Let us now calculate a partial correlation coefficient for real data in order to illustrate the computation procedure and the process of interpreting the results. In Chapter 7, we found that there was a moderately strong correlation ($r = .34$) between adult literacy rates (the independent variable or X_1) and voting turnout (the dependent variable or Y) for 22 selected nations in the Western Hemisphere. Since we also think that a nation's economic development might affect the original relationship, we decide to control for this factor (the control variable or X_2). Using per capita gross national product (hereafter referred to as GNP/cap) as the indicator of economic development,[3] we first compute the simple correlation between GNP/cap

[3] The per capita GNP scores were obtained from Russett, *op. cit.*

and literacy and between GNP/cap and voting turnout. Employing the calculation procedure presented in the previous chapter, we find that $r_{x_2 x_1} = .65$ and $r_{YX_2} = .38$. Given the three simple correlation coefficients, we are ready to calculate the first-order partial between literacy and voting turnout, controlling for GNP/cap:

$$r_{YX_1 \cdot X_2} = \frac{r_{YX_1} - (r_{YX_2} r_{X_2 X_1})}{\sqrt{1 - r_{YX_2}^2} \sqrt{1 - r_{X_2 X_1}^2}}$$

$$= \frac{(.34) - (.38)(.65)}{\sqrt{1 - (.38)^2} \sqrt{1 - (.65)^2}}$$

$$= \frac{.34 - .25}{\sqrt{.93} \sqrt{.58}}$$

$$= \frac{.09}{.71}$$

$$= .13$$

Squaring the partial coefficient, we can state that 2 percent ($.13^2 = .02$) of the variation in voting turnout left unexplained by GNP/cap can be explained by (i.e., is held in common with) adult literacy rates.

How, then, do we interpret this finding? First, let us reexamine the various correlation coefficients and see which causal model they best approximate. All of the simple correlations are non-zero, and when you control for GNP/cap, the original relationship (r_{YX_1}) is sharply reduced (from .34 to .13, or in terms of the proportion of common variation, from 12 to 2 percent) but does not disappear completely. In order to find out whether the alternative cause interpretation is tenable, we must calculate the partial for GNP/cap and literacy, controlling for voting turnout. If this coefficient approximates zero, then the alternative cause model is strengthened. In fact,

$$r_{X_1 X_2 \cdot Y} = \frac{r_{X_1 X_2} - (r_{YX_1} r_{YX_2})}{\sqrt{1 - r_{YX_1}^2} \sqrt{1 - r_{YX_2}^2}}$$

$$= \frac{.65 - (.34)(.38)}{\sqrt{1 - (.38)^2} \sqrt{1 - (.34)^2}}$$

$$= \frac{.65 - .13}{\sqrt{.86} \sqrt{.88}}$$

$$= \frac{.52}{.87}$$

$$= .60$$

Since there is a strong relationship between GNP/cap and literacy independent of their joint relationship to voting turnout ($r_{X_1 X_2 \cdot Y} = .60$), we must reject the alternative model.

Although this decision is straightforward, determining which of the other three causal arrangements is most appropriate is rather difficult since the correlational results come close to both the conditional-intervening and the spurious or intervening patterns. Concentrating on the $r_{YX_1 \cdot X_2}$ partial, the conditional-intervening model predicts that it will be weaker than r_{YX_1} but will not disappear, whereas the correlationally identical spurious and intervening models predict that the partial will approximate zero. In this case, the relationship almost vanishes, but a trace (.13) remains. Thus, there is some statistical evidence for making any one of the following three interpretations:

1. GNP/cap is a conditional-intervening variable. Higher literacy rates cause higher voting turnouts both directly ($r_{YX_1 \cdot X_2} = .13$) and through GNP/cap ($r_{X_1 X_2} = .65$ and $r_{YX_2} = .38$).

2. GNP/cap is a pure intervening variable. The relationship between literacy rates and voting turnout almost vanishes when you control for GNP/cap, so most of the causal influence is transmitted through GNP/cap. Effectively, higher literacy rates cause a higher GNP/cap, which in turn causes higher voting turnout.

3. The original relationship between literacy and voting turnout is spurious: Both are the effects of a common cause—GNP/cap. An increase in GNP/cap causes an increase in literacy rates ($r_{X_1 X_2} = .65$) and an increase in voting turnout ($r_{YX_2} = .38$). The original correlation between literacy and voting turnout ($r_{YX_1} = .34$) is effectively due to their common cause as is seen in the partial of .13 which is very close to zero.

To help cut through this ambiguity, let us reexamine the time-order assumptions made by each interpretation. The first and second explanations—by casting GNP/cap or economic development in the role of the intervening variable—assume that literacy precedes economic development which precedes voting turnout. The spurious interpretation, on the other hand, assumes that GNP/cap precedes both literacy and voting turnout. Since it would seem to make more sense to assume that increases in economic development (as indicated by increases in GNP/cap) precede increases in the literacy rate and indeed are the cause of the latter (possibly through the intervening variable of education expenditures), we might prefer the spurious interpretation.

But if we take this tack, then we should also investigate the possibility that literacy might be a conditional-intervening variable between GNP/cap and voting turnout. To check this out, we need to calculate the partial coefficient between GNP/cap and voting turnout, controlling for literacy ($r_{YX_2 \cdot X_1}$). Recalling the correlational pattern for the conditional-intervening model, this partial should be weaker than the original relationship but should not disappear. In fact, $r_{YX_2 \cdot X_1} = .23$ is less than the original correlation ($r_{YX_2} = .38$) but distinctly greater than zero. Our interpretation would then be that economic development causes increases in voting turnout both directly and indirectly through the intervening variable of literacy. This explanation makes more statistical and theoretical sense than any of the other alternatives. There are still, however, some additional questions to be answered by further analysis. First, does any increase (e.g., very low to low,

low to moderate, moderate to high) in literacy intensify the causal impact of increases in GNP/cap, or is the intervention only important for certain ranges of the literacy variable? As mentioned earlier, we must use physical control to specify the nature of conditional effects since the partial coefficient only summarizes them for the entire range of values. Second, are there any other intervening variables (e.g., urbanization and communication facilities) which should be directly included in the analysis?

This meander around the analytic garden was taken to illustrate the start-stop-adjust character of most data analysis. We started out thinking that literacy was the independent variable and economic development a possible spurious or intervening factor. We ended up, contrarily, having economic development as the independent cause and literacy as a conditional-intervening variable. The lesson is that you should not wed yourself to a single view of causal arrangement for variables, but should be sensitive to possible alternative explanations. Very few of us are right on the first try.

In summary, partial correlation is an elegant mathematical apparatus for controlling one or more metric variables in order to ascertain the impact of those factors on some relationship between two metric variables. Its elegancy resides primarily in the fact that, unlike physical control, one need not worry about the number of cases. Its flaws, when compared to physical control, are that it is imprecise in identifying the specific nature of conditional factors, and that except for dummy variables it measures only linear relationships. Finally, like any method for control, or for that matter like any statistical technique, it must be combined with an intelligent extra-statistical knowledge of the phenomena in order to achieve meaningful and sensible explanations.

MULTIPLE RELATIONSHIPS

Physical controls and partial correlation help us understand the impact of additional variables on the original two-variable relationship, but they do not enable us to measure the multiple influence of two or more independent variables on a dependent variable. If two or more factors together cause the dependent variable, how can we measure that joint impact? When the variables are measured on the nominal or ordinal level, assessing the joint or multiple influence of several factors is extremely difficult. Although there has been and is a great deal of research aimed at developing methods for handling this problem, only tentative approaches have been outlined.[4]

For metric data, however, an extension of the logic underlying simple linear regression, correlation, and partial correlation can be used to measure the multiple impact or correlation of two or more independent variables,

[4] Perhaps this is the best place to point out that statistics, like any academic field, is constantly developing. Most of the techniques presented in this book have been developed in the last century, and we can realistically expect that more breakthroughs will occur in the next few decades.

arriving at an equation which best describes the multiple relationship. As was the case with the two-variable situation, we will use a mathematical approach which measures only the amount of linear relationship; the multiple regression equation describes the relationship and the multiple correlation coefficient reflects how well the equation fits the data. When there were only two variables, we used a two-dimensional scattergram to gain an initial impression of the relationship. With three variables, it is difficult to array the data in two-dimensional space (and with four or more, it is impossible), so we will forego this graphic aid and proceed directly to the mathematical tools.

The form of the multiple regression equation is $Y = a + b_1X_1 + b_2X_2 + \ldots + b_kX_k$ where Y is the dependent variable, the X's are the independent variables (with there being k independent variables), a is a constant, and the b's are the weights assigned to each independent variable. Thus, for example, if $b_2 \ldots b_k$ were all zero (i.e., if there were no linear correlation between $X_2 \ldots X_k$ and Y), then the relationship would reduce to the simple two-variable case ($Y = a + bX$). Calculating the a and b terms for the multiple regression equation is so tedious (and thus, if done by hand, highly error-prone) that the typical practice is to use a computer.[5] Therefore, we will not cover the computational procedures here, but simply mention a few of the technique's applications.

The major use of multiple regression equations in political science is as a mathematical foil for computing multiple correlation coefficients. More often than not, investigators stop after they have measured the degree of the relationship (the multiple correlation coefficient) and do not bother to examine the form of the relationship (the multiple regression equation). Such an analytic practice fails to take full advantage of the available mathematical tools. Since for any single correlation coefficient there are an infinite number of possible forms, it is critical that one also calculate and examine the multiple regression equation in order to know how (and not simply how much) the variables interrelate. Only through the multiple regression equation can you find out what changes in the independent variables are associated with changes in the dependent variable. Moreover, employing the multiple regression equation as a predictor for each individual case (i.e., for each case inserting that case's scores on the independent variables and, using the equation, computing the predicted dependent variable score), one can compare the predicted score with the actual score (the differences between the two scores are called *residuals*). In the two-variable situation, deviant cases could be spotted on the scattergram. When there are many variables, the two-dimensional scattergram is

---

[5] Almost all computer centers have programs designed to perform this task. Students with a knowledge of matrix algebra can find short-cut computational procedures, but even these involve a sizable amount of calculation. For one such shortcut, see Taro Yamane, *Statistics*, New York, Harper & Row, 1967, chap. 22.

no longer available and we are totally reliant on the multiple regression equation to identify cases which do or do not fit the general pattern. As was exemplified in Chapter 7, deviant-case analysis is frequently a fruitful method for furthering our understanding of politics.

The predictive nature of multiple regression equations tempts some individuals to misuse them. Suppose, for example, you wished to forecast the Democratic percentage of the vote by county for an upcoming gubernatorial election. One strategy would be to take, for each county in the last gubernatorial election, the Democratic vote percentage (Y) and measurements on several independent variables (the X's) such as median income and percent urban. You would then calculate the multiple regression equation for the earlier period. Taking this equation, you would next insert the new scores on the independent variables for the current time period and calculate the expected Y values (Democratic vote percentages) for each county. This approach has several defects. First, it assumes that the relationship which existed a number of years ago will continue to hold true. Second and more important to political research, the approach constitutes prediction without understanding. There is no hypothesis-testing, few explicit reasons governing the choice of independent variables, little underlying theory (except for the simplistic assertion that today's relationships will be the same as yesterday's), and no necessary attempt to examine how and how well independent variables relate to the dependent variable or how they interrelate. Instead, we throw everything into the pot, hoping that something in the resulting brew will improve the forecast. Powerful statistical techniques are an aid to, not a substitute for, thoughtful conceptualization.

Mathematically, the multiple correlation coefficient measures how well the multiple regression equation describes the relationship. In order to gain a better understanding of the coefficient, however, let us take a slightly different approach. Our aim is to measure the joint influence of two or more independent variables on a single dependent variable. At first we might think that the multiple correlation coefficient could be obtained by simply adding up the simple correlation coefficients between each independent variable and the dependent variable. For example, if $r_{YX_1} = .20$ and $r_{YX_2} = .35$, we would hold that the multiple $R = r_{YX_1} + r_{YX_2} = .55$. Such an approach, however, is fallacious because each independent variable might be explaining the same part of Y's variation. Let us take a more extreme example to illustrate this point. Suppose that both r_{YX_1} and r_{YX_2} equal 1.0, that both, in other words, are completely correlated to the dependent variable. Would we then conclude that the multiple R is 2.0? Of course not, since one cannot improve on perfection and 1.0 represents perfection. Obviously, both independent variables are explaining precisely the same part of Y's variation, and thus their total or joint impact is still 1.0.

What all of this indicates is that, in order to arrive at a measure of multiple correlation, we must measure each independent variable's unique impact and not simply their total correlation. Fortunately, partial correlation gives us a method for computing the unique influence of an independent variable. Let us examine the formula for the multiple correlation coefficient where there are only two independent variables in order to see how this logic is applied. The equation is

$$R_{Y \cdot X_1 X_2} = |r_{YX_1}| + |r_{YX_2 \cdot X_1}|(1 - |r_{YX_1}|)$$

where R = the multiple correlation coefficient
$\quad Y \cdot X_1 X_2$ = joint impact of X_1 and X_2 on Y
$\quad r_{YX_1}$ = Pearsonian r (or ϕ or r_{pb}) between Y and X_1
$\quad r_{YX_2 \cdot X_1}$ = partial correlation between Y and X_2, controlling for X_1
and $\quad | \ |$ = absolute value, ignoring signs

According to the formula, we begin by measuring the simple correlation between the dependent variable and the first independent variable (r_{XY_1}). (It is immaterial which independent variable is designated as the first.) This influence by definition must be unique, since no other independent variable has as yet been considered. The second term takes what is left to explain $(1 - r_{YX_1})$ and multiplies it by the correlation between the second independent variable and the dependent variable, controlling for the first independent variable. If there were three independent variables, then the third term would take what was left unexplained by the first two independent variables and multiply that by the correlation between the third independent variable and the dependent variable, controlling for the first two independent variables.[6] Throughout the calculation procedure, we are not interested in whether each independent variable is positively or negatively (directly or inversely) correlated with the dependent variable; thus we ignore signs in the computation of R.

The multiple correlation coefficient can range from 0 (no linear-type relationship) to 1 (perfect linear-type relationship). Its square (the coefficient of multiple determination [R^2]) provides the best means of interpretation: the proportion of the variation in the dependent variable jointly explained by the independent variables.

In order to illustrate the computation of the multiple correlation coefficient, let us return to our earlier example involving economic development (X_2), literacy rates (X_1), and voting turnout (Y) for twenty-two nations. For this data,

$$\begin{aligned}
R_{Y \cdot X_1 X_2} &= |r_{YX_1}| + |r_{YX_2 \cdot X_1}|(1 - |r_{YX_1}|) \\
&= .34 + (.23)(1 - .34) \\
&= .34 + (.23)(.66) \\
&= .34 + .15 \\
&= .49
\end{aligned}$$

To interpret this result, we compute the coefficient of multiple determination ($R^2 = [.49]^2 = .24$). Hence, 24 percent of the variation in voting

---

[6] As is evident, the computation procedure for R also gets very tedious for more than two independent variables. Again, standard computer programs exist to do the job.

turnout can be jointly explained by economic development and literacy rates.

NONLINEAR RELATIONSHIPS

Up to now, in discussing the measurement of relationships between and among metric variables, we have used a linear model. Why? There are three reasons. First, the linear model is conceptually the simplest. It is easier to conceive of variables having a one-to-one relationship than any other possibility (e.g., one variable increasing at a decreasing rate vis-à-vis the other variable). As was brought out in Chapter 1, science seeks to simplify the world and, for a geometric representation of relationships, there is nothing simpler than a straight line. Second, the linear correlations and regressions are easier to compute. In the precomputer era, when all computations had to be done by hand or on desk calculators, this was an important consideration. Today, with computers standing by to do the arithmetic, such criteria are less relevant. Third, it appears that more real-world relationships are described by straight lines than by any other single type of curve. (This can be termed the "God-deals-from-a-straight-deck assumption." Recalling your plane geometry, you will remember that a straight line is one member of the curve family.) This is a tentative empirical conclusion, however, and it should be immediately qualified. We might be finding that straight lines are most appropriate because that is what we always test first (i.e., to a certain extent we find what we look for), and even if straight lines are the most useful type of model, there are certainly some relationships which are not linear.

In order to illustrate this last point, examine the scattergram (Figure 8.1) relating age and political participation scores. It is quite evident that these two variables are closely related—that a definite pattern underlies the data; but if you were to compute a linear correlation coefficient for this particular joint distribution, it would be zero or almost zero. (This example also brings home the importance of using scattergrams. If this step had been skipped and one had immediately calculated Pearson's *r*, he might easily [and mistakenly] have concluded that there was no relationship.) The reason why there is no linear relationship is that the underlying pattern is not linear. (Try drawing a straight line through this distribution; no matter how you draw it, it misses a substantial number of the points by a large amount.) On the other hand, a certain curve (⌒)—a type of parabola mathematically described by an equation having the general form $Y = a + b_1X - b_2X^2$—provides an excellent representation of the relationship. As we can see from the scattergram, political participation scores increase as age increases up to middle age, but past this point, they decrease as people get older.

As was mentioned earlier, the calculation of correlation coefficients and regression equations for nonlinear (also known as curvilinear) relationships

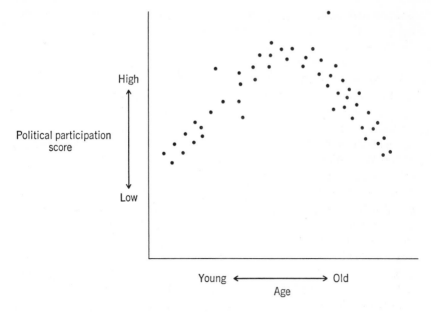

FIGURE 8-1   Scattergram for age and political participation (N = 50)
SOURCE: Hypothetical data.

is beyond the scope of this book. If a relationship appears to be nonlinear, one has two choices. First, he can select some appropriate curve and fit it to the data. Second, he can transform the data so that they better approximate a linear model. Transforming a set of data means performing some constant arithmetic operation (e.g., squaring, taking square roots, finding logarithms) on all the scores. Information on curve fitting is found in Mordecai Ezekiel and Karl A. Fox, *Methods of Correlation and Regression Analysis* (3rd ed., New York, John Wiley, 1959); for an excellent introduction to transformations, see Joseph B. Kruskal, "Transformations of Data," *International Encyclopedia of the Social Sciences* (New York, Macmillan, 1968), vol. 16, pp. 182–193.

CONCLUDING COMMENTS

The heart of any data analysis is determining the causes of a phenomenon, and it is the strategy for probing the heart which we have just covered. The techniques in Chapter 9, while helpful in judging the risks associated with drawing conclusions from data derived from a probability sample, are nothing more than icing on the cake. The "cake" is examining whether this or that independent variable (or both) causes the dependent variable and in attempting to discover the precise causal arrangement. The statistical techniques, as should now be obvious, are not the be-all and end-all of the explanatory process. There is no way that a partial correlation coefficient or a set of physical controls can tell everything about a relationship. The investigator's skilled interpretation must always be heavily involved as well. But, as should also now be evident, statistical techniques can be extremely useful aids in the attempt to understand politics.

EXERCISES

1 Here are twenty cases' (A-T) scores on four nominal variables (I-IV). Each variable has two possible scores: 1 and 2.

Case	Variable I	Variable II	Variable III	Variable IV
A	1	1	1	1
B	2	1	2	2
C	2	2	1	2
D	1	1	1	1
E	1	1	2	2
F	2	2	1	1
G	2	2	2	2
H	1	1	2	2
I	2	1	1	1
J	1	1	1	2
K	1	2	1	1
L	2	2	1	1
M	1	2	2	2
N	2	2	1	2
O	1	2	1	2
P	1	1	1	1
Q	1	2	2	1
R	1	1	1	2
S	2	2	1	1
T	1	1	1	1

Treating Variable I as the dependent variable and Variable II as the independent variable, cross-tabulate these two variables and compute Goodman and Kruskal's tau for the relationship. Next, controlling for Variable III, construct two cross-tabulations of Variables I and II: one for those cases having a score of 1 on Variable III, another for those cases having a score of 2 on Variable III. Compute G-K tau for each cross-tabulation. What effect does a control for Variable III have on the original relationship? Finally, returning to the original relationship between Variables I and II, institute a control for Variable IV by constructing the two cross-tabulations and computing the G-K taus. How does this control affect the relationship between Variables I and II?

2 Designating the dependent variable as Y, the independent variables as X_1 and X_2, we have obtained the following simple correlations: $r_{YX_1} = +.5$, $r_{YX_2} = +.4$, and $r_{X_1X_2} = +.2$. Assuming that Y always occurs after X_1 and X_2 and that the temporal ordering of X_1 and X_2 is unclear, which causal interpretation(s)—alternative, conditional-intervening, intervening, or spur-

ious—make the most sense? Be certain to demonstrate that the simple and partial correlation coefficients support the interpretation.

3 Retaining the same symbols for the variables as were used in Exercise 2, assume that we know that X_1 precedes X_2 which precedes Y and that the simple correlations are: $r_{YX_1} = -.6$, $r_{YX_2} = -.7$, and $r_{X_1X_2} = -.5$. Which causal interpretation(s) are most appropriate?

4 Employing the same symbols and assumptions as Exercise 3, we find that the simple correlations are: $r_{YX_1} = +.4$, $r_{YX_2} = +.8$, and $r_{X_1X_2} = +.5$. Which causal interpretation(s) make the most sense?

5 Compute the multiple correlation coefficient (R) between the two independent variables and the dependent variables in Exercises 2, 3, and 4.

9 MEASURING RISK

Most political research is based on data drawn from probability samples rather than from complete populations. When we find that a non-random relationship exists between two or more variables in a sample, we cannot automatically conclude that there is also a nonrandom relationship in the entire population. Chance factors and nothing more can produce a relationship in the sample even when there is no relationship in the parent population.

To see why this is so let us look at a simple example. Assume that there is a bowl which contains 500 purple marbles, 500 orange marbles, 500 purple swizzle sticks, and 500 orange swizzle sticks. This is our population, and for the entire group there is a zero correlation between color and type of object. Swizzle sticks and marbles are equally likely to be orange or purple, so if we computed Goodman and Kruskal's tau for these two variables (color and type of object), it would equal zero. Suppose you took a probability sample of 100 from this population. Would the correlation between color and type of object in the sample necessarily equal zero? Clearly, no. There is a small, but non-zero, probability that you would get 60 purple marbles and 40 orange swizzle sticks, in which case the correlation (G-K tau) would equal 1.0 (all marbles are purple and all swizzle sticks are orange). In fact, any correlation between zero and one is possible, although as common sense alone would indicate, the probabilities are much higher that the correlation would approximate zero.

There is, then, a danger of being wrong if you infer, on the basis of a non-random relationship in the sample, that there is a nonrandom relationship in the total population. By the same logic, there is a possibility that even if there were no relationship in the sample, there might be one in the population; a zero sample correlation does not necessarily mean that there is also a zero population correlation. Thus, no matter what kind of inference we make concerning the total population based on sample data results, we run a risk of being wrong. If we conclude that there is a nonrandom relationship, it might actually be a random one; if we infer that there is a random relationship, the population relationship might be nonrandom. These two kinds of error are unimaginatively called respectively, Type 1 and Type 2.

What can we do about these inferential risks? We cannot eliminate the chance of making a wrong conclusion, since no matter how hard we try, samples will not always be the same as total populations. We can, however, do more than merely acknowledge the existence of risk by measuring how much risk we are taking in making a specific conclusion. On the whole, we can make a more intelligent decision about inferring the presence of a relationship if we know the precise level of the risk than if we only know that some unspecified risk exists.

In this chapter, we will cover methods for measuring the risks of making a Type 1 error (i.e., concluding that there is a nonrandom relationship in the population when in fact there is none). The next two sections will outline the logic underlying this type of analysis and the following three sections will cover methods for measuring risk (sometimes called *tests of significance*) for nominal, ordinal, and metric relationships. There are several reasons why we will deal only with measuring Type 1 risks. First, if you find that the correlation between the variables in the sample is zero or almost zero, you are not likely to want to infer that there is a nonrandom relationship in the total population. In most instances, you are content to conclude that there is no relationship without worrying about the precise risk (Type 2 error) associated with this conclusion. In terms of research strategy, you are better off examining other possible relationships rather than pursuing to the *n*th analytic degree the precise small probability that a nonrandom relationship does indeed exist in the total population. The best possible evidence that you have says that it does not, so why not be done with it? Second, it is much easier to calculate the chances of making a Type 1 error than it is to compute the probabilities of making a Type 2 error. The third reason—a direct product of the first two—is that investigators rarely calculate the risk of making a Type 2 error. All acknowledge its existence, but few calculate its probability.

THE LOGIC OF MEASURING RISK

In order to understand the logic of measuring the risk of making a Type 1 error, let us first clearly state the question we wish to answer: If there were, in fact, no relationship between the variables in the population, what are the odds that we would get this particular nonrandom relationship in the sample data? We want to know the odds—the precise probability—that you could get such-and-such a relationship in the sample even if there were no relationship in the population. (This probability is often called the level of significance or the significance level.) Once we know the odds, we will have an accurate measure of our risk. For example, if it turns out that we would get the sample relationship 80 percent of the time even when there is no relationship in the total population, then we would have little confidence in the conclusion that there is a nonrandom relationship since the risk of being wrong (i.e., making a Type 1 error) is 80 percent. On the other hand, if our calculations show that we would get the sample relationship less than 1 percent of the time when there is no relationship in the overall population, then there is only a slight risk (i.e., we would make a Type 1 error less than one out of a hundred times) in concluding that a nonrandom relationship exists in the population.

How, then, do we calculate these odds? Although the formulas differ for each level of measurement, the logic of the procedure stays the same:

1. Assume that there is no relationship between the variables in the total population.

2. Using probability theory, construct a frequency distribution of the likelihood (or odds) of each possible degree of relationship in a probability sample drawn from the population described in #1.

3. Based on this frequency distribution, find the frequency with which a relationship as large as or larger than the one actually found in the sample would occur. This value is the likelihood of obtaining the relationship in the sample even if there were no relationship in the population, and it is the measure of the risk involved in concluding that there is a nonrandom relationship between the variables in the population.

The whole procedure, of course, revolves around the frequency distributions derived from probability theory. These theoretical distributions provide the criteria for judging the risk associated with any particular set of results. Without them we would have no way of judging the precise risk, since in order to make precise judgments we need specific criteria. Although there are a large number of different theoretical distributions, we will consider only three: the *chi-square distribution*, the *normal distribution*, and the *F distribution*. These three are used as criteria for, respectively, nominal relationships, ordinal relationships measured by Kendall's tau and Goodman and Kruskal's gamma, and metric relationships.

Since this is not a text in mathematical statistics, we will not prove why certain theoretical distributions (e.g., chi-square) can be applied to certain kinds of relationships (e.g., nominal). You should realize, however, that these distributions are theoretical. They were constructed primarily by using the rational mode of knowing (see Chapter 1) rather than by relying on empirical distributions. Like all mathematical theories, the theory of probability has specific assumptions (e.g., the probability of an event is the relative frequency with which it occurs) and precise rules for manipulation (e.g., the probability of the joint occurrence of two independent events is the product of their separate probabilities of occurring).[1] This body of

---

[1] Since the world in which we all live and which some of us seek to understand seems to be more probabilistic than deterministic, more uncertain than certain, an elementary knowledge of probability theory—a means for systematically dealing with uncertainty—is a helpful tool for clear thinking. For a very readable introduction, see Warren Weaver, *Lady Luck*, New York, Doubleday, 1963.

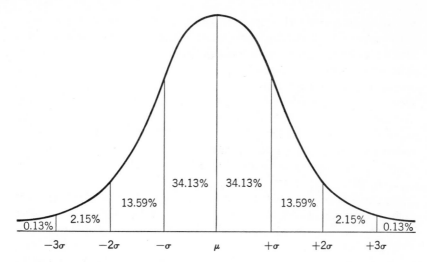

FIGURE 9-1 The normal distribution

theory is then applied to particular kinds of relationships (e.g., nominal) or particular measures of association (e.g., Goodman and Kruskal's gamma) in order to deduce the appropriate theoretical frequency distribution. The distributions we will use to help us measure risk are the fruits of these labors.

Before discussing how risk is computed for nominal, ordinal, and metric relationships, let us take one of these distributions—the normal distribution or, as it is also known, the *normal curve*—and briefly examine some of its major characteristics.

THE NORMAL DISTRIBUTION

The normal distribution is a symmetrical, bell-shaped curve, an example of which is given in Figure 9.1. The points on the horizontal axis beneath the curve represent various scores on a single variable or indicator. As is evident in a normal distribution, scores in the middle range occur most frequently (i.e., the curve is highest at the mean value which, because the distribution is symmetrical, cuts the curve in half), and extremely high and low scores occur least often (i.e., the curve is lowest at both ends).

We need not, however, be content with using value-descriptive terms like "middle range" and "extremely high." If a certain set of scores is normally distributed, a specific proportion of the scores (34.13 percent) will be between the mean score and the mean score plus one standard deviation (i.e., by using the standard deviation as our measuring rod, the proportion of cases between any two scores can be precisely determined).[2] The reason

[2] For an explanation of the mean and the standard deviation, see Chapter 6. The standard deviation's ability to interpret normal distributions is one of the major reasons why it is the preferred measure of variation.

why we are able to calculate these proportions is that a constant proportion of the cases (as graphically represented by the area under the curve) fall between any two scores if we measure the scores in standard deviation units. The proportion of cases between the mean, and plus and minus one, two, and three standard deviations, as well as the proportion between plus and minus three standard deviations and infinity, are all given in Figure 9.1. (We can also determine the proportion for standard deviations falling between these integer values; for example 41.92 percent of the cases fall between the mean and +1.40 standard deviation units. A table which gives the proportion of the area under the curve between the mean and standard deviation units ranging from 0.00 to ±3.00 can be found in Appendix 2.) These percentages represent the proportion of the area under the curve in each section (e.g., 13.59 percent of the area is between plus one standard deviation and plus two standard deviations). Summing all the percentages, we get 100.00 percent of the total area under the curve. For example, if the mean of a set of scores is 100 and the standard deviation is 20 and the scores are normally distributed, 34.13 percent of the scores will be between 100 and 120 (the mean and plus-one standard deviation), 68.26 percent of the scores will fall between 80 to 120 (minus-one standard deviation and plus-one standard deviation), 13.59 percent of the cases will be between 120 and 140 (plus-one standard deviation and plus-two standard deviations), 95.44 percent of the cases will be between 60 and 140 (minus-two standard deviations and plus-two standard deviations), and so forth.

Since we must use standard deviation units (and not simply the original scores) to interpret the normal distribution, the typical practice is to transform the original or raw scores into standard deviation units or Z-scores. To do this, one takes the original scores (X_i), subtracts the mean (μ) from them, and divides by the standard deviation (σ). In formula terms,

$$Z = \frac{X_i - \mu}{\sigma}$$

In our current example, the Z-scores for the original scores of 80 and 140 are

$$Z = \frac{80 - 100}{20} = -1.00 \qquad Z = \frac{140 - 100}{20} = +2.00$$

Now let us see how the normal distribution can be used to measure the risk of inferring that there is a nonrandom relationship in the total population given a specified correlation coefficient (e.g., Kendall's tau of .5) in a sample of a certain size. (Since, all other things being equal, the larger the sample size, the less risky it is to make inferences concerning the entire population, we must take this factor into account in measuring risk.) Recalling the basic assumption, we know that if there were, in fact, no relationship between the two variables in the total population and if an infinite number of random samples of size N were drawn from the population, the correlation coefficients (or some function of the correlation coefficient such as its

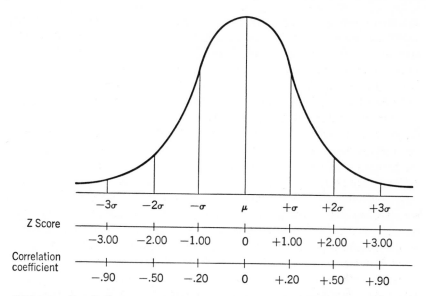

FIGURE 9-2 Hypothetical normal distribution for a correlation coefficient

square root) from all the samples would be distributed normally, with the most likely or mean coefficient being 0 and the least likely being −1 and +1. This distribution is graphically displayed in Figure 9.2. For any particular correlation coefficient (e.g., .5), we can compute the corresponding Z-score (e.g., 2.0).[3] Then, since we know that 95.44 percent of the cases are between the mean and plus-or-minus-two standard deviation units (see Figure 9.1), we can say that 95.44 percent of our infinite number of correlation coefficients from our infinite number of samples would have a Z-score of less than 2.0. By the same token, a correlation coefficient for a sample of size N drawn from a population not having a nonrandom relationship would have a Z-score of 2.0 or higher only 4.56 percent (100.00 percent minus 95.44 percent) of the time. Thus in this hypothetical example, the risk of concluding that the population's relationship is nonrandom is 4.56 percent, since that is the frequency with which a correlation of .5 or higher would occur in a sample of size N when there was not a nonrandom relationship in the total population.

You will note that we used both ends (or tails) of the normal distribution in computing the risk in the above example. We added up the area between minus-two standard deviations and plus-two standard deviations (13.59 percent + 34.13 percent + 34.13 percent + 13.59 percent = 95.44 percent) in computing the proportion of cases where the correlation coefficient would be less than .5; looking at it from the ends of the distribution, we

[3] These figures are hypothetical. Precise formulas for converting correlation coefficients into Z-scores will be given later in the chapter. Here we are concerned only with the logic of the procedure.

added up the area (0.13 percent + 2.15 percent + 2.15 percent + 0.13 percent = 4.56 percent) representing the proportion of samples where the correlation coefficient would be .5 or higher. We followed this procedure because we were only concerned with whether the relationship was nonrandom and not with whether it was positively or negatively nonrandom. We considered only the absolute value of the correlation coefficient (e.g., $|.5|$) and not its sign (+.5 or −.5). We can, however, use the same logical process to measure the risk of concluding that there is a positive (negative) relationship in the total population, given a specified correlation coefficient (e.g., Kendall's tau = +.5) in a sample of size N. To do this, we again compute the corresponding Z-score (e.g., +2.0). Using the normal distribution as our criterion, we ask what proportion of the samples would have a Z-score of +2.0 or higher. Examining Figure 9.1, we see that in only 2.28 percent of the samples (2.15 percent + 0.13 percent) drawn from a population having no relationship would we expect to get a correlation coefficient of +.5 or higher. Thus, the risk of concluding that there is a positive relationship in the total population is 2.28 percent. Note that in this example we made use of only one tail (the right or positive one) for the distribution. This type of risk measurement, where both the size and the direction of the correlation coefficient are taken into account, is thus known as a *one-tailed test*. The previous example, where only the absolute size of the coefficient is considered, is called a *two-tailed test*.

The primary purpose of this section is to show how theoretical distributions are used to measure the risk associated with concluding—on the basis of sample results—that a population relationship is nonrandom, positive, or negative. The theoretical distribution will differ according to the particular correlation coefficient being used, but the logic behind the risk-measurement process remains the same. Before proceeding to a presentation of the computational procedures for measuring risk for relationships measured at different levels, let us mention some other applications of the normal curve since it is the most widely used theoretical distribution. First, as outlined above, it is used for several measures of association including Kendall's tau and Goodman and Kruskal's gamma. Second, the normal distribution forms the major basis for the sampling practices presented in Chapter 4. The means of all random samples drawn from any population will, as the size of the sample increases, approximate a normal distribution which has as its central value the true mean for the entire population. A demonstration of this process was given in Table 4.2. It is this quality of sample means that enables us to measure the accuracy and risk associated with stated levels of variability and sample size. Third, many empirical frequency distributions for political and other variables approximate a normal distribution. To take but one example, some teachers prefer to assume that students' grades often fit the normal pattern; the mystical curve (e.g., "he grades on the curve") mentioned in many bull sessions is none other than the normal curve. The statistically astute student can disguise his failure in a course by telling his parents that he received a high negative Z-score. Fourth, the random errors associated with any process such as measurement will assume a normal distribution.

NOMINAL RELATIONSHIPS

In measuring the degree of association between two nominal variables (see Chapter 7), we used Goodman and Kruskal's tau. Unfortunately, the theoretical distribution underlying tau is not fully developed. Instead, we must calculate a new coefficient—known as chi-square (χ^2)—which does have a developed distribution, appropriately called the chi-square distribution.

The logic underlying the chi-square measure is based on a comparison between the frequencies actually obtained or observed in the cells of the cross-tabulation and the frequencies we would expect to get if the relationship were completely random. We will call the former set observed frequencies (f_o) and the latter set expected frequencies (f_e). If there is a large difference between f_o and f_e in the sample, then it will be less risky to conclude that there is a nonrandom relationship in the total population than if the difference between f_o and f_e is small or nonexistent. What chi-square does is measure the amount of the difference between f_o and f_e, standardize it for the size of the sample, and relate this final figure to a theoretical distribution.

Table 9.1 gives the observed and expected frequencies for the relationship between race and party identification among American Southerners in 1961. The observed frequencies, of course, are those which we get from the original cross-tabulation. In order to calculate the expected frequency for any given cell (i.e., a cell is any single intersection of a row and a column) in the table, we take the total number of cases in the row and multiply it by the proportion of the total number of cases in the sample in that column (the row and column totals are called the marginals). For example,

TABLE 9.1 PARTY IDENTIFICATION OF AMERICAN SOUTHERNERS BY RACE 1961: OBSERVED AND (EXPECTED) FREQUENCIES

Race	Party identification		
	Democrat	Republican	Total
Black	365	86	451
	(357.8)	(93.2)	(451.0)
White	472	132	604
	(479.2)	(124.8)	(604.0)
Total	837	218	1055
	(837.0)	(218.0)	(1055.0)

SOURCE: From *Negroes and the New Southern Politics* by Donald R. Mathews and James W. Prothro, © 1966, by Harcourt Brace Jovanovich, Inc. and reproduced with their permission. Adapted from Table 13-1.

the expected frequency of black Democrats is calculated by taking the total number of blacks (the row total of 451) and multiplying it by the proportion of the sample which is Democrat (837/1,055); the result is

$$f_e \text{ (Black Democrats)} = \frac{(451)(837)}{1,055} = 357.8$$

For the three other cells, the expected frequencies are

$$f_e \text{ (Black Republicans)} = \frac{(451)(218)}{1,055} = 93.2$$

$$f_e \text{ (White Democrats)} = \frac{(604)(837)}{1,055} = 479.2$$

$$f_e \text{ (White Republicans)} = \frac{(604)(218)}{1,055} = 124.8$$

As a check on your calculations, the sum of the expected frequencies should equal the sum of the observed frequencies because we are dealing with the same number of total cases in each situation. As Table 9.2—a summary of the computational process—indicates, the two totals are equal in our example.

The next step in the computational procedure is to find the difference between the observed frequency and the expected frequency for each cell. The results of these subtractions are given in the fourth column in Table 9.2. These differences have two noticeable qualities: They all have the same absolute value (7.2), and their algebraic sum is zero. The first characteristic only necessarily occurs in tables having two rows and two columns, and the reason why it happens in 2×2 tables will be given below. The second quality—the algebraic sum of the differences equaling zero—must by definition occur; if it does not, there has then been an error in the calculations.

Since, unless each and every difference equals zero, some will be positive and others negative, we must use our old stand-by—squaring—to overcome the sign problem. For each cell, as Table 9.2 shows, $(7.2)^2$ equals 51.84. Next we must take the size of the sample into account since the amount of the differences is in part determined by the absolute number of cases in each cell. Even for two tables having an equal degree of relationship, the one with the larger number of cases would have larger $(f_o - f_e)^2$ values. In order to adjust for this fact, we divide each cell's squared differ-

TABLE 9.2 COMPUTING CHI-SQUARE					
Cell	f_o	f_e	f_o-f_e	$(f_o$-$f_e)^2$	$(f_o$-$f_e)^2/f_e$
(a) Black Democrats	365	357.8	7.2	51.84	0.145
(b) Black Republicans	86	93.2	−7.2	51.84	0.556
(c) White Democrats	472	479.2	−7.2	51.84	0.108
(d) White Republicans	132	124.8	7.2	51.84	0.415
Total	1,055	1,055.0	0.0		1.224 (χ^2)

ence by the expected frequency for that cell. For example, for the Black Democrat cell, we divide 51.84 by 357.8 and get as our quotient 0.145. Similarly, for the remaining cells, $51.84/93.2 = 0.556$, $51.84/479.2 = 0.108$, and $51.84/124.8 = 0.145$. Summing these last values, we get chi-square. In this example, $\chi^2 = 1.224$. Summarizing this computational procedure in formula terms,

$$\chi^2 = \sum \frac{(f_o - f_e)^2}{f_e}$$

Before comparing the chi-square value with the theoretical chi-square distribution, there is one additional factor which we must take into account. The more cells there are in the contingency table, the greater the opportunity for the cases' distribution to depart from the random model. For example, if there are only 4 cells in the table, there is a limited number of places for cases to go; conversely, if there are 100 cells (i.e., a 10×10 table), there is a wide variety of possible locations for each case. In order to adjust for this factor, we must measure the amount of distributional freedom associated with tables of different sizes. This measure, called degrees of freedom (df), is calculated by multiplying the number of rows minus one by the number of columns minus one. In the 2×2 table, there is one degree of freedom since $(2 - 1)(2 - 1) = 1$; in a 4×6 table, there are 15 df since $(4 - 1)(6 - 1) = 15$. A reexamination of Tables 9.1 and 9.2 will show the reason why we measure degrees of freedom in this way. In these tables, once the expected frequency for one of the cells was calculated, the others were automatically determined. Given an f_e of 357.8 for the Black Democrat cell, the other f_e's must be 93.2, 479.2, and 124.8 if the expected and observed row and column totals are to be the same. Thus, in the 2×2 table, there is one degree of freedom because only one cell has the freedom to have a wide range of expected frequencies; similarly, in a 4×6 table, 15 of the cells are free to take on different expected frequencies before the f_e's for the remaining 9 cells are determined.

Now we are ready to check our chi-square value of 1.224 against the theoretical chi-square distribution in order to discover the risk of concluding that there is a nonrandom relationship in the overall population. An abridged version of the chi-square distribution is given in Table 9.3.[4] The rows in this table reflect the mathematical import of degrees of freedom. In effect, there is a different chi-square distribution for each number of degrees of freedom; thus, there is one chi-square distribution for one df, another for 2 df, still another for 4 df, and so on. The column values are different risk levels (expressed in probabilities), ranging from a risk of 90 percent to a risk of 1 percent. The numbers within the table are the values of chi-square which must be exceeded if the risk level is to be less than the one at the top of the column.

---

[4] A more detailed chi-square table can be found in Appendix 2.

TABLE 9.3 ABRIDGED CHI-SQUARE DISTRIBUTION

Degrees of freedom	Probability							
	.90	.70	.50	.30	.20	.10	.05	.01
1	0.016	0.148	0.455	1.074	1.642	2.706	3.841	6.635
2	0.211	0.713	1.386	2.408	3.219	4.605	5.991	9.210
4	1.064	2.195	3.357	4.878	5.989	7.779	9.488	13.227
6	2.204	3.828	5.348	7.231	8.558	10.645	12.592	16.812

SOURCE: Table 9.3 is taken from Table IV of Ronald A. Fisher and Frank Yates, *Statistical Tables for Biological, Agricultural and Medical Research,* published by Oliver & Boyd, Edinburgh, and by permission of the authors and publishers.

To read the table, then, one first finds the proper degrees-of-freedom row; in our 2 × 2 example, this is the first row. One then proceeds across the row until he finds the two values which bracket the chi-square for his relationship. In this case, where the chi-square value is 1.224, the bracketing values are 1.074 and 1.642. Next, one finds the probabilities of risks associated with the two bracketing values; in this example, the two probabilities are .30 and .20. One can then conclude that the risk of being wrong in concluding that there is a nonrandom relationship in the entire population based on a chi-square value of 1.224 in a contingency table with one *df* is greater than 20 percent and less than 30 percent. If, in this example, the chi-square were greater than 6.635, the risk of being wrong would be less than 1 percent; if the chi-square were less than 0.016, the risk of being wrong would be greater than 90 percent.

Finally, two points should be kept in mind when using chi-square. First, all other things being equal, the larger the number of cases (or *N*), the larger chi-square will be; in other words, dividing through by the expected frequency does not of and by itself completely adjust for the size of the sample. This of course is as it should be since, as we have already mentioned, the larger the sample, the less the risk in making inferences about the total population. With large samples, however, you should not get carried away when your chi-square calculations tell you that the risk of concluding that the population relationship is nonrandom is less than 1 percent or even 0.1 percent. A relationship can be nonrandom and still have a very low measure of association, and it is the correlation coefficient that is most important for interpreting the phenomena.

Second, the theoretical chi-square distribution assumes that the number of cases is fairly large. If the expected frequency for any cell is five or less, the fairly large assumption is most difficult to make unless there is a large number of cells and only one or two have f_e's of 5 or less. If several cells have low f_e's, then you should collapse categories (e.g., combine strong Democrats and weak Democrats) until most of the f_e's exceed five.

ORDINAL RELATIONSHIPS

As mentioned above, we use the normal distribution and Z-scores to measure risk for both Kendall's tau and Goodman and Kruskal's gamma. In each
instance, we must transform the measure of association into a Z-score, and
then utilizing the normal distribution, ascertain the probability of getting a
Z-score of that size or higher in a sample drawn from a population where
there was no relationship between the two variables. We will first present
the procedures for computing Z-scores for the two coefficients and then
discuss the use of a normal-distribution table to determine the risk probability associated with a certain Z-score.

The formula for computing the Z-score for Kendall's tau is

$$Z\text{-Score (Kendall's tau)} = \frac{\text{Tau}}{\sqrt{\dfrac{4N + 10}{9N(N - 1)}}}$$

where N equals the total number of cases. (The formula is only applicable
in situations where there are few or no ties. If there are many ties, gamma
can be used as the measure of association and the Z-score for gamma can
be employed as the risk measure.) Suppose that for 40 cases there was a
Kendall's tau of +.20. The equivalent Z-score would be

$$Z\text{-score} = \frac{.20}{\sqrt{\dfrac{(4)(40) + 10}{(9)(40)(39)}}}$$

$$= \frac{.20}{\sqrt{\dfrac{170}{14,040}}}$$

$$= \frac{.20}{.11}$$

$$= 1.82$$

The Z-score formula for Goodman and Kruskal's gamma is[5]

$$Z\text{-score (gamma)} = (\gamma)\left(\sqrt{\frac{2(S + D)}{(2N)(1 - \gamma^2)}}\right)$$

where γ = Goodman and Kruskal's gamma
S = the total number of pairs ordered in the same direction
D = the total number of pairs ordered in the opposite direction
and N = the total number of cases

For example, if $S = 550$, $D = 275$, and $N = 60$, then

$$\gamma = \frac{S - D}{S + D} = \frac{550 - 275}{550 + 275} = \frac{275}{825} = .333$$

[5] This is a simplified formula which gives a reasonably accurate estimate of
the risk. For a more complicated formula, see Leo A. Goodman and William H.
Kruskal, "Measures of Association for Cross Classifications, III: Approximate
Sampling Theory," *Journal of the American Statistical Association, 58* (June,
1963), 322–327.

and

$$\text{Z-score } (\gamma) = (.333)\left(\sqrt{\frac{2(550 + 275)}{[(2)(60)] [1 - (.333)^2]}} \right)$$

$$= (.333)\left(\sqrt{\frac{1650}{(120)(.889)}} \right)$$

$$= (.333)\left(\sqrt{15.46} \right)$$

$$= (.333)(3.93)$$

$$= 1.31$$

In order to make it easier to determine the probability of getting any specified Z-score, statisticians have developed a table that gives the proportion of the area under the normal curve which lies between the mean or central value and each Z-score. An abridged version of this normal distribution table is given in Table 9.4. The row headings give the Z-scores in tenths (e.g., 0.0 and 1.8), while the column headings provide the hundredth's digit (i.e., .00 through .09). The table entries are the areal proportions between the mean and each Z-score, and they are expressed in ten-thousandths. For example, 3,186/10,000 (or 31.86 percent) of the area lies between the mean and a Z-score of +0.91. Since the normal curve is symmetrical, we also know that an additional 31.86 percent of the area lies between the mean and a Z-score of −0.91. (To conserve space, the table only gives the area for one-half of the curve.) Thus, the probability of getting a Z-score between 0.00 and +0.91 is .3186 or 31.86 percent, the probability of getting a Z-score between −0.91 and +0.91 is .6372 (.3186 + .3186) or 63.72 percent, and so on. By the same logic, the probability of getting a Z-score of plus-or-minus 0.91 or higher is .3628 (1.0000 − .6372) or 36.28 percent since precisely that portion of the area under the normal curve is outside of the −0.91 through 0.00 to +0.91 Z-score limits.

To use this table to measure risk, we perform the following steps:

1. Using the normal distribution table, find the areal proportion for the Z-score. (Example: For a Z-score of 1.82, the areal proportion is .4656.)

2a. If you are measuring the risk of concluding that there is a non-random relationship in the population (i.e., a two-tailed test), multiply the

					TABLE 9.4	ABRIDGED NORMAL DISTRIBUTION			
Z	.00	.01	.02	.03	.04	.05	.06	.07	.08	.09
0.0	0000	0040	0080	0120	0159	0199	0239	0279	0319	0359
0.9	3159	3186	3212	3238	3264	3289	3315	3340	3365	3389
1.8	4641	4649	4656	4664	4671	4678	4686	4693	4699	4706
2.7	4965	4966	4967	4968	4969	4970	4971	4972	4973	4974

SOURCE: Harold O. Rugg, *Statistical Methods Applied to Education*, Boston, Houghton Mifflin, 1917, pp. 389–390, Appendix Table III, with the permission of the publisher.

areal proportion by two and subtract the product from 1.0000. (e.g., (.4656)(2) = .9312; 1.0000 − .9312 = .0688.)

2b. If you are measuring the risk of concluding that there is a positive (negative) relationship in the population (i.e., a one-tailed test), subtract the areal proportion from .5000. (e.g., 5000 − .4656 = .0344.)

3. In either case, the result is the probability of being wrong in making the conclusion. (Example: In the two-tailed case, the risk is 6.88 percent and, for the one-tailed situation, the risk is 3.44 percent.)

METRIC AND DUMMY RELATIONSHIPS

The theoretical distribution used to measure risk for simple, multiple, and partial linear correlation coefficients is the F-distribution. Because the Pearsonian measures of association deal only with linear relationships, the risk being measured is that of concluding that there is a linear relationship in the total population. We will first give the formulas for computing the F-scores for the different Pearsonian coefficients and then discuss the use of the F-distribution tables to interpret the F-scores.

For the simple Pearsonian r,

$$F = \frac{r^2(N-2)}{1-r^2}$$

where r^2 = simple coefficient of determination
and N = the total number of cases

This F-score, as well as the others to follow, is a ratio between the amount of variation explained by the independent variable(s) and the amount left unexplained, with the ratio adjusted according to the degrees of freedom. In the metric case, there are two kinds of degrees of freedom (df_1 and df_2); the first is a function of the number of independent variables and the second depends on the number of cases. Just as with chi-square, we will need to know the degrees of freedom in order to measure risk since there are different F-distributions for different combinations of df_1 and df_2. For the simple Pearsonian r, df_1 equals the number of independent variables (i.e., it is always one) and df_2 equals the total number of cases minus two $(N-2)$.

For example, if the Pearsonian r were .24 for a sample of 102,

$$F = \frac{(.24)^2(102-2)}{1-(.24)^2}$$
$$= \frac{(.058)(100)}{1-.058}$$
$$= \frac{5.80}{0.942}$$
$$= 6.16$$

The values of df_1 and df_2 are, respectively, 1 and 100.

For multiple correlation coefficients (R's), the formula for F is

$$F = \left(\frac{R^2}{1-R^2}\right)\left(\frac{N-k-1}{k}\right)$$

where R^2 = the multiple coefficient of determination
       N = the total number of cases
and k = the number of independent variables

To compute the degrees of freedom, df_1 equals the number of independent variables (or k) and df_2 equals the total number of cases minus the number of independent variables minus one (or $N - k - 1$).

Applying these formulas to a numerical problem, suppose that for a set of 205 subjects, the multiple R between four independent variables and the dependent variable was .70. Then,

$$F = \left(\frac{(.70)^2}{1-(.70)^2}\right)\left(\frac{205-4-1}{4}\right)$$

$$= \left(\frac{.49}{.51}\right)\left(\frac{200}{4}\right)$$

$$= (.968)(50)$$

$$= 48.40$$

and

$$df_1 = k = 4$$
$$df_2 = N - k - 1 = 200$$

For partial correlation coefficients, the F formula is

$$F = \frac{(\text{Partial } r)^2(N-k-1)}{1-(\text{partial } r)^2}$$

where N = the total number of cases
and k = the number of independent variables and control variables

Similar to the multiple case, df_1 equals the number of independent and control variables (or k) and df_2 equals the total number of cases minus the total number of independent and control variables minus one (or $N - k - 1$).

For example, if for a set of 104 subjects, the partial correlation between the dependent variable and one independent variable, controlling for two other variables (i.e., $r_{YX_1 \cdot X_2 X_3}$) equals .40, then

$$F = \frac{(.40)^2(104-3-1)}{1-(.40)^2}$$

$$= \frac{(.16)(100)}{.84}$$

$$= 19.05$$

and

$$df_1 = k = 3$$
$$df_2 = N - k - 1 = 100$$

Since the level of risk associated with a given metric correlation is the function of three factors (F-score, df_1, and df_2) and since it is impossible to array these three plus risk on a single sheet of paper, we cannot present a single comprehensive F-distribution table. Instead, for each level of risk, we use a separate table which gives, for various df_1 and df_2 values, the minimum F-score which must be achieved in order that the risk be lower than the level designated for that table. For example, Table 9.5 is an abridged version of the F-distribution for the 5 percent level of risk. (Appendix 2 contains a more detailed F-distribution table for four different levels of risk.) The column headings give selected df_1 values, the row labels present different df_2 values, and the table entries are the F-scores which must be equaled or exceeded if the risk of inferring that there is a linear relationship in the total population is to be equal to or lower than 5 percent. Thus, if $df_1 = 1$ and $df_2 = 60$, then F must be equal to or greater than 4.00 in order for the risk to be equal to or less than 5 percent. Although only a relatively few different df_2 values are given, this is not a serious handicap even though the number of cases—the factor which determines df_2— can take on a wide range of values. As a brief inspection of Table 9.5 indicates, there is, for any given df_2 value, only a small difference between the minimum F-value for 30 df_2 and an infinite (∞) df_2. Thus, if the df_2 (or df_1) values for a particular instance are not given in the table, the next higher values provide a very close approximation.

CONCLUDING COMMENTS

All of the risk-measuring methods which have been described in this chapter assume that the data come from a simple random sample, and strictly speaking they should be used only with this one type of sample. Since, however, most proportional and disproportional stratified samples have relatively similar risk and accuracy attributes (see Chapter 4) as simple random samples, these methods provide reasonably accurate risk estimates for these samples as well. For single-stage cluster samples, these

TABLE 9.5   ABRIDGED F-DISTRIBUTION FOR 5 PERCENT RISK

df_1	1	2	3	4	5	6	7	8	9	10	20	∞
df_2												
30	4.17	3.32	2.92	2.69	2.53	2.42	2.33	2.27	2.21	2.16	1.93	1.62
40	4.08	3.23	2.84	2.61	2.45	2.34	2.25	2.18	2.12	2.08	1.84	1.51
60	4.00	3.15	2.76	2.53	2.37	2.25	2.17	2.10	2.04	1.99	1.75	1.39
120	3.92	3.07	2.68	2.45	2.29	2.17	2.09	2.02	1.96	1.91	1.66	1.25
∞	3.84	3.00	2.60	2.37	2.21	2.10	2.01	1.94	1.88	1.83	1.57	1.00

SOURCE: Table 9.5 is taken from Table V of Ronald A. Fisher and Frank Yates: *Statistical Tables for Biological, Agricultural and Medical Research,* published by Oliver & Boyd, Edinburgh, and by permission of the authors and publishers.

risk-measuring formulas will underestimate the risk (i.e., the actual risk of being wrong will be higher than the computed risk). How much they underestimate the risk depends on a comparison of the variability within and between clusters. The more homogeneity within clusters and the greater heterogeneity between clusters, the larger the gap between the actual and the computed risk.

Risk measurements—more frequently called significance tests—can and have been overused. It should always be remembered that they assign precise risk values to specific conclusions. Unfortunately, many investigators treat significance tests as automatic decision-makers and accept or reject hypotheses according to whether the risk is below or above a certain level, known as α (alpha) or the level of significance. The most common cutting point used is .05; that is, if the risk of being wrong is equal to or less than 5 percent, one concludes that there is a nonrandom relationship and, if the chances of error are greater than 5 percent, one infers that no relationship exists in the general population.

To proceed in this manner is to assume that statistical significance equals substantive significance. This kind of significance tester becomes an academic St. Peter who allows the statistically blessed findings (risk less than x percent) to pass into the heaven of important relationships and casts the statistically condemned results (risk greater than x percent) into the hell of ignored research. Such a procedure, which is far from uncommon, is a caricature of the scientific method. Its purported purpose is to prevent the investigator from automatically accepting any relationship as important, to force him to state—prior to any examination of the data— that unless the relationship is significant at the such-and-such level he will conclude that the hypothesis is unsupported by the data. But once the researcher has established a single cutting point, once he has determined that unless the risk is less than, say, .05, he will not accept the substantive hypothesis, then he has performed an unnecessary oversimplification. No matter whether the risk turns out to be .06 or .99, he must, by the dictates of his method, reject his research hypothesis. But, of course, there is a vast amount of difference between a 6 and a 99 percent risk of being wrong and what kind of risk one is willing to take depends on many things (e.g., state of existing knowledge) besides some accepted standard level of significance. You will be doing yourself a great disservice if you divide the universe of all possible results into good (accepted hypotheses) and bad (rejected hypotheses) spheres. Some hypotheses are very well supported by the data, others are moderately or weakly supported, and still others are difficult to interpret at all. Any judgment about the validity of a given hypothesis is tentative and is always subject to further measurement and analysis.

Accordingly, this chapter avoided the use of the conventional terms "significance test" and "level of significance" because the words themselves are misleading. When you employ the logic and techniques presented in this chapter, you are measuring risk and not testing significance. Indeed, to repeat one of this book's principal maxims, no statistical technique can of and by itself tell you whether or not your findings are important or significant.

EXERCISES

1 Assuming that the data in Table 7.2 constitute a random sample of adult American Southerners, what is the risk of concluding that there is a nonrandom relationship between race and party identification in the total population in 1964?

2 In a random sample of sophomores, Kendall's tau between ranks on a liberalism scale and academic class rank for 100 cases equals +.18. What is the risk of inferring that a nonrandom relationship between the two variables exists in the entire sophomore class? Of concluding that a positive nonrandom relationship exists in the overall population?

3 Assuming that the data in Table 7.6 constitute a random sample of all adult Americans, what is the risk of concluding that there is a nonrandom relationship between political efficacy and political participation in the total population? Of concluding that there is a positive nonrandom relationship in the overall population?

4 In a random sample of census tracts in a large metropolitan area, the Pearsonian r between the percentage employed in white-collar occupations and the percentage voting for the Democratic presidential candidate for 62 tracts equals −.32. What is the F-score for this relationship? Is the risk of concluding that there is a nonrandom relationship between the two variables in the total population greater or less than 1 percent? 5 percent? 10 percent? 20 percent?

5 For the same sample as in the preceding exercise, the multiple correlation coefficient (R) between three independent variables (percent white collar, percent homeowners, and percent college graduates) and the dependent variable (percent voting for the Democratic presidential candidate) is −.47. What is the F-score? Is the risk of inferring that there is a nonrandom relationship in the total population greater or less than 1 percent? 5 percent? 10 percent? 20 percent?

6 For the same sample as in the two preceding exercises, the partial correlation between percent white collar and percent voting for the Democratic candidate, controlling for percent college graduates, is −.12. What is the F-score for this partial correlation? Is the risk of inferring that there is a nonrandom relationship in the total population greater or less than 1 percent? 5 percent? 10 percent? 20 percent?

10 PUTTING THINGS TOGETHER

In absorbing all the techniques, approaches, and methods which have been presented in this book, it is easy to lose sight of the research study as an entity and instead to view the presentation as a haphazard collection of interesting and not-so-interesting materials. To help overcome this tendency and to demonstrate how analytic tools can be merged into a viable attempt to understand some aspect of politics, this chapter portrays a single research project. This description will follow the same order as the entire book, moving from the research plan or design through measurement, sampling, data collection, coding, and data analysis. Thus, in addition to exemplifying many of the topics considered earlier, the chapter will also serve as a review of the research process.

PLANNING THE RESEARCH

The five steps in planning a research investigation are choosing a topic, reviewing previous studies, stating the hypothesis, operationalizing the concepts, and developing a strategy for testing the hypothesis. In one sense, planning is the most crucial stage, since unless we plan well, we will not be able to execute well.

Several individuals intent on reforming the cities have bemoaned the fact that many citizens apparently do not concern themselves with the area's problems as a whole but instead restrict their attention to their own narrowly conceived group interest. Such a disposition, it appears, makes it extremely difficult to institute comprehensive new programs since such efforts generally do not have any strong interest-group appeals. Put another way, these programs try to aid everybody a little rather than help a few a lot. Regardless of individual positions on the desirability of public policies directed at the entire area, the fact that such programs frequently face strong opposition cannot be denied. In city after city, proposals to restructure metropolitan government, improve area-wide planning and the like have been defeated by the voters. All of this leads to the question: Why do some people support area-wide policies while others will only back special-interest programs; or at a more basic level, why do some people think in area-wide terms while others limit their perspective to their own lives?

Although there is insufficient space here to do a complete review of the relevant literature, we can outline the major areas to be searched and relate a small portion of the earlier investigations to our study. At a minimum, an adequate review would examine case studies of attempts to approve area-wide programs in order to help identify factors which had an impact on the success or failure of such efforts.[1] Although analyses of single cases are not scientific generalizations, they can be a fruitful source of hypotheses for further testing. Second, a review would examine any systematic studies made heretofore of certain types of policies in order to ascertain the variables associated with their approval or disapproval.[2] Third, it might be useful to look at some sociological and social-psychological analyses of human motivations relevant for community issues; certain attitudinal dimensions might be independent or intervening causes of an area-wide perspective. Finally and most obviously, any review should closely scrutinize studies which relate some independent variable(s) to individuals' voting on, opinions about, or evaluations of local public policies.

Among this last group, two studies seem especially relevant. James Wilson and Edward Banfield, after analyzing precinct voting patterns on several referenda (e.g., new zoo, expanded sewer facilities) in Cleveland and Chicago during the late 1950s and early 1960s, concluded that

... voters in some income and ethnic groups are more likely than voters in others to take a public-regarding rather than a narrowly self-interested view of things—i.e., to take the welfare of others, especially that of "the community" into account as an aspect of their own welfare. We offer the additional hypothesis that both the tendency of a voter to take a public-regarding view and the content of that view . . . are largely functions of his participation in a subculture that is definable in ethnic and income terms. Each subcultural group, we think, has a more or less distinctive notion of how much a citizen ought to sacrifice for the sake of the community as well as of what the welfare of the community is constituted. . . . According to this hypothesis, the voter is presumed to act rationally; the ends he seeks are not always narrowly self-interested ones, however. On the contrary, depending upon his income and ethnic status they are more or less public-regarding.[3]

---

[1] One such case study is Henry J. Schmandt, Paul G. Steinbicker, and George D. Wendel, *Metropolitan Reform in St. Louis*, New York, Holt, Rinehart and Winston, 1961.

[2] One example of this type of investigation is Robert L. Crain, Elihu Katz, and Donald B. Rosenthal, *The Politics of Community Conflict*, Indianapolis, Ind., Bobbs-Merrill, 1968.

[3] James Q. Wilson and Edward C. Banfield, "Public Regardingness as a Value Premise in Voting Behavior," *American Political Science Review*, 58 (December, 1964), 885.

By ethnic, the investigators meant individuals of Czech, Irish, Italian, and Polish descent living in precincts having a high proportion of the same nationality group. Precincts inhabited by these ethnic types were less likely to be public-regarding on referenda than Anglo-Saxon, Jewish, or Negro precincts. The income variable was positively related to public-regardingness (i.e., the higher a precinct's median income, the higher its public-regarding vote), although income was felt to be secondary to the ethnic factor.

Second, a random-sample survey of 181 registered voters in Nashville and Davidson County, Tennessee, indicated that support of metropolitan organization (an area-wide issue) was positively "associated with (1) voter dissatisfaction with services, (2) the non-anticipation by voters of higher taxes stemming from reorganization, (3) voter education levels higher than grade school, and (4) voter understanding of 'metropolitan.' "[4] The same study found that, when education was controlled, income had no independent effect on support for metropolitan reorganization.

In addition to making use of these substantive findings in the planning of our study, we can also utilize some of the methods and concepts. In particular, Banfield and Wilson's distinction between public-regarding and private- or self-regarding can be helpful for differentiating between area-wide rationales and special-interest positions.

Both of the above studies dealt with voting behavior on area-wide issues and did not directly examine the degree of concern with these issues beyond the electoral context. In order to get away from any possible extraneous effects caused by the idiosyncracies of electoral campaigns, let us make our dependent variable the manner (public-regarding or self-regarding) in which local issue concerns are evaluated. For our independent variable, let us combine the income and education factors mentioned in the above investigations into a broader social-class variable. (Possible conditional, intervening, and alternative factors will be discussed below.) Thus, our working hypothesis is: *The higher an individual's social class, the more likely he is to evaluate local issues in a public-regarding manner.*

What are some possible ways of finding empirical indicators for public-/self-regardingness and social class? Public-/self-regardingness can be dissected as follows:

Variable I: Objective perspective

Indicator I*A*: The more the policy affects every citizen to an equal extent, the more public-regarding it is.

Indicator I*B*: The larger the number of individuals for whom the benefits (to be received from the policy) exceed the costs of the policy, the more public-regarding it is.

---

[4] Brett W. Hawkins, "Public Opinion and Metropolitan Reorganization in Nashville," *Journal of Politics*, 28 (May, 1966), 418.

Variable II: Subjective perspective

Indicator II*A*: The more the policy is perceived by individuals as affecting every citizen to an equal extent, the more public-regarding it is.
Indicator II*B*: As perceived by individuals, the more people for whom the benefits to be received by the policy exceed the costs of the policy, the more public-regarding it is.

The two breakdowns—objective and subjective—are the same except for the method by which the public-regarding character of policies is judged. Variable I's indicators rely on some outside evaluation according to standardized criteria, while Variable II's indicators depend on the evaluation of each individual subject. The subjective tack seems more appropriate for our purposes, since we are primarily interested in the manner in which individuals judge policy and not the objective impact of those policies. Moreover, an objective analysis of the impact or cost-benefit ratio of a large number of policies would be a time-consuming (and thereby an expensive) task, and in some instances the measurement of these characteristics might be quite unreliable (i.e., two analysts might assign widely different cost-benefit ratios to the same policy).

The one possible ambiguity in choosing the subjective approach is that an individual can support a public-regarding policy (objective definition) for self-regarding reasons (subjective definition) or support a self-regarding policy (objective definition) for public-regarding reasons (subjective definition). Even this potential difficulty, however, can be turned to our advantage, because if we wish, we can go ahead and objectively categorize policies as public- or self-regarding, and examine the extent to which the subjective reasons for supporting or opposing these policies are the same as the policies' objective classification. In other words, as a by-product of this study, we could test the hypothesis that public-regarding policies tend to be supported or opposed for public-regarding reasons and self-regarding policies tend to be supported or opposed for self-regarding reasons. Although we will not follow up this notion here, note how studies can be used for hypotheses other than the ones they were designed to test. By thinking ahead, we can sometimes multiply the utility of a single investigation by including a few more items, and thereby at one and the same time, collect data to test several hypotheses.

Our operationalization of public-/self-regardingness, then, will rely on the individual subject's evaluative manner. If his position on a policy is justified in terms of its affecting every citizen to an equal extent or according to the number of people for whom the benefits exceed the cost or both, then we will call him *public-regarding*. If his position on a policy is justified in terms of its impact on a specific segment of the population, then we will call him *self-regarding*.

One somewhat sketchy breakdown for the social-class concept would be:

Variable I: Education

Indicator IA: Number of years an individual attended school.
Indicator IB: Number of social science courses completed.

Variable II: Income

Indicator IIA: Family income for the current year.
Indicator IIB: Current monetary value of family assets.

Variable III: Occupation

Indicator IIIA: Standardized prestige ranking assigned by national sample.
Indicator IIIB: Amount of physical (as opposed to mental) effort required.

Variable IV: Self-defined social class

Indicator IVA: Individual's evaluation of his own social class.
Indicator IVB: Individual's evaluation of his father's social class.

In selecting an operational definition for social class based on this dissection, we have two choices. We can form an index based on some combination of the first three variables, or we can rely on the individual's own opinion of his social class. Although the latter choice would make for easier measurement in that it would only require asking the individual a single question, past studies show that when asked to give their social class, most Americans answer either "middle class" or "working class." In other words, when measured this way, the variable does not vary much, and as we have already seen, an indicator with low variation is a handicap when one wishes to measure covariation. Consequently, we will use a combination of education, income, and occupation as our measure of social class. For each of these three, we will employ the A indicator, because in each case it is either a less costly or a more reliable method of measuring the variable. Individuals are more apt to remember how many years they attended school than they are to recall how many social-science courses they had. In addition, one would have to define "social science," and this clarification would lengthen interview time. Similarly, family income is less ambiguous than family assets, and placing price tags on all the various assets would be extremely difficult. Finally, standardized prestige rankings for occupations can be readily obtained, while determining the amounts of physical and mental effort involved in a particular occupation would be very difficult. These operational definitions, of course, are not yet measuring instruments. We still must develop actual mechanisms for defining and gathering the scores, a task which will be performed after we develop our research strategy.

The first step in formulating a strategy is to specify the study subjects. In this project, the hypothesis clearly refers to individual human beings, so that is the level of analysis. Since we would like our results to apply to as large a population as possible, we want to take some kind of probability sample. Moreover, since the independent variable is social class, we need a population which has a reasonable amount of variation in class levels. This latter requirement would rule out the use of a high-income suburb or a low-income slum. Hence we decide to take a probability sample of a city large enough to have a socioeconomically diverse population and a variety of policy issues. Because our funds are limited, we choose the closest large city (River City) and restrict our completed sample size to 400.

Next, we must consider the three requirements for inferring a causal relationship: temporal order, covariation, and the elimination of other possible causes. The first two conditions should present no problem in our study. It makes much more sense to assume that an individual's social class precedes his manner of evaluating public policies than vice versa, and both social class and public-/self-regardingness should vary enough to enable a satisfactory measurement of their covariation. One can, however, foresee many possible contaminating factors; since randomization is not a feasible strategy in this project (among other things, there is no way to randomly assign social-class values to the study subjects), these factors must be identified and their scores included in the investigation.

Let us take each of the major types of confounding factors (intervening, conditional, alternative, and spurious) and discuss how they might relate to the present investigation. To check out possible intervening factors, let us ask if social class directly influences the manner of policy evaluation or if there is some intervening step which must be taken in order for social class to have an impact. We could argue that a higher social class does not, of and by itself, make a man more public-regarding but that it does so largely or solely because it increases his local political involvement, which in turn makes him more public-regarding. Thus we have as a possible intervening factor: *degree of local political involvement.*

Are there any circumstances where we would expect social class to have more or less than its usual impact on public- and self-regardingness? One possibility is that the surrounding neighborhood's social-class composition will have a reinforcing or debilitating influence on the original relationship depending on whether it is the same as or different from the individual's own social class. According to this line of thinking, a person in a high social class would be more likely to be public-regarding if he lived in a high-social-class neighborhood and less likely to be public-regarding if he resided in a low-social-class neighborhood; similarly, a low-social-class individual would be less likely to be self-regarding if his neighborhood were upper-social-class and more likely to be self-regarding if his neighborhood were largely lower-social-class. Thus we have as a possible conditional factor: *neighborhood social class.*

In searching for alternative causes, we should ask ourselves what else besides social class might affect the manner in which local public policies are evaluated. Wilson and Banfield clearly nominate ethnicity for strong consideration. If an individual is a member of one of several ethnic groups, he is more likely to be self-regarding. It is important that we include this factor in our study in order that we might compare our results with previous research. Such a cumulative strategy is the process by which scientific research builds a coherent body of findings. Thus we have as a possible alternative cause: *ethnicity.*

Finally, we must ask if there is any factor that might be a mutual cause of social class and public-/self-regardingness and thereby produce a spurious relationship. Since such a factor must logically occur before the original independent and dependent variables, this narrows the list of possibilities. One candidate for the spurious role is father's social class. Conceivably, both an individual's social class and his degree of public-regardingness might be caused by his father's social class. A father with a high social class would provide the resources (e.g., a good education) for his offspring to achieve a high social class and instill in them the necessity for evaluating issues in a public-regarding manner. Thus we have as a possible spurious factor: *father's social class.*

Diagrammatically, these four possibilities, along with the original relationship, can be expressed as follows, where SC is social class, PSR is public-/self-regardingness, LPI is local political involvement, NSC is neighborhood social class, E is ethnicity, and FSC is father's social class:

SC ⟶ PSR (Original relationship)

SC ⟶ LPI ⟶ PSR (Intervening case)

When NSC = SC, SC ⟶ PSR (Conditional case)

SC ⟶ PSR (Alternative case)
E ⟶

FSC ⟶ PSR (Spurious case)
⟶ SC ⟶

In addition, we can combine many of the possibilities to obtain still different causal arrangements. For example, by combining the intervening and conditional cases, we get

When NSC = SC, SC ⟶ LPI ⟶ PSR

Since we have four new variables (local political involvement, neighborhood social class, ethnicity, and father's social class), our next step normally would be the operationalization of these concepts. Again, in order to conserve space and because the social-class concepts have effectively already been operationally defined, we will bypass this step here. We will, however, consider the measurements of these variables in the next section.

MEASURING THE VARIABLES

Now that we have developed a plan for the research study, we must next decide on specific measuring devices for each variable. As mentioned above, the operationalization process gives us the criteria for measurement but we still need concrete indicators for obtaining the scores. For example, we know that our social-class measure will have educational, income, and occupational components and that certain criteria (e.g., annual family income) will be used for each component, but we still must determine how to combine these components and how to measure them (e.g., income can be measured in dollars or in percentiles).

In Chapter 3, we discussed a method for constructing a socioeconomic status index having education, income, and occupation components. We will use a similar index to measure an individual's social class in this study. The initial education measure will be the number of years a person attended school, the income indicator will be the annual family income (in dollars) for the current year, and the occupational measure will be the prestige ranking (from 0 to 100) of the job of the head of the household as gathered from a national sample of American adults.[5] Since we cannot add years, dollars, and prestige units to form an overall index, we must transform the education and income indicators into quasi-prestige rankings. This is done by determining the relative standing vis-à-vis the national adult population of each educational and income level and then measuring that ranking on a 0 to 100 scale (i.e., in percentiles). For example, if an individual has 15 years of formal education and if only 14 percent of American adults have had that much education, then he is higher than 85 percent of all Americans, and his percentile score is 86. To obtain the final social-class score, we decide to weight each component equally, and thus the formula is

$$\text{Social class score} = \frac{\text{Education score} + \text{Income score} + \text{Occupational score}}{3}$$

Dividing the score by 3 is done in order to keep the final score on an esthetically pleasing 0 to 100 scale.

To obtain a neighborhood social-class score, we can use an equivalent approach. Indeed, in order to maintain conceptual comparability, a similar index is highly desirable. To measuure neighborhood social class then, we first determine the census tract in which the individual lives, and for that

---

[5] The prestige rankings are found in Albert J. Reiss, Jr. et al., op. cit., pp. 262–275; we will assume that all members of a single household receive their occupational status from that of the household head.

tract, we find the median school years completed and the median family income.[6] These two indicators can be transformed into percentile scores by the same method used for individuals. A more elaborate procedure is necessary to obtain an occupational score since the census tract statistics give only the male job distribution by nine broad categories. (Since our original occupation score was based on the household head's job and since most heads are males, we will use only the male job distribution in computing the neighborhood occupational score.) Fortunately, however, the Reiss volume has prestige rankings for these census categories, and an overall 0 to 100 score for the tract can be calculated. To do this, we take the number of individuals in each category (e.g., 402 in the sales-worker group), multiply it by the prestige score for that category, add up the products for all the categories, and divide by the total number of employed males. To get the overall neighborhood social-class score, we use the same formulas as for the individual social-class index.

In attempting to measure the social class of an individual's father, we confront a recall problem. Although a person is likely to remember his father's educational level and almost certain to recall his occupation, any income estimate he might make is apt to be highly unreliable. Moreover, given inflation and changes in the typical standard-of-living levels over the past fifty years, comparing incomes from various points in time is highly hazardous. Thus, our best strategy might be to drop the income component, and base the father's social-class index entirely on education and occupation. Since income is highly correlated with education and occupation, this compromise should not have much impact on the study's results. We still, however, have a problem with what criterion to use in assigning prestige scores to each educational level. For example, some of our respondents' fathers will have grown up in the late nineteenth century when a high school education was a relatively rare achievement, while others' fathers will have been born in the twentieth century when a high school diploma was not nearly so uncommon. In cases like these, it would clearly be inaccurate to assign the same educational score to an 1890 and a 1935 high school graduate. (We are of course ignoring this problem in calculating the social-class score for each individual, although a little reflection would show that the two situations are not entirely comparable since we are assuming that the study subjects are all members of the same generation.) Each individual should be compared to his own generation instead, but this would involve an enormous amount of work since separate rating scales would have to be developed for each decade or two.

In order to save time and trouble, we will rely solely on the father's occupation as the indicator of his social class. Moreover, we will assume that the occupational prestige rankings have remained roughly constant during the past century so that we can use the same prestige scores for all the subjects' fathers.

---

[6] For an explanation of census tracts, see Chapter 5.

Since our measure of public-/self-regardingness is conceptually based on the manner in which a person evaluates a policy, the best measurement tactic would be to let the individual evaluate a policy and then categorize his answer (according to the operational definitions given in the preceding section) as public-regarding, self-regarding, both, or neither. Accepting this as a proper procedure, should we allow the individual to pick his own policy or policies, or should we provide all the subjects with a standard list? The former approach has the advantage of allowing the individual to evaluate things that he cares about, but it might impair comparability since it is easier to give a public-regarding rationale for certain kinds of policies; two individuals might be equally public-regarding, but one might be more concerned about area-wide policies and thereby appear more public-regarding. The second approach—giving the respondents a single list—solves the comparability problem but might be rather artificial since there is the danger that many of the subjects will not have given much thought to some or all of the listed policies. We can, however, partially counteract this artificiality by using policies that have recently been in the news in River City.

Which approach should we use? Since each one has its advantages and disadvantages, since it is extremely important to get the best possible measurement of the dependent variable, and since using one does not necessarily exclude using the other, we shall include both in the study. There is no need to make hard choices unless it is absolutely necessary.

For each approach we must still develop a scoring scheme. In the first case, we will let the subject mention up to three policies, and for each policy allow him to give as many reasons as he wishes. If the reason is public-regarding, we will assign it a score of 2; if it is partially public-regarding and partially self-regarding, we will score it as 1; and if it is self-regarding, we will assign a zero score. Rationales which do not have a public- or self-regarding content will be ignored. In order to prevent the number of reasons mentioned from affecting the overall score, we will divide the total score by the number of mentions having a public- or self-regarding content. For example, if a person gives two public-regarding responses and two self-regarding responses, his overall score would be $(2 + 2 + 0 + 0)/4$ or 1.0. If the person gives less than two reasons, no score will be calculated.

We will use the same 2–1–0 scoring scheme for the evaluations of the standardized list of policies, and again we will let the subject offer as many reasons as he desires. In this case, the subject must give at least three reasons in order to be included in the analysis. Our list should include a variety of policies which have been publicly discussed during the past six months. Based on a careful reading of the newspapers for this period, we first make up a list of all policies which have received a good deal of attention, and from this large list select a balanced set of five policies: air pollution, city and county government consolidation, elementary and secondary school aid, law enforcement, and welfare payments.

In measuring an individual's degree of local political involvement, it is preferable to use actual behavior rather than an abstract self-rating. Directly asking the subject to evaluate his involvement might lead him to describe how involved he wished to be or thought he should be, rather than his actual involvement. Thus, we should take an indirect approach by asking the subject how often he performs certain activities implying local political involvement. Two activities that meet this requirement are: reading and listening to news about local politics and discussing local politics with one's friends and associates. For each of these two forms of behavior, we can develop a four-point scale. If the activity is performed nearly every day, the score is 3; once or twice a week, 2; from time to time, 1; never, 0. Summing the two scores, we get a local political involvement index ranging from 0 to 6.

To compare our findings with those of Wilson and Banfield, our measurement of ethnicity should be similar to theirs. Their definition of ethnic—based in part on that of the Bureau of the Census—is any person born abroad or whose father or mother (or both) was born abroad; they exempt from this group any Jew, Negro, or British immigrant. Using this definition, we will score a person as 1 if he meets the ethnic criteria and as 0 if he does not.

Since the kinds of statistical techniques we will be able to employ depend on the levels at which the study variables have been measured, we should briefly review the measurement levels of each of the variables. The individual and neighborhood social-class variables are a mixture of metric (percentiles for education and income) and ordinal (prestige ranks for occupation), while father's social class is ordinal since it is based entirely on occupational prestige. Since there are a large number (100) of prestige ranks, we can assume that each prestige unit is roughly equal, however, and thereby treat all the social-class variables as metric measures. Ethnicity is a dummy variable, with the presence of the attribute scored as 1 and the absence as 0. Both the public-/self-regardingness and the local political-involvement factors are measured at the ordinal level, although we can again use metric statistical techniques (e.g., partial correlation) if we are willing to assume that the regardingness- and involvement-units are equal. Since the other factors are metric or dummy variables, we will make this assumption so that we might apply metric analytic tools to the entire study.

Finally, we should consider our measurement's reliability and validity. Do they consistently measure the phenomenon from case to case and are they really measuring what we think they are measuring? In selecting our measurements, we have been keeping these factors in mind. For example, we used father's occupation as the sole indicator of his social class since we thought that individuals would not reliably remember their fathers' incomes or educational experiences. A concern for validity caused us to use two measures for public- and self-regardingness. We always need to remember that unless we measure well, our later analysis will be worthless.

SELECTING THE SUBJECTS

We have already decided that we need a sample of 400 River City adults. Moreover, we want to have a probability sample in order that we can make inferences with calculable levels of risk and accuracy about the entire universe. In order to draw this sample, we must first precisely define the universe or population. Our definition will be all persons 21 years of age or older who currently reside in noninstitutional dwelling units in River City. People living in prisons, hospitals, old-age homes, dormitories, and the like are excluded in order to simplify the sampling process.

We then compute the number of contacts which must be made in order to have a completed sample of 400. If our pessimistic expected completion rate is 60 percent (i.e., only 60 percent of the people in the original sample will ultimately be interviewed), we will require an initial sample of 667 (400 times 100/60).

Since there is no list of the population, we must use a multistage approach. In addition, since our funds are limited we must cluster the sample in order to reduce travel costs. As the first stage in our multistage sampling procedure, we obtain a list of census tracts from the appropriate Bureau of the Census publication for River City. Assuming there are 50 tracts, we assign each one as many unique numbers as it has adult noninstitutional residents. Using a table of random digits, we select 20 census tracts; with 20 sampling points, we can achieve a moderate amount of concentration without unduly limiting the sample's representativeness. If we chose only 4 or 5 tracts, the odds that these areas would not be representative of the entire city would be much higher than when we select 20 tracts.

Next, we obtain a map of all streets and dwelling units from the River City Planning Department, and for each selected census tract we assign a unique number to each square block. If a block has an extraordinarily large or small number of dwelling units, we divide or combine so that each block has a roughly equal number of dwelling units. Again using a table of random digits, we select 11 blocks in each of the 20 census tracts. For each selected block, we assign unique numbers to each dwelling unit and, again using the random-digits table, select 3 dwelling units. Finally, for each selected dwelling unit, we use the household-selection-decision table (see Table 4.3) to pick the respondent. Reviewing the stages, we have 20 census tracts, 11 blocks per tract, 3 dwelling units per block, and 1 person per dwelling unit or (20)(11)(3)(1) or 660 contacts.

COLLECTING THE DATA

In this stage of the research process, we must design the questionnaire, brief the interviewers, code the collected data, and calculate the index scores for the variables. Since our subjects are individual persons whose modes of policy evaluation and social class are not publicly available, we must use a survey as our collection device. (The neighborhood social-class data will be obtained from Census sources.) Moreover, since the subjects are scattered throughout the city, since not all of them have telephones, and since many are not sufficiently motivated or literate to complete a written form, neither a group-administered nor a telephone or mail survey is appropriate. We must use face-to-face interviews, and our questions should be able to be understood by all types of people. Following the question-writing guidelines presented in Chapter 5, we construct the following questionnaire:[7]

Hello, I'm (*Name of Interviewer*) from the River City University Survey Research Bureau. We're conducting a survey of River City citizens about their attitudes toward civic affairs. First, could you tell me how many people live here? Anyone else in the family? (PAUSE) Anyone else living here who is not related to you? I'd like to know the ages of the people. How old is (*Mention First Name*)? (*Continue getting the ages for all the persons mentioned. Assign a number to each person 21 years of age or older in the following order: males from oldest to youngest, then females from oldest to youngest. Using the respondent selection table, identify the appropriate respondent. If the respondent is the person you are talking with, go ahead with interview. Otherwise, ask to speak to the appropriate person. If he or she is not at home, try to arrange an appointment.*)

1A. What do you personally feel are the most important problems which the government in River City should try to take care of? (*Probe for up to three problems*)

1B. (*For each problem*) Why do you feel that way?

2A. Some people think that the River City government should do more to control air pollution. Others think more government action isn't necessary. Have you been interested enough in this to favor one side over the other? (*If NO, go to 3A*)

2B. (*If YES to 2A*) Which do you think?

2C. Why do you feel that way?

3A. Some people say that the River City and Bridge County governments should be joined together. Others say that they should be kept apart. Have you been interested enough in this to favor one side over the other? (*If NO, go to 4A*)

3B. (*If YES to 3A*) Which do you think?

3C. Why do you feel that way?

4A. Some people think that more money should be spent on River City grade and high schools. Others think that enough money is being spent now. Have you been interested enough in this to favor one side over the other? (*If NO, go to 5A*)

4B. (*If YES to 4A*) Which do you think?

4C. Why do you feel that way?

5A. Some people think more money should be spent by the River City government to control crime. Others think that enough money is

---

[7] Most of these questions are adapted from standard University of Michigan Survey Research Center items. The typical questionnaire would also have space for recording the answers.

being spent now. Have you been interested enough in this to favor one side over the other? (*If NO, go to 6A*)

5B. (*If YES to 5A*) Which do you think?

5C. Why do you feel that way?

6A. Some people think that the River City government should spend more money to increase welfare payments. Others think that enough money is being spent now. Have you been interested enough in this to favor one side over the other? (*If NO, go to 7*)

6B. (*If YES to 6A*) Which do you think?

6C. Why do you feel that way?

7. Do you follow the accounts of River City political and governmental affairs? Would you say that you follow them nearly every day, once or twice a week, from time to time, or almost never?

8. What about talking about River City political and governmental affairs with other people? Do you do that nearly every day, once or twice a week, from time to time, ar almost never?

9. What is (your/the head of the household's) occupation? I mean, what kind of work (do you/does he) do? (*If not clear or obvious*) What exactly (do you/does he) do on (your/his) job? What kind of business is that? (*If head of household is unemployed*) What kind of work (do you/does he) usually do? (*If head of household is retired*) What kind of work did (you/he) do before (you/he) retired?

10. What kind of work did your father do for a living while you were growing up? (*If not clear or obvious*) What exactly did he do on his job? What kind of business is that?

11. How many grades of school did you finish?

12. Many people don't know their exact income for this year yet; but would you tell me as best you can what you expect your income for this year to be——before taxes?

13A. Where were you born?

13B. (*If respondent is not black and nor foreign-born*) Were both your parents born in this country? (*If NO*) Which country was your father born in? Which country was your mother born in?

13C. Are you Protestant, Roman Catholic, or Jewish? Thank you for your cooperation.

The linkage between the questions and the variables is fairly obvious. Question 1A provides the lead-in for the open-ended measure of public-/self-regardingness (1B). Questions 2A, 3A, 4A, 5A, and 6A set the stage for the closed-ended measures of public-/self-regardingness and filter out those respondents who do not have an opinion on the particular issue. The B series in Questions 2–6 asks the respondent to take a position, and the C series probes for the mode of evaluation. Questions 7 and 8 measure local political involvement, Questions 9 through 12 cover the social-class components, and Questions 13A–C measure ethnicity.

In addition to familiarizing themselves with the questions and reviewing the standard interviewing procedures, the interviewers should be aware of the study's objectives. In particular, all answers to the evaluation items

(Questions 1B and 2C–6C) should be recorded verbatim, and the respondent should be encouraged to discuss fully his reasons for supporting a certain position. We want to get as much information as possible on these items in order to maximize our ability to assign accurate public-/self-regardingness scores.

In coding the data, we must first construct a codebook listing the column location of each variable on the IBM card and giving the possible codes for each variable. An abbreviated version of our codebook is:

Columns	Variable	Coding scheme
1–3	Respondent identification number	Unique number for each respondent (e.g., 001–400)
4–5	First problem (Q. 1A)	Two-digit number for each problem (e.g., water pollution = 11), with no answer = 00
6	First problem: PSR (Q. 1B)	Self-regarding reason = 0 Mixed public and self = 1 Public-regarding reason = 2 No regarding implication = 8 No answer = 9
7–8	Second problem (Q. 1A)	Same as Columns 4–5
9	Second problem: PSR (Q. 1B)	Same as Column 6
10–11	Third problem (Q. 1A)	Same as Columns 4–5
12	Third problem: PSR (Q. 1B)	Same as Column 6
13	Air pollution (Q. 2A–2B)	Should do more = 1 Pro-Con = 2 More action isn't necessary = 3 No opinion = 4 No answer = 9
14	Air pollution: PSR (Q. 2C)	Same as Column 6
15	City-county merger (Q. 3A–3B)	Should join together = 1 Pro-Con = 2 Kept apart = 3 No opinion = 4 No answer = 9
16	City-county merger: PSR (Q. 3C)	Same as Column 6
17	School aid (Q. 4A–4B)	Spend more = 1 Pro-Con = 2 Spending enough = 3 No opinion = 4 No answer = 9
18	School aid: PSR (Q. 4C)	Same as Column 6
19	Crime control (Q. 5A–B)	Same as Column 17
20	Crime control: PSR (Q. 5C)	Same as Column 6
21	Welfare payments (Q. 6A–6B)	Same as Column 17
22	Welfare payments: PSR (Q. 6C)	Same as Column 6
23	Media involvement (Q. 7)	Almost never = 0 From time to time = 1 Once-twice a week = 2 Nearly every day = 3 No answer = 9
24	Conversational involvement (Q. 8)	Same as Column 23

(Continued)

Columns	Variable	Coding scheme
25–26	Head of household occupation (Q. 9)	Two-digit code adapted from Survey Research Center code
27–28	Father's occupation (Q. 10)	Same as Columns 25–26
29–30	Respondent's education (Q. 11)	Actual number of grades completed with no answer = 99
31–32	Family income (Q. 12)	Actual income (in thousands) with no answer = 00 and all incomes over $100,000 coded as 99
33–34	Respondent's country of birth (Q. 13A)	Two-digit code adapted from Survey Research Center code
35–36	Father's country of birth (Q. 13B)	Same as Columns 33–34
37–38	Mother's country of birth (Q. 13C)	Same as Columns 33–34
39	Respondent's religion	Protestant = 1 Roman Catholic = 2 Jewish = 3 Other = 4 No answer = 5
40	Respondent's race	White = 1 Black = 2 Other = 3

Up to this point, all we have done is to code the responses actually given to the questions. In most instances, however, these initial responses are not the same as the final variables; for example, the ethnicity score is based on country of birth (non-U.S.), religion (non-Jewish), and race (non-black). Thus, we must provide locations for the intermediate and final forms of these variables:

Columns	Variable	Coding scheme
41–42	PSR score: open-ended	Actual score to one decimal place (e.g., 1.2 coded as 12); if insufficient answers for score, code as 99
43–44	PSR score: closed-ended	Same as Columns 41–42
45–46	Respondent's occupational prestige rank	01 to 99; if no answer, code as 00
47–48	Respondent's educational percentile	Same as Columns 45–46
49–50	Respondent's income percentile	Same as Columns 45–46
51–52	Respondent's social class score	Same as Columns 45–46
53–54	Father's occupational prestige rank (and social class score)	Same as Columns 45–46
55–62	Neighborhood social class measures	Same as Columns 45–52
63	Local political involvement score	0–6; if no answer to one or both questions, code = 9
64	Ethnicity	Nonethnic = 0 Ethnic = 1

The next step is to code (on coding sheets) each respondent's answers to the questionnaire items. For the evaluation questions ("Why do you feel that way?"), two persons independently code the responses in order to minimize code bias and maximize reliability. If the two coders agree on how a particular evaluation should be categorized (e.g., as public-regarding), then their decision is accepted; if they disagree, then they, along with a third person, mutually discuss the response and arrive at a common decision.

Following the coding of the original questions, the prestige and percentile ranks for the social-class components (respondent, father, and neighborhood) are entered on the coding sheet. These codes are then punched onto IBM cards and checked by repunching the codes on an IBM verifier. Finally, an index-construction computer program is used both to compute the social class, public-/self-regardingness, local political involvement, and ethnicity scores and to enter these scores into the appropriate columns on the IBM cards.

Note that we have been careful to retain the responses to the original questions even though, as the study is now planned, we will rely entirely on the index scores. The reason for this policy is that, if we change our minds about how an index should be constructed (e.g., if we decide to assign occupation a stronger weight in the social-class score or we want to consider blacks as ethnics instead of nonethnics), the data necessary for making the new calculations are readily available. Moreover, data which are now incidental to our study objectives (e.g., which problems were mentioned to the first question or the direction of preferences on the policies) can be easily incorporated if we so desire.

DESCRIBING EACH VARIABLE
Our primary concern here is to see if each factor varies sufficiently to warrant its being included in an analysis of covariation. If everybody is public-regarding or has a high social-class score, there is little point in going further. To check out the variation of each measure, all we need do is to examine its frequency distribution; there is no need, in this particular study, to calculate any precise measure of variation (e.g., standard deviation).

Table 10.1 gives the frequency distributions for the two public-/self-regardingness indexes. For both measures, the amount of variation is quite sufficient; no interval (except for "insufficient responses") has more than 26 percent of the cases and none has less than 12 percent. Similar frequency distributions for the other variables also reveal an adequate amount of variation.

DESCRIBING TWO-VARIABLE RELATIONSHIPS
Before measuring the amount of covariation between the independent variable (subject's social class) and the dependent variable (public-/self-

TABLE 10.1 FREQUENCY DISTRIBUTIONS FOR TWO MEASURES OF PUBLIC-/
SELF-REGARDINGNESS (PSR) FOR RIVER CITY ADULTS

Scores[b]	PSR I[a]	PSR II[a]
0.0–0.4	51 (12.8%)	57 (14.2%)
0.5–0.8	80 (20.0%)	84 (21.0%)
0.9–1.2	96 (24.0%)	101 (25.2%)
1.3–1.6	66 (16.5%)	76 (19.0%)
1.7–2.0	53 (13.2%)	61 (15.2%)
Insufficient responses	54 (13.5%)	21 (5.2%)
Total	400 100.0	400 99.8[c]

[a] The PSR I measure is based on problems mentioned by the respondent; PSR II is based on a standard set of five problems.
[b] High scores indicate high public-regardingness, while low scores indicate high self-regardingness.
[c] Percentage totals do not always equal 100.0 percent because of rounding.
SOURCE: The data are hypothetical.

regardingness), we must decide which one of the two measures of the dependent variable to use in the analysis. We could, of course, perform two complete analyses, first using one measure and then the other. But this will not be necessary if the two public-/self-regardingness indicators correlate highly. If they are strongly interrelated, then either one can be employed since both would yield approximately the same results.

To see if this can be done, we must measure the degree of association between the two measures. Although we can reasonably assume that these two variables are metric, there is no need to do so at this point; all we require is a measure of association, and Kendall's tau is preferable for this one purpose, since unlike Pearson's r it does not demand that we assume a linear relationship. Using either a standard computer program or the more laborious paper-and-pencil method, we find that Kendall's tau equals +.91. Since the maximum value for this coefficient is +1.0, this means that almost all the pairs are ordered in the same direction and that the two indicators are very highly correlated. (In addition, this high correlation increases our confidence in the validity of the indicators since two different ways of measuring the concept yielded very similar results.) Since we can employ either indicator, we select PSR II because more subjects are scored on it than on PSR I (see Table 10.1).

In measuring the amount of variation between public-/self-regardingness and the subject's social class, we will use Pearson's r, so that in the later analysis involving additional variables (e.g., ethnicity) we can employ partial correlation coefficients; if we employed ordinal measures of association, we would then have to use physical controls later, and given the fact that there are only 400 subjects, we would run a strong risk of having too few cases in some analyses. After constructing a scattergram (not shown here) for the joint relationship between the two variables and finding out that the pattern of the dots supports the linear assumption, we compute an r of

+.57. To interpret this coefficient, we square it (the coefficient of determination); in this instance, $r^2 = .32$. This means that 32 percent of the variation between individuals' social-class scores and their public-/self-regardingness scores is held in common. Our hypothesis that the two variables are positively related is reasonably supported by the results. Although the covariation is by no means complete (if it were, both r and r^2 would equal 1.0), it is a good deal greater than zero. We must still, however, check out the impact of additional variables on this basic two-variable relationship.

DESCRIBING MULTIVARIATE RELATIONSHIPS

The first two criteria for inferring causality have now been established. The independent variable temporally precedes the dependent variable (an individual's social class precedes his manner of evaluating local issues), and the independent and dependent variables vary together in a consistent, nonrandom manner ($r_{PSR,SC} = +.57$).[8] Our third task is to specify more precisely the causal arrangement by examining whether there are any intervening, conditional, alternative, or spurious factors. We will first check out the four causal arrangements outlined in the strategy-formulation section, and depending on what we discover from this inquiry, perform further analyses before making any conclusions.

Let us first see whether local political involvement is an intervening factor between social class and public-/self-regardingness. If indeed social class affects public-/self-regardingness only by causing an increase in local political involvement that in turn causes an increase in public-regardingness, we would predict that there would be positive correlations—between social class and local political involvement and between local political involvement and public-/self-regardingness; the original correlation ($r_{PSR,SC} = +.57$) would then reduce to zero or almost zero. Calculating the two simple correlations (for these and the following simple correlations where both variables are metric, we first construct scattergrams to test the appropriateness of the linear model), we find that $r_{LPI,SC} = +.62$ and that $r_{PSR,LPI} = +.45$; thus the first condition is met. We must compute the partial correlation next:

$$r_{PSR,SC \cdot LPI} = \frac{r_{PSR,SC} - (r_{LPI,SC})(r_{PSR,LPI})}{\sqrt{1 - (r_{LPI,SC})^2} \sqrt{1 - (r_{PSR,LPI})^2}}$$

$$= \frac{(.57) - (.62)(.45)}{\sqrt{1 - (.62)^2} \sqrt{1 - (.45)^2}}$$

$$= \frac{.29}{(.79)(.89)}$$

$$= .41$$

The original simple correlation between social class and public-/self-regardingness (+.57) does not reduce to zero but only to +.41 when we

[8] In this section, we will use the variable abbreviations adopted earlier in the chapter.

control for the effects of local political involvement. Thus at this stage, we can conclude that although local political involvement plays an intervening role (the correlation is reduced from $+.57$ to $+.41$), it is not a pure intervening factor (the partial correlation of $+.41$ does not approximate zero).

Our second causal arrangement holds that when a person's own social class coincides with his neighborhood's typical social class, the original relationship between social class and public-/self-regardingness is intensified. Conversely, when there is a discrepancy between the two social-class factors, the original relationship is weakened. In order to check out this notion, we employ a physical control. We divide the sample into two groups: those having similar individual and neighborhood social-class scores and those having dissimilar scores. If the difference between the two scores (both of which are measured in percentiles) is 10 or less, we will consider them as similar; if the difference is 11 or more, we will define them as dissimilar. For each of these two groups, we compute the Pearsonian r's. For the similar group, $r_{PSR,SC} = +.59$; for the dissimilar group, $r_{PSR,SC} = +.56$. Although there is a very slight tendency for the similar group to have a stronger relationship than the dissimilar group, the difference is quite minor, and the most sensible conclusion is to reject the idea that degree of similarity between neighborhood and individual social class systematically affects the original relationship.

The third causal arrangement based on the Wilson-Banfield study states that ethnicity is an alternative cause of public-/self-regardingness; specifically, an ethnic person is less likely to be public-regarding than is a non-ethnic individual. If this causal situation holds, we should find that there is a positive simple correlation between social class and public-/self-regardingness, a negative simple correlation between ethnicity and public-/self-regardingness, and a zero or near-zero partial correlation between social class and ethnicity when controlling for public-/self-regardingness; since if social class and ethnicity are independent alternative causes, their only interrelationship would be the product of their mutual association with public-/self-regardingness. Since we have already calculated the Pearsonian r between social class and public- and self-regardingness, we know that the positive correlation condition for this relationship is fulfilled: $r_{PSR,SC} = +.57$. Computing the point biserial correlation between ethnicity and public-/self-regardingness, we find that $r_{PSR,E} = -.39$; thus the second condition is also met. Next we compute the point biserial correlation between social class and ethnicity ($r_{SC,E} = -.72$), and using all three of the above simple correlations, calculate the partial correlation between social class and ethnicity controlling for public- and self-regardingness:

$$r_{SC,E \cdot PSR} = \frac{(-.72) - (.57)(-.39)}{\sqrt{1 - (.57)^2}\, \sqrt{1 - (-.39)^2}}$$

$$= \frac{-.50}{(.82)(.92)}$$

$$= -.67$$

The third condition is not met; instead of reducing to zero, the partial correlation is very close to the original correlation between social class and ethnicity (−.72). Thus we must reject the alternative cause interpretation.

We cannot, however, eliminate ethnicity from the analysis. Clearly, it is playing some part in the causal scheme since it is moderately correlated with public-/self-regardingness (−.39) and strongly associated with social class (−.72). Assuming that public-/self-regardingness must always be last in the temporal order, four other causal structures involving these three variables are logically possible: ethnicity might be an intervening variable between social class and public-/self-regardingness, social class might be an intervening variable between ethnicity and public-/self-regardingness, ethnicity might be the mutual cause of both social class and public-/self-regardingness (and thus the relationship between the latter pair would be spurious), and social class might be the mutual cause of ethnicity and public-/self-regardingness (and thus, again, the latter relationship would be spurious).

Since it does not make sense to conceive of social class occurring before ethnicity (how can one's income, for example, affect the nationality of his parents), we can reject the first and fourth possibilities on time-order grounds. Turning to the third alternative, if ethnicity is producing a spurious relationship between social class and public-/self-regardingness, then we would expect, first, non-zero simple correlations between ethnicity and each of these two variables and a zero or near-zero partial correlation between social class and public-/self-regardingness controlling for ethnicity, since the only relationship between this pair would be the product of their mutual dependency on ethnicity. As we have already seen, the first condition is met; $r_{SC, E} = -.72$ and $r_{PSR, E} = -.39$. To test the second condition, we must compute:

$$r_{PSR,CE \cdot E} = \frac{(.57) - (-.39)(-.72)}{\sqrt{1 - (-.39)^2} \ \sqrt{1 - (-.72)^2}}$$
$$= \frac{.29}{(.92)(.69)}$$
$$= +.46$$

The ethnicity control does not have much effect on the relationship between social class and public-/self-regardingness; the original two-variable correlation is +.57, and the controlled measure of association is +.46. Thus we can reject the proposition that ethnicity is causing a spurious relationship between social class and public-/self-regardingness.

This leaves us with the second alternative—that social class is an intervening variable between ethnicity and public-/self-regardingness. The correlational pattern corresponding to this causal model would be: first, non-zero simple correlations between ethnicity and social class and between social class and public-/self-regardingness, and second, a zero or near-zero partial correlation between ethnicity and public-/self-regardingness controlling for social class since, if social class is a pure intervening factor, all or nearly all of ethnicity's influence on public-/self-regardingness would flow through social class. We already know that the first condition is satisfied since $r_{SC, E} = -.72$ and $r_{PSR, SC} = +.57$. All we must do now is calculate the partial:

$$r_{E,PSR \cdot SC} = \frac{(-.39) - (.57)(-.72)}{\sqrt{1 - (.57)^2} \ \sqrt{1 - (-.72)^2}}$$

$$= \frac{.02}{(.82)(.69)}$$

$$= +.04$$

As predicted, the partial correlation approximates zero and we can conclude that social class is a nearly complete intervening factor between ethnicity and public-/self-regardingness. If a person is an ethnic, he is less likely to have a high social-class score and thereby less likely to be public-regarding; conversely, if an individual is not an ethnic, he is more likely to have a high social class score and thereby more likely to be public-regarding.

Before examining the role of father's social class in our explanatory schema, let us summarize our findings up to this point. We have found that social class correlates positively with public-regardingness, that local political involvement is a partial intervening factor between the two original variables, that the degree of similarity between neighborhood and individual social class does not affect the original relationship, and that social class is an almost pure intervening factor between ethnicity and public-/self-regardingness. In diagrammatic terms, this intermediate set of findings can be expressed:

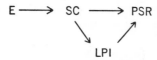

There are several ways in which father's social class could fit into the above causal arrangement. First, as we mentioned in the strategy formulation stage, father's social class might be causing a spurious relationship between social class and public-/self-regardingness. If this is the case, then we would predict, first, non-zero simple correlations between father's social class and each of the two original variables and, second, a zero or near-zero partial correlation between social class and public-/self-regardingness when controlling for father's social class. In checking the first condition, we calculate the Pearsonian r's and find that $r_{SC, FSC} = +.65$ and $r_{PSR, FSC} = +.32$; thus this stipulation is met. Next, we compute the partial correlation coefficient:

$$r_{PSR, SC \cdot FSC} = \frac{(.57) - (.32)(.65)}{\sqrt{1 - (.32)^2} \ \sqrt{1 - (.65)^2}}$$

$$= \frac{.36}{(.95)(.76)}$$

$$= +.50$$

Since controlling for father's social class only slightly reduces the strength of the original relationship ($r_{PSR, SC} = +.57$ and $r_{PSR, SC \cdot FSC} = +.50$), the partial correlation does not support the spurious interpretation.

Second, father's social class might be a cause of an individual's social class which in turn influences public-/self-regardingness. In other words, social class might be a partial or complete intervening variable between father's social class and public-/self-regardingness. In order for this interpretation to be valid, the simple correlations between father's social class and social class and between social class and public-/self-regardingness must be non-zero, and the partial correlation between father's social class and public-/self-regardingness controlling for social class must be zero or almost zero (complete intervening) or, if not near-zero, somewhat less than the simple correlation between father's social class and public-/self-regardingness (partial intervening). As we have already seen, $r_{SC, FSC} = +.65$ and $r_{PSR, SC} = +.57$, so that the first condition is satisfied. Computing the partial correlation coefficient, we find that

$$r_{PSR, FSC \cdot SC} = \frac{.32 - (.57)(.65)}{\sqrt{1 - (.57)^2} \sqrt{1 - (.65)^2}}$$

$$= \frac{-.05}{(.82)(.76)}$$

$$= -.08$$

The control for social class does cause the simple correlation ($r_{PSR, FSC} = +.32$) to reduce to almost zero ($r_{PSR, FSC \cdot SC} = -.08$), so that the conclusion that social class is a nearly complete intervening variable between father's social class and public-/self-regardingness seems a good one.

As of now, our correlational analysis suggests the following causal pattern:

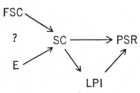

Father's social class and ethnicity influence the individual's social-class score which in turn influences public-/self-regardingness both directly and through local political involvement. The one remaining ambiguity involves the manner in which father's social class and ethnicity relate to each other and to social class. Ignoring, for the moment, the arrows to the right of social class and assuming that ethnicity temporally occurs before father's social class (again, it would be difficult to see how an individual's occupation or income or education could determine his parents' country of origin), three possible causal arrangements are: (1) ethnicity and father's social class are alternative causes of social class; (2) father's social class is a pure intervening factor between ethnicity and social class; and (3) ethnicity produces a spurious relationship between father's social class and social class. In graphic terms, these three causal structures are:

(1)   (2)   (3)

Although all three causal models imply that the simple correlations between all three variable pairs are non-zero, a point already substantiated in two cases ($r_{SC, FSC} = +.65$ and $r_{SC, E} = -.72$) and, after calculating the point biserial coefficient between ethnicity and father's social class, supported in the third instance ($r_{FSC, E} = -.93$), each causal arrangement implies a different partial correlation.

The alternative-cause formulation argues that the partial correlation between father's social class and ethnicity controlling for respondent's social class should be zero or almost zero since, if the former two factors are independent causes, their mutual association should be the product of their joint causation of social class. Computing this partial, we discover that

$$r_{FSC,E \cdot SC} = \frac{(-.93) - (.65)(-.72)}{\sqrt{1 - (.65)^2} \ \sqrt{1 - (-.72)^2}}$$

$$= \frac{-.46}{(.76)(.69)}$$

$$= -.88$$

Instead of reducing to zero, the partial coefficient ($-.88$) is almost as large as the simple correlation ($-.92$); thus, we must reject the alternative-cause interpretation.

The intervening model implies that, if father's social class is a pure intervening factor, the partial correlation between ethnicity and social class controlling for father's social class should be zero or almost zero. When we compute the partial, we find that

$$r_{SC,E \cdot FSC} = \frac{(-.72) - (.65)(-.93)}{\sqrt{1 - (.65)^2} \ \sqrt{1 - (-.93)^2}}$$

$$= \frac{-.12}{(.76)(.37)}$$

$$= -.43$$

Since the partial coefficient does not, as predicted, reduce to zero, we can reject the idea that father's social class is a pure or complete intervening factor between ethnicity and social class. There is, however, a fairly substantial drop in the relationship between ethnicity and social class when we control for father's social class ($r_{SC, E} = -.72$ and $r_{SC, E \cdot FSC} = -.43$), so that we might consider the possibility that father's social class is a partial intervening factor between the other two variables. Before entering into a detailed analysis of this possibility, let us investigate the spurious causal model.

If the relationship between father's social class and social class is a spurious product of their joint dependency on ethnicity, then we would predict that the partial correlation between the two social-class variables controlling for ethnicity would be zero or almost zero. Calculating this coefficient, we find that

$$r_{SC.FSC \cdot E} = \frac{.65 - (-.72)(-.93)}{\sqrt{1 - (-.72)^2}\ \sqrt{1 - (-.93)^2}}$$

$$= \frac{-.02}{(.69)(.37)}$$

$$= -.08$$

The original simple relationship between father's social class and respondent's social class ($r_{SC, FSC} = +.65$) almost vanishes when we control for ethnicity ($r_{SC, FSC \cdot E} = -.08$). The correlational results support the spurious interpretation more than any other alternative explanation; thus, we will not go back to consider the partial-intervening model and instead accept the spurious arrangement.

Summarizing our conclusions, we have found that if an individual is an ethnic, he (and his father) is likely to have a low social-class status, which, in turn, makes him less likely (both directly and because a low social-class status makes him less likely to be involved in local politics) to evaluate policies in a public-regarding manner. Conversely, if a person is a non-ethnic, he (and his father) is more likely to possess a high social-class status which, in turn, makes him more likely (both directly and because a high social-class status makes him more likely to be involved in local politics) to evaluate policies in a public-regarding fashion. In graphic terms, our final causal formulation is:

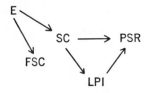

MEASURING RISK

Since our data come from a sample, we should measure the risk of inferring that the nonrandom relationships which we have discovered in the sample also occur in the total population (all River City adults). Because the risk-measurement methods presented in Chapter 9 are based on a simple random sample, and because we have used a multistage cluster sample in this study, we must either adjust the formulas to take the clustering effect into account or, at a minimum, treat the risk figures we get from the simple random-sample formulas as conservative estimates of the risk in this situation. Let us take the latter (and simpler) course and, if we find that the risk is very slight, we will not bother to employ the more complicated calculation procedures for cluster samples.

The critical correlation coefficients in our causal structure are those between ethnicity and social class, ethnicity and father's social class, social class and local political involvement, local political involvement and public-/self-regardingness, and social class and public-/self-regardingness controlling for local political involvement. These are the paths that the causal flow follows. For these coefficients, the appropriate risk-measurement model is the F-distribution. For the four simple correlations, the F formula is

$$F = \frac{r^2(N-2)}{1-r^2}$$

and for the one partial correlation the F equation is

$$F = \frac{(\text{partial } r)^2(N-k-1)}{1-(\text{partial } r)^2}$$

In each instance, N denotes the total number of cases on which the correlation coefficient is based and, in the latter case, k stands for the total number of independent and control variables. (Since we do not have a score on every variable for every member of the sample, N will vary from one test to the next and, in this study, will always be less than the total sample size of 400.)

Applying these formulas to the five correlation coefficients, we get

$$F(r_{SC,E}) = \frac{(-.72)^2(391-2)}{1-(-.72)^2} = \frac{201.658}{.4816} = 418.725$$

$$F(r_{FSC,E}) = \frac{(-.93)^2(369-2)}{1-(-.93)^2} = \frac{317.418}{.1351} = 2349.504$$

$$F(r_{LPI,SC}) = \frac{(.62)^2(368-2)}{1-(.62)^2} = \frac{140.690}{.6156} = 228.541$$

$$F(r_{PSR,LPI}) = \frac{(.45)^2(365-2)}{1-(.45)^2} = \frac{73.508}{.7975} = 92.173$$

$$F(r_{PSR,SC \cdot LPI}) = \frac{(.41)^2(364-2-1)}{1-(.41)^2} = \frac{60.684}{.8319} = 72.946$$

For the four simple correlations, $df_1 = 1$ and $df_2 = N-2$; for the partial coefficient, $df_1 = 2$ and $df_2 = 361$. Examining the F-distribution table for 1 percent risk in Appendix 2, we find that, for a df_1 of 1 and a df_2 of infinity, the F-value must be equal to or exceed 6.64; when $df_1 = 2$ and df_2 equals infinity, the F-value must be equal to or greater than 4.60. Since all of the F-values for these five coefficients are substantially greater than these two scores (the smallest obtained F is 72.946), the risk of being wrong by inferring that there is a nonrandom relationship in the total population is well under 1 percent.

WHERE DO WE GO FROM HERE?

Once we have finished our study, what comes next? To answer this question, let us return to the outline of the scientific method given in Chapter 1. There we divided the scientific process into five stages: getting an idea, getting the facts, summarizing the facts, explaining the facts, and testing the explanation. In this sample research study, we have performed the first three stages, and in this book we have concentrated on procedures for getting and summarizing the facts.

In deciding what to do next, we can choose one of two alternatives. First, we can seek an improved summarization of the facts or a better generalization of the causal structure underlying the manner in which local public policies are evaluated. We can conduct our study in other cities in order to test the generalization's universality; we can try to improve the reliability and validity of the measurements in order to make the link between our theoretical concepts and the empirical world as close and unambiguous as possible; and we can seek out other alternative, conditional, intervening, and spurious factors in order to make our causal structure more accurate.

The second course of action is to go on to the fourth and fifth stages of the scientific method—to seek an explanation for our generalization and, once we have found it, to test its inductive implications to the full. Why do ethnics tend to evaluate local policies in a self-regarding manner? Can we base our explanation on differing types of culture having different ways of viewing society? Or does the explanation lie in the way ethnics raise their children? Whatever the preferred explanation, what testable hypotheses can be deduced from it? When we collect and summarize the facts, do they support these hypotheses? If so, how might we explain the explanation and how might we interrelate it with other explanations of different political phenomena? If the explanation does not agree with the facts, have we tested poorly or is the explanation truly inadequate? If the tests are poor, how can we improve them? If the explanation is deficient, what other explanation might work?

The questions never stop because the search for knowledge never ends. Although we discover more and more, there is more and more to know.

EXERCISES

1   Like any research project, the one described in this chapter can be improved. Write a critique of this attempt and suggest means for improving it. At a minimum, the essay should cover the operationalization of the key concepts, the inclusion or exclusion of possible confounding factors, the measurement instruments, the data-collection methods, and the data-analysis techniques.
2   Perform a similar critique for any political research project in an area of interest. The bibliographic sources given in Chapter 2 can help locate such a study.

APPENDIX 1. CALCULATORS, UNIT RECORD EQUIPMENT, AND COMPUTERS

Just as modern housewives no longer cook the evening meal over an open fire, present-day investigators no longer rely on paper, pen, and memory to manipulate data and compute statistical coefficients. Whatever its adverse by-products, technology has relieved us of the more tedious tasks of data analysis, and for this we can be thankful. Unless one is a very unusual person, he does not derive any great joy from counting, adding, taking square roots, and the like. Moreover, precisely because these activities are so boring, most of us become very error-prone if we are forced to perform them for any length of time. This appendix will mention the various machines available for analysis tasks and briefly state the kinds of operations they can execute. Because of the wide differences both within and between types of data-analysis equipment, no specific operating instructions will be presented here. For this information, you should consult the manuals supplied by the manufacturers and the machines' custodians.

DESK CALCULATORS

There are three types of hand-operated calculating machines: adding machines, electromechanical calculators, and electronic calculators. Adding machines, which come in both mechanical and electromechanical models, are mainly useful for adding long series of scores. For this one function, however, the electromechanical adding machine is better than other more advanced calculators, since it not only provides the final sum but also prints all the scores.[1]

Electromechanical calculators have been the workhorses of the desk-calculating group during the past two decades, although they are gradually being replaced by the more versatile electronic models. The electromechanical machines that use electricity to power mechanical dials can add, subtract, multiply, and divide; most models are capable of expressing up to twenty digits on their bank of mechanical dials. The electronic calculators, which rely almost exclusively on electronic circuitry, can not only perform the same operations as their electromechanical counterparts, but they can also take square roots, automatically place the decimal point, and store a limited number of intermediate results and constants.

UNIT RECORD EQUIPMENT

Although when we think of a punchcard, we naturally think of a computer, several electromechanical machines, referred to as unit record equipment,

---

[1] Most of the descriptive statements in Appendix 1 are subject to a few qualifications. Thus, for example, a few electronic calculators do provide printed output.

have been developed to prepare and manipulate punchcard data. These machines are useful for preparing data for computer analysis as well as performing certain simple operations such as the construction of cross-tabulation tables.

The major types of unit record equipment are the keypunch, the verifier, the reproducer, the collator, the interpreter, the tabulator, and the counter-sorter. The keypunch and the verifier, which were discussed in Chapter 5, are used, respectively, to enter or punch the data on the cards and to check the punches' accuracy. The reproducer, as its name implies, can produce duplicate copies of any punchcard or set of punchcards. In addition, this machine can transfer data from one or more columns on one punchcard into a different set of columns on another punchcard. The collator can compare data on two sets of punchcards to see if the punches are identical, combine data on two sets of punchcards into one merged set of cards, select specified punchcards from an entire set, and check the identification number columns to ascertain whether the ID's rise or fall in correct (i.e., one-by-one) order.

Although the keypunch normally prints the punches in each column at the top of that column, punchcards which have been produced by the reproducer, collator, or the computer do not have the printed data on the card. The interpreter, however, can read the punches and print the appropriate values on the card although, because of space limitations, the values normally do not appear immediately above the column in which they are punched. Indeed, if printed values are needed for more than the first sixty columns the punchcards must be run through the interpreter a second time. If you want the data printed on paper, the tabulator will do the job. Although the computer can also provide printed output paper, it is frequently easier and less expensive to use the tabulator. The tabulator is also known as the accounting machine and is capable of performing certain basic arithmetical operations. Since the advent of the computer, however, its use for these latter purposes has declined.

The counter-sorter can, for any column on a set of punchcards, sort the cards according to which row is punched (e.g., all the cards with "1" punches in one stack, all with "2" punches in another stack, and so forth) and count the number of punchcards in each stack. It can, in other words, perform a frequency distribution for any column. Moreover, since a cross-tabulation is a two-stage frequency distribution, the counter-sorter can also be employed to build these tables. After sorting the cards for the column containing the independent variable, each stack (i.e., each value or category of the independent variable) is separately run through the counter-sorter on the column containing the dependent variable.

COMPUTERS

Although the term *computer* can be applied to any calculating device (e.g., slide rules), it is most commonly applied to machines which can both store data (e.g., variable scores) and instructions (e.g., add Variable A to Variable B) and independently execute the instructions. Within this general framework, computers can be classified according to whether they are analog or digital and whether they are special-purpose or general-purpose. An analog computer uses some physical phenomenon (e.g., flow of an electrical current) to represent the data; the stronger the electrical current, the higher the score on some variable. Digital computers, on the other hand, employ specified combinations of off-on electrical circuits to represent different integers (e.g., the integer 8 is represented by "on-off-off-off"). Special-purpose computers can only perform a limited set of operations (e.g., operate a home furnace), while a general-purpose machine can perform almost any calculating task. With only rare exceptions, social scientists use general-purpose digital computers, and it is this class of machine which we will discuss. Although general-purpose digital computers come in all shapes and sizes, almost all can perform the tasks that political researchers assign them. Thus, in the following discussion, we will not distinguish between large and small machines.

The great advantage of computers over desk calculators is the former's ability to store information and to act without constant human intervention. With a desk calculator, you must enter each score and perform each arithmetical (e.g., add) and logical (e.g., do not calculate a score for this subject because he did not answer the appropriate survey question) operation; each time, you must personally intervene by pressing some button. With a computer, conversely, the data and the set of instructions (or *program*), written in one of many special languages mutually comprehensible by man and machine, can, through the medium of punchcards,[2] be read into the machine and, while you go about your other business, the computer will perform all the operations and print out the results. (This happy outcome occurs only when the set of instructions is logically unambiguous and conforms to the computer language rules.) Moreover, in addition to performing the typical arithmetical operations, the computer can make a limited number of logical comparisons (Example: Is A greater than, equal to, or less than B?) which give it a great deal of versatility in conducting involved series of manipulations and calculations.

Although, from the above description, it might seem that you must learn one or more of the special computer languages (e.g., FORTRAN) in order to utilize the computer, this is not so. Because many operations (e.g., calculating means, constructing cross-tabulation tables, computing regression coefficients) are performed frequently, certain standard or *library* programs have been developed to carry out these tasks. To use these library programs, one need prepare only a limited number of relatively simple instruction cards. Most university computer centers have either developed their own set of library programs for manipulating and statistically analyzing social science data or they have adapted a set of programs written at another computer installation. Three sets of library programs widely used in political research are the Biomedical Computer Programs (BMD or BIMED) developed at the University of California at Los Angeles; OSIRIS, prepared at the University of Michigan and especially well-suited for Inter-University Consortium for Political Research data; and the Statistical Pack-

---

[2] Other common forms of entering data and instructions into computers are special typewriters, magnetic tapes, and magnetic disks.

age for the Social Sciences (SPSS), developed at Stanford University. Although it takes some time to learn how to utilize these library routines, the sharp decrease in tedious work and the great increase in accuracy make the investment worthwhile.

Although computers are a boon to political researchers, they can be and often are misused. First, because the machine is so good at performing complicated calculations, some are tempted to employ statistical techniques which they do not really understand. Someone tells you that, in order to achieve your research objectives, you should use a principal-components factor analysis with a varimax rotation. Even though you have only the foggiest notion of what factor analysis is all about and no idea what *principal components* and *varimax rotation* mean, you can obtain a library program to do the calculations and, presto, you have some results. But you do not have an adequate understanding of the substantive implications of the results nor do you know how a different version of factor analysis (or some other technique) might alter the findings. The lesson is clear: Do not use techniques you do not understand even if the computer knows how to calculate them.

A second temptation encouraged by the computer's calculational potency is to correlate everything with everything. Instead of conducting a carefully designed study, you simply collect as many measurements as possible for your subjects, place them on punchcards, put them into the computer, and let it grind out every possible intercorrelation. This type of procedure, known as a *fishing expedition*, is a postcomputer phenomenon. Previously, no sensible person would have invested the time and energy to calculate one coefficient after another in a search for a few high correlations. Although this strategy has some minimal value as a preliminary searching device for finding worthwhile hypotheses for future testing, its disadvantages generally outweigh its advantages. Even if you discover some relatively high correlations, what have you learned? If you calculate 100 correlation coefficients, chance alone would predict that some will be high. Which ones were chance occurrences and which reflect some causal relationship? To answer this question, you obviously must structure a study which considers time-order, other possible causes, reliability and validity, and so on. In short, you must do what you should have done in the first place: conduct a well-planned study instead of a random search.

A third danger, especially prevalent among neophyte researchers, is to treat computer-printed output as TRUTH. Human beings collect the data and human beings interpret the results, and the fact that the data, at some intermediate point in the research process, happened to pass through the bowels of a computer cannot change the very simple but essential point that research is a human activity. Computers can help guarantee that your results will be arithmetically accurate, but they can do nothing to make them more empirically sensible.

APPENDIX 2.
STATISTICAL TABLES

TABLE A2.1   TABLE OF RANDOM DIGITS

---

73 32 73 91 15 20 92 67 46 98 36 66 67 41 89 73 05 32 03 11 63 55 71 10 59

18 89 43 49 96 32 42 73 48 31 55 08 24 80 31 42 71 89 44 21 85 14 77 34 67

59 80 79 20 28 10 82 53 65 37 60 73 45 65 12 36 56 02 26 56 05 27 52 16 57

59 83 44 59 73 65 22 15 05 42 70 51 31 61 91 08 35 63 61 95 93 24 08 02 57

90 06 43 68 71 75 86 79 98 34 37 86 03 95 12 74 14 07 15 24 69 07 58 29 21

05 05 50 02 87 24 24 56 36 11 39 64 93 93 01 39 73 44 04 28 63 08 47 48 77

49 80 41 89 07 48 08 84 26 36 61 34 80 32 82 01 90 49 85 96 25 47 72 12 57

54 03 78 32 30 60 87 97 48 98 96 55 70 49 04 53 33 01 57 65 59 07 96 50 76

98 05 88 20 28 74 75 91 21 01 01 17 36 07 44 56 46 07 54 75 23 67 52 32 04

67 54 65 51 37 49 25 19 69 89 57 95 10 20 08 20 35 43 02 38 61 45 03 01 09

26 49 64 44 46 78 33 69 27 64 59 27 39 66 77 19 39 49 14 77 54 14 36 11 23

75 97 40 13 56 14 15 17 22 14 18 08 68 04 75 78 53 72 09 60 23 81 47 17 25

49 87 38 46 20 33 99 89 26 14 61 29 66 52 25 72 62 95 34 74 02 79 96 22 66

56 69 17 38 38 36 41 14 71 42 06 23 22 89 15 82 57 00 80 65 38 00 87 76 80

84 10 65 96 53 69 82 27 99 92 12 45 84 75 67 36 76 26 79 25 78 34 37 43 55

09 87 41 68 37 23 59 37 31 38 04 41 42 39 32 16 76 65 02 30 09 21 68 05 98

46 15 37 23 08 81 05 72 08 28 93 56 90 00 05 94 90 12 30 85 49 41 24 28 29

05 35 36 82 06 43 55 09 13 27 30 52 43 32 56 24 14 80 71 67 27 22 88 76 38

03 50 53 21 27 98 72 51 82 54 24 86 92 88 83 59 78 43 70 00 82 93 71 19 77

94 21 10 38 38 03 00 69 24 31 01 09 27 37 40 62 22 44 14 54 14 21 72 87 82

10 48 91 79 22 74 42 22 98 73 24 69 90 68 87 00 14 29 23 58 53 61 37 15 87

83 59 58 32 96 81 19 28 80 88 94 22 29 67 98 37 31 74 18 13 02 60 68 84 02

96 43 73 97 06 84 93 19 99 12 47 85 85 29 37 69 63 62 55 15 47 76 07 36 98

75 00 64 08 35 15 53 22 26 65 89 87 76 27 19 42 14 53 99 94 22 28 73 62 45

10 01 87 91 90 79 01 02 91 38 97 88 78 13 66 69 53 80 33 41 95 66 89 40 18

70 08 22 28 11 66 80 31 90 98 43 54 94 56 74 39 43 16 20 07 66 94 51 19 00

Table A2.1, Continued

59 38 22 23 21 22 32 30 76 29 15 93 03 75 02 64 62 18 00 46 71 10 09 57 98

87 91 93 65 44 49 24 39 40 18 82 53 05 78 88 96 21 99 00 72 50 88 86 32 28

72 68 44 22 39 12 16 68 19 11 97 91 72 24 03 38 62 11 97 27 86 56 76 86 39

93 64 82 84 72 63 02 31 75 18 55 60 18 65 49 35 26 43 28 15 97 77 19 21 24

99 68 83 55 23 87 88 98 43 12 32 06 28 05 80 90 63 31 12 51 79 87 67 45 47

18 03 39 97 87 21 53 82 05 21 34 62 36 13 04 11 60 73 79 60 91 19 97 58 95

66 41 16 39 65 64 38 08 27 42 44 35 54 52 12 41 21 63 58 04 54 87 15 04 46

62 91 35 74 12 28 05 06 17 98 18 24 95 76 25 06 07 89 63 31 61 62 90 66 28

77 38 49 79 47 74 79 49 57 91 63 58 61 38 31 99 16 30 74 22 01 62 37 08 40

50 86 56 29 73 63 54 11 66 68 66 44 54 34 67 68 19 61 74 25 58 45 30 62 87

48 61 96 07 67 26 81 72 69 84 70 61 12 84 45 27 31 44 45 16 31 91 94 22 46

30 61 08 85 73 81 24 96 36 32 41 46 84 64 68 63 20 36 87 37 34 85 55 78 84

37 13 78 39 34 12 70 76 43 69 68 56 38 96 34 91 42 31 03 51 58 14 21 36 27

27 55 56 58 72 72 34 76 97 60 22 35 37 55 85 22 86 97 16 59 92 22 96 92 47

78 87 11 81 67 63 60 40 92 48 36 87 55 92 10 51 84 68 86 61 61 96 16 65 92

18 61 02 92 64 23 74 53 37 90 59 77 51 77 13 36 37 43 52 30 56 98 57 94 07

33 14 16 54 71 29 11 21 28 22 87 13 78 68 63 55 83 98 94 13 21 79 75 07 95

60 54 67 88 26 31 97 15 37 78 93 83 17 44 71 64 26 31 31 33 59 62 41 49 79

12 80 02 12 47 77 81 58 19 71 52 38 20 17 24 66 70 46 54 57 44 64 38 77 86

26 09 94 73 09 48 37 76 12 62 10 12 80 22 79 30 67 49 24 10 74 79 06 27 24

38 23 46 31 26 91 57 82 08 41 70 31 42 68 39 59 90 05 03 28 42 34 29 51 58

83 22 84 00 25 28 57 73 94 33 07 45 11 28 67 53 25 03 18 60 23 49 03 39 30

80 30 38 35 82 91 25 38 43 16 66 80 54 79 40 24 03 91 95 91 38 82 21 13 35

10 55 32 92 91 08 73 49 68 43 95 93 06 07 83 30 21 71 47 33 38 33 21 16 46

86 53 87 06 05 47 45 13 48 38 93 07 10 27 23 77 92 84 96 01 29 82 28 24 98

40 57 96 19 65 94 42 80 39 75 81 25 99 88 57 36 74 18 40 92 32 47 65 41 07

81 06 71 54 04 82 52 09 28 64 93 39 64 09 66 25 77 26 65 36 07 68 58 89 18

32 51 68 88 59 12 42 84 85 84 28 24 29 81 96 67 91 47 88 32 12 52 15 78 81

16 72 78 28 86 33 02 65 34 37 90 55 79 12 89 63 36 90 01 52 42 17 24 74 61

62 05 38 41 28 62 05 01 82 38 98 13 79 76 87 53 59 19 84 67 21 22 50 89 17

55 11 76 67 59 82 57 93 70 21 21 49 95 27 54 29 97 92 35 75 91 60 99 40 14

94 39 57 74 71 55 55 42 38 18 22 17 93 65 53 38 95 70 40 61 34 19 04 77 27

Table A2.1, Continued

```
82 54 19 31 19 66 07 70 99 04 42 11 06 90 03 16 24 42 20 51 61 81 78 29 94
90 85 67 55 56 65 37 23 15 93 72 64 63 42 66 95 15 37 36 40 27 32 53 87 16
47 99 29 95 83 94 35 47 26 45 24 29 77 06 52 34 64 14 20 17 34 15 06 21 88
90 21 53 63 95 83 03 76 70 93 28 05 02 20 90 21 22 73 96 86 79 24 81 39 70
88 32 00 88 90 86 22 37 96 38 81 72 50 06 13 79 43 43 24 57 77 15 37 49 67
44 66 76 88 25 73 39 83 74 06 49 45 82 15 57 73 73 26 22 40 57 86 69 31 97
17 81 00 96 22 14 31 06 98 10 26 23 35 11 18 01 23 45 03 23 47 57 01 08 13
15 18 68 73 48 42 30 23 87 49 19 38 18 41 96 06 26 87 97 00 63 30 37 40 25
88 13 76 98 65 24 29 42 59 75 56 23 86 92 65 58 36 01 17 65 53 51 03 80 59
06 11 84 10 31 38 84 27 64 95 05 05 49 73 86 94 44 54 27 28 82 96 76 04 52
39 91 28 93 67 79 14 98 28 26 89 57 06 50 58 74 66 16 15 62 19 70 25 52 48
73 04 88 68 46 18 73 65 06 62 47 68 83 61 98 92 20 63 29 85 35 70 67 19 09
27 76 44 19 30 62 53 12 65 30 27 33 71 39 57 88 57 52 92 64 78 71 18 61 99
11 82 23 52 65 96 21 03 76 26 41 57 49 10 08 61 38 64 51 04 06 03 52 79 94
31 49 30 88 23 81 72 57 66 45 92 71 89 31 53 45 41 17 52 24 07 25 83 16 21
72 93 24 94 90 57 48 47 27 21 83 57 08 06 13 27 43 52 10 12 53 44 39 63 32
80 81 35 58 97 75 36 68 03 56 16 87 37 77 72 34 56 65 99 45 62 25 54 24 09
32 47 03 21 11 41 68 73 93 85 69 12 79 09 02 53 95 80 75 00 94 19 68 56 06
43 43 44 35 20 87 17 74 47 91 92 03 62 94 52 91 31 97 29 14 19 21 45 99 30
76 64 59 28 26 70 36 84 17 41 36 36 35 40 22 19 68 69 18 56 74 94 56 86 76
84 60 79 25 40 10 85 11 47 70 60 17 80 52 62 31 45 81 04 37 69 14 25 93 23
82 58 03 59 56 81 55 99 81 67 91 81 95 55 23 96 88 06 35 96 73 60 06 40 35
83 37 31 22 49 75 92 09 26 92 50 99 26 36 09 81 42 04 50 47 76 13 15 30 32
39 99 72 72 53 60 71 28 71 78 45 47 75 98 26 96 46 45 61 58 67 25 50 90 09
17 51 63 61 19 41 01 70 57 56 04 02 66 65 46 33 67 73 09 42 33 05 71 92 02
12 99 79 24 92 56 41 77 07 17 78 10 85 27 55 51 21 74 66 42 14 49 25 23 13
79 67 61 17 05 58 27 06 67 31 90 65 58 13 53 32 21 85 76 77 22 45 13 81 77
35 57 60 51 15 19 24 74 72 91 24 37 30 82 05 41 37 09 87 93 79 14 30 45 82
40 21 05 12 51 66 27 05 35 26 55 49 80 89 18 58 30 21 91 10 46 76 56 81 71
66 29 56 33 81 96 16 52 86 84 54 22 70 37 09 81 66 32 18 49 04 52 45 87 55
74 72 28 39 88 36 18 19 64 98 51 76 31 12 30 86 30 95 31 93 66 80 28 90 86
95 08 80 05 90 59 73 20 25 60 60 32 29 67 17 36 54 33 90 07 27 41 95 24 78
```

Table A2.1, Continued

29 15 05 74 00 07 78 22 51 91 91 73 20 00 60 73 07 38 33 49 49 96 57 11 05

30 29 85 03 75 31 20 45 95 40 06 76 37 95 23 14 28 72 36 80 56 35 05 76 51

06 00 94 44 00 49 60 74 61 89 34 05 59 09 40 89 04 12 74 57 58 38 09 40 55

32 54 04 23 33 75 87 42 46 17 55 88 89 60 55 96 99 70 37 37 64 13 23 97 96

85 00 50 34 33 72 15 39 97 53 65 96 60 00 15 78 54 95 25 78 83 88 13 33 46

17 02 63 02 56 53 77 64 67 68 02 43 18 27 62 44 12 55 52 20 15 05 45 36 66

06 48 13 74 79 34 78 66 24 70 25 76 46 66 69 33 64 33 72 47 45 75 71 65 86

76 10 98 29 12 64 07 10 27 67 94 35 27 53 35 88 69 30 68 70 69 96 74 80 49

75 78 14 69 75 68 95 87 09 87 75 10 63 60 66 06 78 20 15 13 64 67 38 06 94

92 34 37 90 85 83 47 64 92 02 67 45 38 95 16 66 50 50 75 47 45 92 78 58 49

52 22 20 78 74 02 65 79 98 19 80 29 63 30 11 39 71 89 61 02 13 12 01 82 11

48 14 61 73 05 50 91 43 80 54 41 77 92 43 57 63 30 34 05 73 21 82 71 78 41

03 73 43 31 92 63 31 79 70 04 39 84 81 07 90 38 39 10 03 95 78 78 43 69 29

10 55 53 33 67 11 78 40 74 78 22 19 12 80 86 01 70 09 93 00 23 32 55 87 35

42 12 24 02 68 57 81 33 19 31 24 17 46 09 37 38 24 04 31 55 77 21 49 82 27

74 50 00 35 92 74 89 73 52 93 85 18 28 45 77 19 07 24 48 85 68 53 90 26 05

78 98 18 18 51 92 87 07 72 02 07 06 72 64 44 69 57 94 54 90 05 34 15 57 34

82 23 42 72 19 93 75 76 62 82 84 83 72 45 27 14 83 78 55 21 55 85 75 29 90

86 45 88 10 48 92 37 74 44 01 39 09 40 22 29 35 37 03 60 14 67 43 67 30 68

22 65 01 91 24 59 80 69 39 31 90 76 55 81 17 30 60 54 29 70 51 94 87 15 66

02 36 37 93 30 36 63 20 82 47 21 32 87 07 74 94 53 69 78 46 04 30 09 99 98

79 68 30 54 80 25 39 41 07 27 08 04 17 39 42 96 58 55 34 38 51 91 23 40 41

15 85 11 56 29 93 27 08 74 23 54 24 78 86 22 06 67 62 97 35 57 19 86 42 75

03 10 34 99 23 78 89 07 88 18 99 72 74 30 93 04 35 78 14 20 33 76 87 41 39

40 16 43 35 99 63 18 08 26 01 30 87 80 12 13 44 12 16 48 23 95 42 06 87 64

49 46 05 01 47 94 96 51 79 83 60 66 54 91 62 53 95 39 71 13 79 57 49 62 29

39 25 98 36 65 52 49 39 88 33 71 35 46 90 98 17 89 14 87 37 37 27 74 11 51

08 15 97 38 92 81 98 79 72 12 07 64 37 31 23 04 74 64 94 25 59 78 04 38 83

41 61 49 00 42 39 44 45 53 86 95 67 56 38 02 09 75 69 01 85 35 84 25 58 04

41 03 61 59 37 59 95 13 46 10 09 44 23 24 93 46 98 79 80 87 24 20 45 95 95

57 21 58 43 87 80 62 30 75 21 52 80 53 52 85 84 35 33 40 98 18 02 03 83 39

Table A2.1, Continued

```
95 87 77 12 05 47 16 40 88 79 99 29 40 35 71 77 78 97 79 26 42 85 10 31 99
77 34 72 38 99 31 80 20 36 60 72 95 29 95 56 81 88 06 09 81 53 33 09 91 03
64 61 22 47 93 16 07 23 07 04 28 83 54 81 59 81 23 92 16 04 79 45 97 06 86
95 91 14 38 75 81 11 48 87 93 91 50 57 67 98 71 55 35 67 12 35 99 53 21 42
26 13 15 26 37 62 58 48 48 32 17 97 75 73 92 41 41 16 64 00 78 31 15 05 13
74 43 02 63 46 60 68 53 29 03 23 61 80 80 12 86 68 69 44 19 71 24 41 02 63
39 28 74 95 83 96 63 82 16 19 92 49 51 58 99 53 51 78 75 58 12 67 70 89 98
98 81 81 18 45 39 11 92 43 17 32 50 49 12 46 98 80 55 85 72 78 67 84 54 26
80 42 07 83 68 63 08 94 45 48 14 01 67 61 68 39 38 65 33 98 59 09 06 75 61
40 39 71 09 48 79 59 09 56 74 31 90 26 26 16 33 20 14 00 31 02 03 51 85 43
37 50 65 56 74 03 68 38 86 79 10 28 06 47 03 97 45 10 34 48 51 93 58 90 02
91 90 78 75 90 85 29 10 98 34 11 45 87 44 59 87 71 06 21 39 71 62 88 53 11
64 25 90 83 64 86 31 88 98 35 66 32 28 95 29 00 71 22 04 03 48 32 55 86 74
99 20 06 37 29 42 72 81 77 09 44 66 28 28 55 02 57 06 70 08 53 56 75 02 36
61 53 22 09 41 67 02 46 72 48 41 18 26 05 69 42 09 38 51 10 08 48 99 12 72
98 34 21 58 57 66 81 70 61 23 23 22 09 96 33 79 14 22 48 54 41 66 83 92 32
66 79 75 19 36 87 06 19 25 57 02 71 86 37 71 33 31 31 70 56 52 75 14 05 63
25 26 21 05 00 76 39 71 49 51 46 27 62 52 90 16 71 38 03 09 36 13 06 02 25
62 60 85 09 71 85 44 50 99 81 17 68 54 86 69 26 75 70 18 22 95 77 69 57 00
52 94 19 76 62 52 07 99 85 11 56 13 98 95 22 12 69 51 04 25 89 18 06 47 93
57 91 05 23 61 08 79 71 24 72 48 80 10 11 10 18 68 64 48 03 39 60 10 64 95
00 17 05 93 41 98 56 00 28 21 09 45 79 18 28 68 00 60 07 27 22 35 88 56 51
17 97 98 74 93 80 54 58 69 12 85 72 13 60 27 40 37 76 53 61 72 86 70 23 19
65 86 71 53 82 52 13 67 34 43 94 93 49 14 26 94 33 88 28 74 48 77 60 26 76
96 45 33 34 71 95 19 86 61 46 90 46 54 21 84 30 21 28 76 02 56 09 70 64 31
71 63 19 07 75 46 79 69 22 45 23 99 15 65 38 22 48 88 90 50 92 09 72 96 89
44 55 10 56 02 62 80 52 08 80 01 24 91 94 83 79 43 31 09 93 37 97 40 67 01
26 94 23 06 47 21 67 60 75 51 79 13 32 29 59 38 48 01 62 76 96 18 09 23 08
89 76 45 41 37 53 01 74 79 34 34 83 92 10 91 63 47 14 78 88 35 77 65 96 45
```

SOURCE: The RAND Corporation, *A Million Random Digits*, Glencoe, Ill., Free Press, pp. 56 58, with the permission of the RAND Corporation.

TABLE A2.2 DISTRIBUTION OF CHI-SQUARE

					Probability					
df	.90	.70	.50	.30	.20	.10	.05	.02	.01	.001
1	.0158	.148	.455	1.074	1.642	2.706	3.841	5.412	6.635	10.827
2	.211	.713	1.386	2.408	3.219	4.605	5.991	7.824	9.210	13.815
3	.584	1.424	2.366	3.665	4.642	6.251	7.815	9.837	11.341	16.268
4	1.064	2.195	3.357	4.878	5.989	7.779	9.488	11.668	13.277	18.465
5	1.610	3.000	4.351	6.064	7.289	9.236	11.070	13.388	15.086	20.517
6	2.204	3.828	5.348	7.231	8.558	10.645	12.592	15.033	16.812	22.457
7	2.833	4.671	6.346	8.383	9.803	12.017	14.067	16.622	18.475	24.322
8	3.490	5.527	7.344	9.524	11.030	13.362	15.507	18.168	20.090	26.125
9	4.168	6.393	8.343	10.656	12.242	14.684	16.919	19.679	21.666	27.877
10	4.865	7.267	9.342	11.781	13.442	15.987	18.307	21.161	23.209	29.588
11	5.578	8.148	10.341	12.899	14.631	17.275	19.675	22.618	24.725	31.264
12	6.304	9.034	11.340	14.011	15.812	18.549	21.026	24.054	26.217	32.909
13	7.042	9.926	12.340	15.119	16.985	19.812	22.362	25.472	27.688	34.528
14	7.790	10.821	13.339	16.222	18.151	21.064	23.685	26.873	29.141	36.123
15	8.547	11.721	14.339	17.322	19.311	22.307	24.996	28.259	30.578	37.697
16	9.312	12.624	15.338	18.418	20.465	23.542	26.296	29.633	32.000	39.252
17	10.085	13.531	16.338	19.511	21.615	24.769	27.587	30.995	33.409	40.790
18	10.865	14.440	17.338	20.601	22.760	25.989	28.869	32.346	34.805	42.312
19	11.651	15.352	18.338	21.689	23.900	27.204	30.144	33.687	36.191	43.820
20	12.443	16.266	19.337	22.775	25.038	28.412	31.410	35.020	37.566	45.315
21	13.240	17.182	20.337	23.858	26.171	29.615	32.671	36.343	38.932	46.797
22	14.041	18.101	21.337	24.939	27.301	30.813	33.924	37.659	40.289	48.268
23	14.848	19.021	22.337	26.018	28.429	32.007	35.172	38.968	41.638	49.728
24	15.659	19.943	23.337	27.096	29.553	33.196	36.415	40.270	42.980	51.179
25	16.473	20.867	24.337	28.172	30.675	34.382	37.652	41.566	44.314	52.620
26	17.292	21.792	25.336	29.246	31.795	35.563	38.885	42.856	45.642	54.052
27	18.114	22.719	26.336	30.319	32.912	36.741	40.113	44.140	46.963	55.476
28	18.939	23.647	27.336	31.391	34.027	37.916	41.337	45.419	48.278	56.893
29	19.768	24.577	28.336	32.461	35.139	39.087	42.557	46.693	49.588	58.302
30	20.599	25.508	29.336	33.530	36.250	40.256	43.773	47.962	50.892	59.703
40	29.051	34.872	39.335	44.165	47.269	51.805	55.759	60.436	63.691	73.402
50	37.689	44.313	49.335	54.723	58.164	63.167	67.505	72.613	76.154	86.661
60	46.459	53.809	59.335	65.227	68.972	74.397	79.082	84.580	88.379	99.607

SOURCE: Table A2.2 is abridged from Table IV of R. A. Fisher and F. Yates, *Statistical Tables for Biological, Agricultural and Medical Research*, 6th ed., 1963, published by Oliver & Boyd, Edinburgh, by permission of the authors and publishers.

TABLE A2.3 AREAL PROPORTIONS UNDER THE NORMAL CURVE[a]

Z	.00	.01	.02	.03	.04	.05	.06	.07	.08	.09
0.0	0000	0040	0080	0120	0159	0199	0239	0279	0319	0359
0.1	0398	0438	0478	0517	0557	0596	0636	0675	0714	0753
0.2	0793	0832	0871	0910	0948	0987	1026	1064	1103	1141
0.3	1179	1217	1255	1293	1331	1368	1406	1443	1480	1517
0.4	1554	1591	1628	1664	1700	1736	1772	1808	1844	1879
0.5	1915	1950	1985	2019	2054	2088	2123	2157	2190	2224
0.6	2257	2291	2324	2357	2389	2422	2454	2486	2518	2549
0.7	2580	2612	2642	2673	2704	2734	2764	2794	2823	2852
0.8	2881	2910	2939	2967	2995	3023	3051	3078	3106	3133
0.9	3159	3186	3212	3238	3264	3289	3315	3340	3365	3389
1.0	3413	3438	3461	3485	3508	3531	3554	3577	3599	3621
1.1	3643	3665	3686	3718	3729	3749	3770	3790	3810	3830
1.2	3849	3869	3888	3907	3925	3944	3962	3980	3997	4015
1.3	4032	4049	4066	4083	4099	4115	4131	4147	4162	4177
1.4	4192	4207	4222	4236	4251	4265	4279	4292	4306	4319
1.5	4332	4345	4357	4370	4382	4394	4406	4418	4430	4441
1.6	4452	4463	4474	4485	4495	4505	4515	4525	4535	4545
1.7	4554	4564	4573	4582	4591	4599	4608	4616	4625	4633
1.8	4641	4649	4656	4664	4671	4678	4686	4693	4699	4706
1.9	4713	4719	4726	4732	4738	4744	4750	4758	4762	4767
2.0	4773	4778	4783	4788	4793	4798	4803	4808	4812	4817
2.1	4821	4826	4830	4834	4838	4842	4846	4850	4854	4857
2.2	4861	4865	4868	4871	4875	4878	4881	4884	4887	4890
2.3	4893	4896	4898	4901	4904	4906	4909	4911	4913	4916
2.4	4918	4920	4922	4925	4927	4929	4931	4932	4934	4936
2.5	4938	4940	4941	4943	4945	4946	4948	4949	4951	4952
2.6	4953	4955	4956	4957	4959	4960	4961	4962	4963	4964
2.7	4965	4966	4967	4968	4969	4970	4971	4972	4973	4974
2.8	4974	4975	4976	4977	4977	4978	4979	4980	4980	4981
2.9	4981	4982	4983	4984	4984	4984	4985	4985	4986	4986
3.0	4986.5	4987	4987	4988	4988	4988	4989	4989	4989	4990

[a] Each entry in this table represents the proportion of cases, with a base of 10,000, which lie between the mean and various standard deviation units (Z-scores). For example, 1,554/10,000 of the cases lie between the mean and 0.40 standard deviation units.

SOURCE: Harold O. Rugg, *Statistical Methods Applied to Education*, Boston, Houghton Mifflin, 1917, pp. 389–390, Appendix Table III, with the permission of the publisher.

TABLE A2.4 DISTRIBUTION OF F

Risk = .20

$df_1 = 1$	2	3	4	5	6	8	12	24	∞
df_2									
1	9.47	12.00	13.06	13.64	14.01	14.26	14.58	14.90	15.24	15.58
2	3.56	4.00	4.16	4.24	4.28	4.32	4.36	4.40	4.44	4.48
3	2.68	2.89	2.94	2.96	2.97	2.97	2.98	2.98	2.98	2.98
4	2.35	2.47	2.48	2.48	2.48	2.47	2.47	2.46	2.44	2.43
5	2.18	2.26	2.25	2.24	2.23	2.22	2.20	2.18	2.16	2.13
10	1.88	1.90	1.86	1.83	1.80	1.78	1.75	1.72	1.67	1.62
20	1.76	1.75	1.70	1.65	1.62	1.60	1.56	1.51	1.45	1.37
30	1.72	1.70	1.64	1.60	1.57	1.54	1.50	1.45	1.38	1.28
40	1.70	1.68	1.62	1.57	1.54	1.51	1.47	1.41	1.34	1.24
60	1.68	1.65	1.59	1.55	1.51	1.48	1.44	1.38	1.31	1.18
120	1.66	1.63	1.57	1.52	1.48	1.45	1.41	1.35	1.27	1.12
∞	1.64	1.61	1.55	1.50	1.46	1.43	1.38	1.32	1.23	1.00

Risk = .10

$df_1 = 1$	2	3	4	5	6	8	12	24	∞
df_2									
1	39.86	49.50	53.59	55.83	57.24	58.20	59.44	60.70	62.00	63.33
2	8.53	9.00	9.16	9.24	9.29	9.33	9.37	9.41	9.45	9.49
3	5.54	5.46	5.39	5.34	5.31	5.28	5.25	5.22	5.18	5.13
4	4.54	4.32	4.19	4.11	4.05	4.01	3.95	3.90	3.83	3.76
5	4.06	3.78	3.62	3.52	3.45	3.40	3.34	3.27	3.19	3.10
10	3.28	2.92	2.73	2.61	2.52	2.46	2.38	2.28	2.18	2.06
20	2.97	2.59	2.33	2.25	2.16	2.09	2.00	1.89	1.77	1.61
30	2.88	2.49	2.28	2.14	2.05	1.98	1.88	1.77	1.64	1.46
40	2.84	2.44	2.23	2.09	2.00	1.93	1.83	1.71	1.57	1.38
60	2.79	2.39	2.18	2.04	1.95	1.87	1.77	1.66	1.51	1.29
120	2.75	2.35	2.13	1.99	1.90	1.82	1.72	1.60	1.45	1.19
∞	2.71	2.30	2.08	1.94	1.85	1.77	1.67	1.55	1.38	1.00

Risk = .05

$df_1 = 1$	2	3	4	5	6	8	12	24	∞
df_2									
1	161.4	199.5	215.7	224.6	230.2	234.0	238.9	243.9	249.0	254.3
2	18.51	19.00	19.16	19.25	19.30	19.33	19.37	19.41	19.45	19.50
3	10.13	9.55	9.28	9.12	9.01	8.94	8.84	8.74	8.64	8.53
4	7.71	6.94	6.59	6.39	6.26	6.16	6.04	5.91	5.77	5.63
5	6.61	5.79	5.41	5.19	5.05	4.95	4.82	4.68	4.53	4.36
10	4.96	4.10	3.71	3.48	3.33	3.22	3.07	2.91	2.74	2.54
20	4.35	3.49	3.10	2.87	2.71	2.60	2.45	2.28	2.08	1.84
30	4.17	3.32	2.92	2.69	2.53	2.42	2.27	2.09	1.89	1.62
40	4.08	3.23	2.84	2.61	2.45	2.34	2.18	2.00	1.79	1.51
60	4.00	3.15	2.76	2.52	2.37	2.25	2.10	1.92	1.70	1.39
120	3.92	3.07	2.68	2.45	2.29	2.17	2.02	1.83	1.61	1.25
∞	3.84	2.99	2.60	2.37	2.21	2.10	1.94	1.75	1.52	1.00

Table A2.4, Continued

				Risk = .01					
$df_1 = 1$	2	3	4	5	6	8	12	24	∞
df_2									
1	4052.	4999.	5403.	5625.	5764.	5859.	5982.	6106.	6234.	6366.
2	98.50	99.00	99.17	99.25	99.30	99.33	99.37	99.42	99.46	99.50
3	34.12	30.82	29.46	28.71	28.24	27.91	27.49	27.05	26.60	26.12
4	21.20	18.00	16.69	15.98	15.52	15.21	14.80	14.37	13.93	13.46
5	16.26	13.27	12.06	11.39	10.97	10.67	10.29	9.89	9.47	9.02
10	10.04	7.56	6.55	5.99	5.64	5.39	5.06	4.71	4.33	3.91
20	8.10	5.85	4.94	4.43	4.10	3.87	3.56	3.23	2.86	2.42
30	7.56	5.39	4.51	4.02	3.70	3.47	3.17	2.84	2.47	2.01
40	7.31	5.18	4.31	3.83	3.51	3.29	2.99	2.66	2.29	1.80
60	7.08	4.98	4.13	3.65	3.34	3.12	2.82	2.50	2.12	1.60
120	6.85	4.79	3.95	3.48	3.17	2.96	2.66	2.34	1.95	1.38
∞	6.64	4.60	3.78	3.32	3.02	2.80	2.51	2.18	1.79	1.00

SOURCE: Table A2.4 is abridged from Table V of R. A. Fisher and F. Yates, *Statistical Tables for Biological, Agricultural and Medical Research*, 6th ed., 1963, published by Oliver & Boyd, Edinburgh, by permission of the authors and publishers.

INDEX

71 72 73 74 7 6 5 4 3 2 1